MARTIN R. DELANY'S CIVIL WAR
⸻ AND ⸻
RECONSTRUCTION

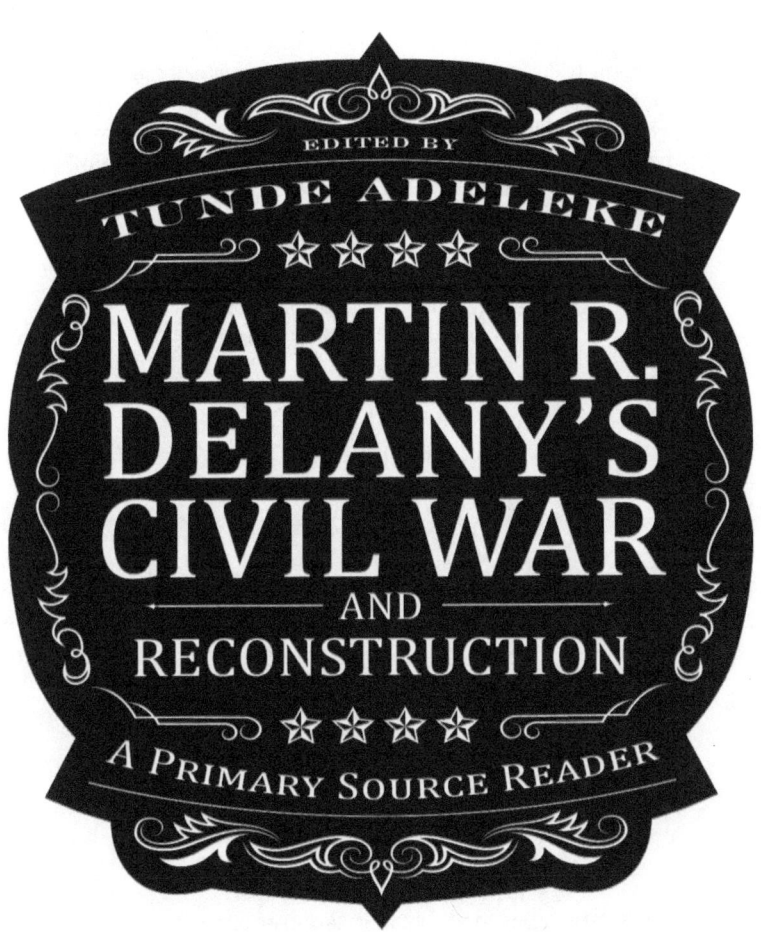

EDITED BY
TUNDE ADELEKE

MARTIN R. DELANY'S CIVIL WAR AND RECONSTRUCTION

A PRIMARY SOURCE READER

UNIVERSITY PRESS OF MISSISSIPPI / JACKSON

The University Press of Mississippi is the scholarly publishing agency of
the Mississippi Institutions of Higher Learning: Alcorn State University,
Delta State University, Jackson State University, Mississippi State University,
Mississippi University for Women, Mississippi Valley State University,
University of Mississippi, and University of Southern Mississippi.

www.upress.state.ms.us

The University Press of Mississippi is a member
of the Association of University Presses.

Copyright © 2020 by University Press of Mississippi
All rights reserved
Manufactured in the United States of America

First printing 2020
∞

Library of Congress Cataloging-in-Publication Data

Names: Adeleke, Tunde, editor.
Title: Martin R. Delany's Civil War and Reconstruction : a primary source
reader / Tunde Adeleke.
Description: Jackson : University Press of Mississippi, 2020. | Includes
bibliographical references.
Identifiers: LCCN 2019026484 (print) | LCCN 2019026485 (ebook) | ISBN
9781496826633 (hardback) | ISBN 9781496826640 (paperback) | ISBN
9781496826657 (epub) | ISBN 9781496826664 (epub) | ISBN 9781496826671
(pdf) | ISBN 9781496826688 (pdf)
Subjects: LCSH: Delany, Martin Robison, 1812–1885. | Reconstruction (U.S.
history, 1865–1877)—Sources. | Reconstruction (U.S. history,
1865–1877)—South Carolina.
Classification: LCC E185.2 .M37 2020 (print) | LCC E185.2 (ebook) | DDC
973.8—dc23
LC record available at https://lccn.loc.gov/2019026484
LC ebook record available at https://lccn.loc.gov/2019026485

British Library Cataloging-in-Publication Data available

THIS ONE IS FOR
GLORIA ADANMA ADELEKE
MY WIFE AND FRIEND
WITH GRATITUDE

Contents

Acknowledgments..xi
Introduction..3

CHAPTER 1
THE BLACK MAJOR

    Introduction.. 27
1 Delany to Secretary of War, December 15, 1863................... 30
2 The Secretary of War of the United States of America............ 31
3 C. W. Foster to Capt. Henry Keteltas, February 27, 1865......... 32
4 C. W. Foster to Delany, February 27, 1865....................... 33
5 Delany to C. W. Foster... 33
6 C. W. Foster to Rufus Saxton, February 27, 1865................. 34
7 Delany to C. W. Foster, March 24, 1865.......................... 35
8 C. W. Foster to Delany, March 27, 1865.......................... 36
9 Attention, Charlestonians! Rally Round the Flag!................ 36
10 Black National Defenders....................................... 38
11 Delany Counsels Freedmen....................................... 39
12 H. J. Hawkins on Delany, August 13, 1865....................... 44
13 Delany to C. W. Foster, February 5, 1867....................... 45
14 Delany to C. W. Foster, April 4, 1867.......................... 46

CHAPTER 2
Freedmen's Bureau Sub-assistant Commissioner

Introduction 47
1 Prospects of the Freedmen of Hilton Head Island 1 52
2 Prospects of the Freedmen of Hilton Head Island 2 52
3 Prospects of the Freedmen of Hilton Head Island 5 54
4 Prospects of the Freedmen of Hilton Head Island 6 56
5 Prospects of the Freedmen of Hilton Head Island 7 58
6 Triple Alliance: The Restoration of the South—Salvation of
    Its Political Economy 62
7 Homes for the Freedmen 1, March 7, 1871 63
8 Homes for the Freedmen 2, March 23, 1871 64
9 Homes for the Freedmen 3, May 1, 1871 66
10 Special Orders No. 372 68
11 Delany's Freedmen's Bureau Report, December 1865 69
12 Delany's Freedmen's Bureau Report, March 1867 70
13 Delany's Freedmen's Bureau Report, September 1867 74
14 Delany's Freedmen's Bureau Report, May 1868 79
15 A Typical Contract between Freedmen and Planters
    in Delany's District 83
16 D. E. Sickles to Gen. E. D. Townsend on Delany, January 30, 1866 85
17 Excerpts from an Editorial of the *New South* 86
18 R. K. Scott to Gen. O. O. Howard, July 22, 1868 87

CHAPTER 3
The Conservative Republican

Introduction 89
1 Delany's Advice to Black Leaders, February 22, 1866 101
2 Delany to President Andrew Johnson, July 25, 1866 103
3 Delany to Rev. Henry H. Garnet, July 27, 1867 105
4 Colored Officials 106
5 Delany to L. S. Langley, February 5, 1868 109
6 Thoughts for the Colored People 110
7 University Pamphlets: A Series of Four Tracts on National Polity 112
8 On a Black Man's Party 122
9 Ward Meeting at Military Hall 122
10 Mass Meeting of Republicans 124
11 Side Issues 126

12	The Appeal to Race	128
13	Republican Meetings—Ward 6	129
14	Grand Mass Meeting: Edgefield Alive; 10,000 People Present	130
15	The Fourth in Charleston	130
16	A Card to the Editor of the *Republican*	131
17	Meeting at Military Hall	132
18	A Political Review: Delany to Frederick Douglass, August 14, 1871	133
19	Frederick Douglass to Delany, August 31, 1871	141
20	S. N. Gailliard on Delany	146
21	The *News and Courier* on Delany to Frederick Douglass, August 17, 1871	148
22	The *News and Courier* on Delany to Frederick Douglass, August 18, 1871	152
23	The *News and Courier* on Delany to Frederick Douglass, August 19, 1871	156
24	Major Delany's Letter: Refuting Delany's Allegation of Republican Party Bias	159
25	South Carolina Obligations 1: Delany to the Editor of the *New York Times*, September 25, 1872	161
26	South Carolina Obligations 2: Delany to the Editor of the *New York Times*, September 30, 1872	162
27	Rev. R. H. Cain to Gov. Franklin J. Moses, May 18, 1873	163
28	Delany to Justice Jonathan Wright, February 10, 1874	164
29	The *New York Times* on Delany's Letter to Justice Wright	166
30	Minority Representation: A Colored Advocate in Favor of It in South Carolina	167

CHAPTER 4
The Independent Republican

	Introduction	169
1	Independent Republicans: Conservatives and Republicans in a Common Cause	173
2	The Independent Republican State Nominating Convention, Hibernian Hall	174
3	The Independent Republican State Convention	176
4	Green and Delany	177
5	A Voice from the Mountains	180
6	The Cause of Fair Dealing and Peace in Chester	181
7	The *News and Courier* on Major Delany	182

CHAPTER 5
TRIAL AND CONVICTION

Introduction 183
1 Delany to Frederick Douglass: Trial and Conviction,
   February 28, 1876 186
2 The Charges against M. R. Delany. 204
3 C. C. Bowen to Gov. D. H. Chamberlain, April 3, 1876 205
4 *The State vs. Martin R. Delany*: Judge's Recommendations 206
5 Petition for Delany's Pardon 206
6 Rev. N. N. Hunter to Delany, April 22, 1876 208
7 Delany to W. R. Jones, Esq., May 18, 1876 208
8 R. S. Tharin to Gov. D. H. Chamberlain, June 1, 1876 209
9 Delany to W. R. Jones. 210
10 *The State vs. M. R. Delany*: Pardon Granted. 212
11 Delany to Gov. D. H. Chamberlain, September 1, 1876 212

CHAPTER 6
A NEW DEPARTURE

Introduction 215
1 The Black Man's Political Movement: Delany to Rev. Garland H.
   White, September 18, 1876 218
2 The Campaign in the City: The Colored Democracy of Ward 4 220
3 The Campaign in the City: Meeting of the Colored Democratic
   Club of Third Ward, October 21, 1876 221
4 The Campaign in the City: Meeting in Hibernian Hall 222
5 Union of the Two Races: What Prevents It? 223
6 Negative Report on Delany by Attorney St. Julian Jervey 224
7 Petition to Dismiss Delany as Trial Justice. .225
8 Delany to Gov. Wade Hampton, April 2, 1878 226
9 Counter-Petition to Retain Delany as Trial Justice. 226
10 Delany to Hon. H. R. Latrobe, July 8, 1878 227
11 Delany to William Coppinger, August 18, 1880 229
12 Delany to William Coppinger, December 18, 1880 232

Selected Bibliography 235
Index 241

ACKNOWLEDGMENTS

This is a collection of letters, speeches, contemporary nineteenth-century newspaper articles, commentaries, and reports written by, and about, Martin R. Delany (1812–85). These primary sources cover his Civil War and Reconstruction career in South Carolina. There are a total of ninety-two documents, the vast majority of which have not been previously published. The few that have been published were mostly published as excerpts and not as full documents. They are presented here in their entirety. I began collecting Delany's Reconstruction letters, articles, Freedmen's Bureau reports, and correspondence with South Carolina Governors and State officials, including articles and commentaries about him in local newspapers and magazines, in the early 1980s. Most of these documents are public records preserved in files and electronic formats (microfilms) in libraries, archives, and private collections in the United States and Canada. It was a painstakingly slow process of deciphering and transcribing Delany's cursively handwritten letters and reports, speeches, articles, and other documents preserved in nineteenth-century newspapers, magazines, and journals. Transcription was particularly challenging due to the age and delicate nature of several of the documents. It was simply impossible to decipher some words. I have used ellipses to indicate missing words or phrases. Fortunately, there are not too many of these, and they do not obscure the central messages or ideas in the documents.

Work on this project has taken more than three decades. I began transcribing and editing the documents in 1986 while teaching at the University of Maiduguri, Nigeria. Unfortunately, due to extenuating circumstances, I had to suspend work on the project and did not return to it until 1990, when I moved to the United States and began teaching at Ohio State University in Columbus, Ohio. There is nothing as challenging and daunting as attempting to transcribe and edit papers and documents of, and about, an individual of such acclaimed and profound complexity (some would say contradiction). Most critics agree that Martin Delany exemplified complexity and multidimensionality both as a person and in his professions and endeavors. His life struggles interspersed with major episodes in American and African Diaspora history: slavery, abolition, colonization, emigration, Black Nationalism, pan-Africanism, Civil War, and Reconstruction. Although overwhelming, the task of collecting and editing Delany's documents is equally enriching and rewarding. His life and struggles are lenses through which to acquire deeper understanding of, and appreciation for, the enormity and complexity of the challenges blacks confronted and endured in nineteenth-century America, as well as the adaptation, survival, and resistance strategies and institutions they developed. To study Martin Delany, therefore, is to gain critical insight into the dynamics, complexities, and forces that shaped the nineteenth-century black American experience. He both experienced and influenced experiences that defined major phases in American and African diaspora history.

As with any academic endeavor, this has not been a one-person accomplishment. I would not have been able to acquire the bulk of these documents without the assistance of the staff of the many libraries and archives I visited during my research. They all deserve due acknowledgment and credit for facilitating my research and, in a few cases, for granting permission to publish the documents. I am indebted to the South Carolina Department of Archives and History for Delany's Freedmen's Bureau files and papers, Reconstruction correspondence, and the papers of the Reconstruction governors and other state officials with whom he corresponded; the South Caroliniana Research Library of the University of South Carolina for microfilm of the various state Reconstruction newspapers and magazines as well documents on, and about, Delany; the Charleston Historical Society Library in Charleston for Delany Files and other documents and for permission to publish his *Trial and Conviction*; the Wilson Library of the University of North Carolina, Chapel Hill, for the Dawson Pamphlets Collections and for permission to publish Delany's *University Pamphlets: A Series of Four Tracts on National Polity*. I am also grateful to the following for assistance with Delany files and documents in their collections: the Western Pennsylvania Historical Society in Pittsburgh; the Hilton Head Island Public Library in Hilton Head, South Carolina; the Carnegie Library in Pittsburgh, Pennsylvania; the War Records Offices of the Library of Congress and the National Archives in Washington, DC; the Moorland-Spingarn Research Center, Howard University, Washington, DC; the Kent County Historical Society Library, Chatham, Ontario, Canada; the Cross Cultural Learners Center Library, London, Ontario, Canada; Xenia Public Library, Xenia, Ohio; and Wilberforce University Library, Wilberforce, Ohio. I want to specially extend my gratitude to the staff of the Interlibrary Loans Department of the D. B. Weldon Library of the University of Western Ontario for assistance with acquisition of several Delany documents, and the staff of the library's Special Collection Room for giving me access to the then–newly acquired but uncatalogued Boyd B. Stutler Papers. I also want to acknowledge the following for responding to my letters of inquiry and requests for Delany documents and papers in their collections: the Library Company of Philadelphia, Philadelphia, Pennsylvania; the Boston Public Library, Boston, Massachusetts; the American Antiquarian Society, Worcester, Massachusetts; the Western Reserve Historical Society, Cleveland, Ohio; and the Francis A. Countway Library of Medicine, Harvard University, Cambridge, Massachusetts.

Last but certainly not the least, I thank the editorial staff of the University Press of Mississippi for their interest in publishing Delany's documents. I would be remiss not to acknowledge my appreciation for the comments and suggestions of the Press's two anonymous external reviewers. I found their comments constructive and most helpful.

MARTIN R. DELANY'S CIVIL WAR AND RECONSTRUCTION

Introduction

I

To engage Martin Robison Delany (1812–1885) is to confront the complexities and paradoxes of nineteenth-century black American leadership. He embodied the utilitarianism and pragmatism that the late August Meier described as the defining attributes of nineteenth-century black leadership.[1] He refused to confine his life and struggles within the Manichaean good-versus-evil framework. There was no absolute good or absolute evil in Delany's worldview. On the contrary, in crucial historical moments and contexts, Delany acknowledged only complex contending forces and interests, each with discernible merits and demerits. By characterizing Delany as someone who could not be classified "with either the good guys or the bad guys," Delany aficionado Victor Ullman captured his ambiguity, or what many of Delany's contemporaries perceived as his behavioral eccentricity.[2] In Delany's judgment, no choice or condition was absolute or sacrosanct. His decisions were determined not so much by dogmatic adherence to some ideologically or racially defined considerations but by the dictates of what his *conscience* and *reason* determined to be in the interest of blacks. Delany made this poignant declaration early in his abolitionist career; "I care little for precedent, and therefore, discard the frivolous rules of formality, conforming always to principle, *suggested by conscience, and guided by the light of reason.*"[3] In other words, he gauged situations and events through the prism of his utilitarian and pragmatic lenses.

To his nineteenth-century contemporaries (black and white alike), Delany evoked and conjured conflicting images, perceptions, and emotions. To some, he was the quintessence of blackness.[4] His friend and fellow abolitionist, with whom he collaborated as coeditor of the *North Star*, Frederick Douglass, underscored Delany's racial essentialist character when he observed that while Douglass merely thanked God for making him a man, Delany always thanked God for making him a black man.[5] Bishop Daniel Payne of the African Methodist Episcopal Church once described Delany as someone who had far greater love for his race than he had for humanity. He was, in Bishop Payne's words, "too intensely African to be popular and thereby multiplied enemies where he could have multiplied friends."[6] The white abolitionist William Lloyd Garrison portrayed Delany as "so black as to make his identity with the African race perfect."[7] One contemporary, Nelson Grant of Circleville, Virginia, identified Delany "among the finest of men."[8] Others, however, offered far less flattering portraits. Two of them reflected the ambivalence Delany evoked. To William H. Burleigh of Allegheny, Pennsylvania, Delany was both "a man who is as black as the ace of spade . . . who can make a good speech" and also someone who "lacks common sense."[9] Responding to a request for reference on Delany's character, William M. Shim of Pittsburgh wrote,

> Mr. Delany . . . was well known as an intelligent, active, energetic, zealous and uncompromising abolitionist. . . . I am constrained to express the opinion that he is not a man to be relied on for any great Christian or missionary enterprise. He is one of several who was at different times proposed to fill vacancies in the Board of Trustees of the college, against whom Mr. Avery set his face firmly and decidedly. . . . Affirmatively he has the reputation of being visionary and officious and negatively . . . lacks some of the indisputable requisite of such character as you seem to be in search of.[10]

After listening with great apprehension to a public lecture Delany delivered to Freedmen on Saint Helena Island, South Carolina, in the early phase of Reconstruction, Edward M. Stoeber, first lieutenant with the 104th United States Colored Troops, reported to the assistant adjutant general that he considered Delany "a thorough hater of the white race."[11] And yet it was precisely during this period that some highly placed white conservative introduced Delany as "the honest exemplar of the honest colored men of South Carolina."[12] Another described Delany as an educated man, a true patriot, and statesman who acquitted "himself so completely alongside the first gentlemen of South Carolina."[13]

These mixed and conflicting perceptions mirrored the deeper and larger conflicts, ambivalences, or what Theodore Draper aptly termed "dualities" of Delany's public life.[14] At some times, especially during the mid-nineteenth-century phase of his career, Delany espoused militant nationalist and anti-American ideas and values. Later, however, during the Civil War and Reconstruction period, he publicly disavowed such militancy, opting for racial reconciliation, compromises, and accommodation. That Delany's life and struggles embodied such "dualities" was not unique. In fact, this was a defining attribute of black leadership orientation to America in the nineteenth century.[15] As August Meier explained, "Overall, the typical late nineteenth-century black political leader in the South was a moderate. All were practical men who saw the necessity of compromise. They were also ambitious men who needed white support to advance themselves and the interests of their black constituents. Even the most militant spokesmen ... found astute compromise essential to obtain the benefits desired either personally or for the race."[16] Delany was therefore no exception.

Yet despite his complex, ambivalent, and at times conflicting dispositions and idiosyncrasies, the portrait of Delany that came to dominate twentieth-century black American memory was of the ideologue, the racial essentialist, uncompromising, and anti-European Black Nationalist. This was the Delany glamorized in twentieth-century Black Nationalist discourses. There was hardly an acknowledgment or awareness of his "dualities" and ambivalences. A major historiographical challenge for Delany scholarship, therefore, remains the dominance of a personality that reflected only a dimension of his life and struggles (the radical, militant, anti-establishment character; the quintessence of blackness). There is no acknowledgment of the other conservative, accommodating, and pro-establishment personality. Thus, Delany is memorialized as an implacably militant and uncompromising ideologue of the black struggles.

Emphasis on his radicalism could be attributed to the ideological and instrumentalist slant of the context of his historical rebirth. Twentieth-century reconstruction of Delany's life coincided with the upsurge of instrumentalist historiography in the late 1960s and early 1970s.[17] Black history was then driven by what Peter Walker (in a different context) characterized as "selective perception syndrome," in which only data or information that reinforced a certain ideological disposition were isolated and highlighted. This informed how Delany was conceptualized.[18] Consciously or subconsciously, those who studied Martin Delany tended to steer toward, and highlight only, aspects of his life and thoughts that dovetailed with the radical and anti-establishment ethos of instrumentalist history. This was clearly, as Peter Walker rightly observed (again, in a different context) an attempt "to resolve the problem of human unruliness ... by avoiding it."[19] Delany's authorized biographer, Frank (Frances)

Rollin set the tone by describing Delany as someone "who conformed to no conservatism for interest's sake nor compromises for the sake of party or expediency... His sentiments partaking of the most *uncompromising radicalism.*"[20] Rev. Theodore J. Holly of the Episcopal Church of Haiti portrayed Delany as "manly and independent," someone who "refused to play second fiddle to whites on issues relating to the black struggle . . . his devotion to his race was such that he would *not compromise with whites*, always preferring to 'be himself', alone in 'solitary grandeur' against republican radicalism, corruption, evincing foresight that enabled him anticipate the demise of reconstruction."[21]

Delany was therefore exalted as the ideological father of black radicalism, and his values and idiosyncrasies were magnified for adaptation. In other words, Delany became the exemplar of implacable militancy in the iconography of twentieth-century black resistance. However real, this militant persona was not Delany's one and only personality trait. Despite the existence of Bill McAdoo's critical and damning portrait of Delany's nationalist ideas published in 1966 and subsequent revisionist publications in the last decade and half about Delany's ambivalence and pragmatism, the ideological and instrumentalist portrait has remained dominant.[22] There appears to be both a reluctance and failure on the part of most modern scholars to acknowledge that Delany's life was not just one long chapter of indefatigable militancy, but a set of complex historical experiences and contexts that mirrored his ambivalent values and thoughts.

For more than two decades after the publication of Victor Ullman's and Dorothy Sterling's pioneering biographies of Delany and subsequent works by Floyd J. Miller and Cyril Griffith, black American historiography ignored the crises and contradictions of Delany's life and thoughts.[23] Few are willing to engage the phenomenon of "dualities" that Theodore Draper much earlier identified as crucial to understanding Delany's life and thoughts or even acknowledge the ambivalence Victor Ullman suggested when he described Delany as someone who could not be classified "with either the good guys or the bad guys." Delany seemed frozen in an ideological twilight zone: a one-dimensional, radical, anti-establishment character. Although there have been studies that highlight the complexities of Delany's life and thus raise questions about the instrumentalist genre, critics in both scholarly and popular discourses reject and delegitimize any interpretation or portraits of Delany other than the ideological and instrumentalist. Consequently, Delany has been, and remains, the victim of what the late Walter Rodney (in a different context) termed the "grand singular" narrative or discourse, a strictly ideological and binary discursive mode that is devoid of nuance.[24] He'd been compartmentalized and fitted with ideological straitjacket often by scholars who either have not taken time to study his life and writings, or have only sketchily read portions of his writings without an understanding of their historical contexts. Others simply relied on interpretations by so-called Delany scholars whose objective is to advance Delany as an ideological arsenal for twentieth-century Black Nationalist resistance. They invent and popularize a dehistoricized personality. The ambiguities and nuances of his life and thoughts are either deemphasized or jettisoned, reproducing, in the process, a distorted portrait. These "Delany scholars and experts" pontificate dogmatically about the instrumentalist and nationalist worldview while refusing to acknowledge anything about Delany that contradicted the ideological and nationalist worldviews they defended.

The Delany historiography is at a crossroads and has been for decades. Conflicting interpretations and genres compete for authentication. There are unresolved questions. Was Delany militant and uncompromising? Or, was he, like leading blacks of his times, pragmatic, utilitarian, accommodating, and at times conservative? Or, better still, could Delany have been a combination of some or all of the above attributes? In other words, did he manifest complex and conflicting dispositions (radical, conservative, ideologue, pragmatist, utilitarian, accommodating, and compromising)? How do we address these questions? One practical approach would be to afford Delany greater latitude for self-representation by bringing readers within earshot of his voice. In other words, the historical reconstruction of Delany must include giving readers unfiltered access to his writings and speeches. The objective here is to let Delany speak for himself, with little authorial intervention; to allow the reader full access to his ideas and writings, and a glimpse into the mind of this "other Delany"; and thus gain informed knowledge and understanding of the neglected and marginalized dualities and ambivalences of his life and thoughts. No medium has proven more effective in bringing subject and readers within communicative proximity, thus bridging decades, if not centuries, of historical time, space, and distance, than the documentary genre.

The availability of original papers and documents has tremendously enriched the historiographies of black leaders such as Frederick Douglass, Booker T. Washington, W. E. B. Du Bois, Henry McNeal Turner, Alexander Crummell, and many others.[25] These documentary anthologies provide direct and unrestricted insights into these leaders' minds and thought processes. A major challenge of the Delany historiography, however, has been assembling his scattered documents. Robert Levine has taken the lead in tacking this difficult task, and his published anthology is indeed welcome and long overdue.[26] That it took more than three decades after the publications of the first modern biographical studies of Delany in the early 1970s before his collection of documents was published underscores the difficulty associated with Delany's papers. Acquiring and publishing Delany's speeches and writings, scattered in libraries, archives, and private collections across the globe, is a daunting task. Another consideration was the devastating loss of hundreds of Delany papers in the fire that engulfed Wilberforce College in 1866. As a trustee, Delany maintained a personal library on the third floor, which was completely destroyed.[27]

The potency of the instrumentalist genre and its shortcomings compel "hearing" directly from Delany. Levine's anthology is a step in the right direction and a work of immense historiographical significance. For the first time, readers have access to Delany's own words and writings. This is important, given the dominant ideological context within which Delany has been constructed since the 1960s. A major shortcoming of the Levine anthology, however, is the sketchy and inadequate representation of the crucial Civil War and Reconstruction phase of Delany's life and struggles. While Levine's anthology satisfies a critical need, the poor representation of the Civil War and Reconstruction leaves a gaping hole. The few documents Levine selected for this period neither illuminate the complexities of Delany's ideas and activities nor reflect the depth of the crises that his advent into politics provoked in South Carolina. Also, the documents Levine presented are mostly brief excerpts, not full documents. This shortcoming, therefore, compromises understanding of both the complexities of Delany's ideas and his location within the ideological spectrums of black leadership in American history.

Regardless of how others viewed his actions, Delany perceived himself first and foremost as a laborer "in the cause of humanity." He underscored this universalistic character of his vision at crucial moments in both the antebellum and postbellum eras. First, in the vast majority of reports, letters, and commentaries he published in the *North Star* during his brief collaboration with Frederick Douglass (1847–49), Delany closed with "Yours for God and Humanity."[28] Second, in his 1871 landmark letter to Douglass in which he rendered a lengthy and damning review of Radical Reconstruction and what he characterized as its destructive impacts on Black America, he closed with "Your friend and co-laborer *in the cause of Humanity.*"[29] Delany's repeated construction of his struggles within the broader universalistic as opposed to a racialist purview was not coincidental. He was deliberate in opting to define himself within a "universalistic" frame at a time when, he felt, leading blacks were duped into embracing and endorsing racialized, culturally provincial, and divisive *Weltanschauung*. This is a portrait of Delany that some critics have yet to acknowledge. This universalism was most vividly demonstrated during his advent into politics in Reconstruction South Carolina.

Martin R. Delany's Civil War and Reconstruction, therefore, bridges a critical gap in the Delany historiography. It is imperative that readers have not only direct engagement with Delany's writings and speeches but also full and unrestricted access. Authorial interventions in the selection process in the form of either summarizing or downsizing of documents, as is the case with Levine's book, have been significantly responsible for the twin faults of misrepresentation and misunderstanding of Delany. Readers' understanding and constructions of Delany have thus far been compromised by such "disruptive" (for want of a better concept) selection process, which often compromised the opportunity to more directly and fully engage and understand Delany. To mitigate this, therefore, the documents in this study are presented in their entirety.

Another important aspect of this publication is the contextualization of Delany's ideas and speeches. Wherever possible, the documents are presented along with whatever critical responses and reactions they evoked and provoked among his contemporaries. Thus, it is not just Delany's writings and speeches that are presented here but also his contemporaries' responses. Juxtaposing Delany's writings and speeches with the reactions they provoked facilitates not only greater understanding of their full import and significance but also, and perhaps more importantly, appreciation of the magnitude of the power and influences Delany wielded. The documents underscore his political suaveness and the utilitarian, pragmatic, complex, and complicated nature of his political thought. Regardless of the ideological, primordial, or cosmopolitan values and idiosyncrasies one associates with Delany, there is a certain consistent and irrefutable attribute he embodied: Delany loved his race and was unashamedly proud of his African ancestry and heritage. Yet he loved America as well and was as deeply passionate about America as he was about Africa. In Martin Delany this double consciousness, though at times conflicted, was not necessarily irreconcilable. Being African and American reinforced each other. Both identities were fundamental to Delany's sense of being, to his existential fulfillment.

A primary objective of this documentary study is to help bring clarity to what I consider the existential problematic of the Delany historiography: Who was the real Martin Delany? Was the real Delany militant, anti-establishment, uncompromising, and perhaps even anti-white and anti-America? Or could the real Delany be the conservative, utilitarian, and pragmatist who reached across the racial divide and explored diverse political and social reform strategies? Will the real Martin Delany please rise? In essence, the central and still-unresolved challenge of the Delany historiography remains the inability to agree on the central defining attributes of the man. This is the challenge at the core of this collection of Martin Delany's Civil War and Reconstruction papers. To gain clarity and understanding of Delany and possibly resolve the existential problematic of the historiography, it is necessary to engage Delany's own writings and speeches directly. In other words, the reader needs to access Delany more directly through his speeches and writings, not through interpretations and filters provided by others. There are several intellectual benefits to reading Delany's speeches and "listening" to and "hearing" his voice, not the least of which is the acquisition of informed understanding of the dynamics of, and appreciation for, the dualities or ambivalences and contradictions of his life and thought. Delany was clear and unambiguous about his self-definition, the ideas and values he cherished, and his goals and visions for blacks and for America. One need only read his Civil War and Reconstruction writings and speeches to appreciate his complexities.

This study is divided into six chapters representing the key phases of Delany's Civil War and Reconstruction career. The documents in chapter 1 introduce readers to Delany's services as a recruiting agent and the first combat black major in the Union Army during the Civil War. They embody his visions, hopes, and aspirations for blacks in postslavery America. They offer glimpses into his patriotic fervor and leadership abilities. In chapter 2, the documents relate to Delany's next major assignment after the Civil War: as a Freedmen's Bureau sub-assistant commissioner in Hilton Head Island, South Carolina. Delany described in detail his views and opinions on what could and should be done to ensure that freedmen had the resources and opportunities to fully explore the meaning of freedom and the benefits of doing so. The documents also highlight some of the critical problems and challenges freedmen confronted, as well as Delany's strategic efforts and the solutions he proposed that enabled him to create a successful working relationship between freedmen and planters (former slaves and former slaveholders) in his bureau district, a feat that was not matched by bureau agents in other districts.

Documents in chapter 3 introduce readers to the intricacies of the first phase of Delany's entry into the politics of Reconstruction South Carolina. They elucidate, among others, Delany's political philosophy and visions, his conflicted and ambivalent views on black political rights, his controversial stand on the subject of social equality, his attempts to curtail black political aspirations, and his insistence that blacks attained some "pre-qualification" before aspiring for certain political positions. The documents also reveal the reactions and responses of contemporaries across the ideological spectrum (radicals and conservatives) to Delany's controversial and often provocative views on Radical Reconstruction, his scathing assessment of black political participation and performances in Reconstruction, his critique of Republicanism and its challenges, his unease and disillusionment with the Radical Republican Party in South Carolina, his relentless and scathing rebuke of what he characterized as the Party's corruptive and destructive influence on blacks. Finally, they reveal the reactions of the Republican Party and its black political allies to Delany's persistent calls for politics of moderation and compromise. Overall, the documents in this chapter underscore not only the conflicts Delany's ideas provoked with the ruling Radical Republicans but also the essential and underlying pragmatism of his thoughts. Delany explained the rationale for his advocacy of accommodation and compromise and persistent opposition to what he characterized as the destructive ideological and doctrinal rigidity of Radical Republicanism. The resultant political divergence and controversies became the grounds for Delany's decision to quit the Republican Party and join the Democratic Party (party of ex-slaveholders and ex-Confederates) in 1876.

The documents in chapter 4 shed further light on the dynamics of Delany's controversial views on social equality and racial reconciliation, his prescriptions and strategies for attaining justice and equity, the shortcomings and failures of Radical Republicanism, the pitfalls of the Black–Radical Republican Party alliance, and further reactions of ideological opponents to his ideas. The documents also expound on the circumstances leading to Delany's brief alliance with South Carolina conservatives, independents, and ex-Confederates in an abortive attempt to wrench political power from the Radical Republicans and turn Reconstruction along a more reconciliatory and moderate course. Known as the Independent Republican Movement (IRM), this alliance between Delany and South Carolina conservatives and ex-Confederates exemplified the duality and ambivalence Theodore Draper and Victor Ullman both drew attention to, as well as the compromise August Meier identified as a defining attribute of nineteenth-century black leadership. Equally significant, the IRM also underscored the utilitarian and conflicted nature of Delany's political thought.

In chapter 5, the documents elucidate the crises of Delany's conservatism. Here, Delany provided detailed explanations for his persecution by, and ultimately alienation from, the Radical Republicans. He emphasized the political nature of the persecution and elaborated on the circumstances leading to it and to his trial and conviction for grand larceny. The documents also include the commentaries and reaction of contemporaries to Delany's predicament. Overall, this chapter illuminates the challenges Delany confronted, especially the desperate and difficult political and socioeconomic retributions he experienced during the closing years of Reconstruction. The documents in this chapter also engage the reader more intimately with the dynamics of Delany's political conservatism, as well as the political and socioeconomic ramifications. Delany offered readers explanations for the grand larceny charge and subsequent trial and conviction. He portrayed the entire episode as politically instigated in retaliation for his conservative ideas and persistent opposition to Radical Republicanism. What is particularly revealing in this chapter is Delany's introduction of the outline of ten "offenses" he alleged Radical

Republicans had charged him with, which served as justifications for the grand larceny prosecution. Undoubtedly, Delany wanted to publicize these offenses in order to expose the political and vindictive nature of the episode and thus generate public sympathy for his predicament.

The documents in chapter 6 address the underpinnings of Delany's growing frustration with Radical Republican rule in South Carolina and his momentous decision to switch to the Democratic Party in the epochal election of 1876. In some of the documents, Delany explained the circumstances of his decision to switch Party allegiance and the political and economic costs and consequences. Furthermore, in his correspondence with officials of the American Colonization Society, Delany summarized the negative and vindictive reactions his political conservatism provoked, and the new direction he envisioned in the aftermath of the failure of his political aspirations: emigration and renewed quest for the Black/African nationality.

Overall, this documentary study embodies the complexities, trials, and tribulations of Delany's postbellum career. The book takes readers through the major phases and transitions of that career: his time as black major, sub-assistant commissioner of the Freedmen's Bureau, conservative Republican, and independent Republican, his trial and conviction; his transition to a new departurist Democrat, and finally back to his stance on emigration and Black Nationalism.

II

Martin Delany was a free black, the youngest of seven children born to Samuel and Pati Delany on May 6, 1812, in Charlestown, Virginia (now in West Virginia). Situated on the valley of the Shenandoah River, Charlestown had fewer than a thousand inhabitants when Delany was born. Delany inherited his free status from his mother, who was free. Under Virginian law, mothers passed their status on to their children. Like most free blacks, however, freedom did not confer any special rights or privileges. Consequently, Delany's childhood experiences mirrored the ugly and dehumanizing realities of slavery and racism. From the start he encountered a hostile world and acquired firsthand knowledge of slavery through the experiences of his slave father, Samuel. His grandparents were also slaves. His maternal grandparents, Shango and his wife, Graci, had been captured in Africa sometime in the late eighteenth century and transported across the Atlantic. They were finally sold to a planter near Richmond, Virginia. In fact, the society into which Delany was born and raised mirrored the broader contradiction or paradox of American democracy. Jeffersonian Virginia nurtured contradictory and potentially explosive experiences. On the one hand, there was the leisurely, affluent, and elegant lifestyle of the aristocratic ruling class and slave owners. At the other extreme were the dull, poverty-stricken, and dehumanizing experiences of blacks. One authority described the Shenandoah in the early nineteenth century as an agreeable and hospital environment that fulfilled the hopes and aspirations of the early Germans, Scots-Irish, and English immigrants. For these settlers, many of whom, like the Scots-Irish, had escaped persecution elsewhere, the Shenandoah was indeed a promised land.[30] For blacks, however, slave and free alike, the Shenandoah was anything but idyllic.

The early settlers supposedly dispensed with slavery. This would change with the arrival of English migrants in the second half of the eighteenth century.[31] There is still disagreement on the experiences of these early slaves. Soon, however, with the increase in slave population, slavery assumed its distinctive and *peculiar* character. Slaves were poorly fed and clothed, brutalized, and dehumanized. Such inhumane practices as burning, maiming, and whipping were common. Free blacks, on the other hand, had to contend with the emptiness and fragility of freedom. They were denied all the vestiges of American citizenship, including the right to vote and access to education. These free blacks held desperately and precariously to a fragile freedom that was very often revoked through reenslavement.[32] Delany's parents were soon compelled to flee Virginia for the relative safety of Chambersburg, Pennsylvania. But Chambersburg was no haven, and the persistence of racism and discrimination only reinforced Delany's growing unease and indignation. In July of 1831, at the age of nineteen, and determined to resist and overcome the debilitating weight of oppression and discrimination, Delany left his parents and headed for Pittsburgh.[33] This decision reflected both his growing maturity and his inner determination to become more actively involved in the emerging black abolitionist movement.

By the early nineteenth century, Pennsylvania was fast becoming the seedbed of black abolitionism. The liberal atmosphere and reputation of Pennsylvania had attracted black migrants from other parts of the country. Pittsburgh had in fact become a metropolis of the black struggle, where migrants who were escaping oppressive conditions elsewhere had congregated for years. When Delany arrived, therefore, there was already a nucleus of black abolitionism in formation. These blacks were drawn together by a determination to forge concerted efforts toward meaningful freedom and equality. They had created miniature structures and institutions for self-improvement and cooperative development. Delany also arrived at a momentous time, when blacks were agitated and invigorated by the abortive Nat Turner insurrection in Southampton, Virginia. Although it failed, the episode assumed mythic proportion among blacks. Delany began his education at the African Methodist

Episcopal Church Cellar school organized by "Daddy Ben" Richards, a wealthy realtor and butcher, and Reverend Lewis Woodson, a fugitive from Virginia.[34] Although Delany met other notable and influential blacks, two individuals profoundly shaped his ideological outlook: Woodson and William Whipper. Whipper was a native Pennsylvanian from Little Britain in Lancaster County. Both men discussed and explained moral suasion ideas and values in black newspapers and soon became the leading philosophical advocates of the ideology of moral suasion that shaped black abolitionism for the first half of the nineteenth century.[35] Delany quickly immersed himself in the struggles and, according to his authorized biographer, registered his vow against the enemies and oppressors of his race.[36]

Since Delany's formative years and ideological mentoring and development coincided with the first phase of the Negro National Convention Movement that emerged in Pennsylvania in the early 1830s, his role in these early conventions was minimal. However, within a few years, he rose to become a leading advocate and crusader for moral suasion. Delany arrived Pittsburgh in 1831 and immediately embraced the bourgeoning antislavery and reform activities, especially the struggle for blacks to gain unrestricted access to education. His efforts resulted in the creation of the African Education Society of Pittsburgh. Delany also helped found the Theban Literary Society for improvement in the literary and intellectual endeavors of blacks. By 1834, less than five years after he arrived, Delany became active member of the Pittsburgh moral suasion reform efforts, a secretary of the Temperance Society of the People of Color of Pittsburgh, and a founding member of the Young Men's Moral Reform Society of Pittsburgh.

These reform initiatives among blacks in Pittsburgh and other parts of Pennsylvania in the 1830s were extensions of a growing national movement. The black church, the black press, and the convention movement became institutions and signifiers of organized black abolitionism in the early 1800s. These were crucial avenues (albeit conflicted and ambivalent with respect to the church) for the dissemination of antislavery and moral suasion ideas.[37] In 1787 in Philadelphia, Reverends Richard Allen and Absalom Jones and a few other blacks withdrew from the Saint George's Methodist Episcopal Church in protest of the established practice of confining blacks to segregated pews during worship. Subsequently, Allen and Jones founded the Free African Society, which became a precursor to the African Methodist Episcopal Church. The founding of the AME Church birthed the independent black church movement, which spread to other states.[38] In 1827 John Russwurm, a Jamaican immigrant and graduate of Bowdoin College, founded the first black newspaper, *Freedom's Journal*. He believed that blacks needed to be heard and should be more actively involved in articulating their interests and needs. As Russwurm underscored in the inaugural issue of the paper, "We wish to plead our cause. Too long have others spoken for us. Too long has the publick been deceived by misrepresentations, in things which concern us dearly." Black abolitionists generally agreed on the need for a strong newspaper to articulate black interest and disseminate ideas and values that would advance black community efforts at self-improvement. Other black newspapers soon followed, including the *Colored American* and the *North Star*.[39]

The call for black unity in the face of mounting anti-black violence that reached a frightening proportion in Cincinnati, Ohio, in 1829 birthed the convention movement. Helmed in by restrictive and discriminatory laws and besieged by racial violence, free blacks finally decided to launch the convention movement as an organizational framework for proactive and concerted efforts.[40] By 1834 they had adopted moral suasion as a guiding philosophy. Moral suasion reflected blacks' faith in the Protestant work ethic and the promises of the American Dream. Moral suasion derived from the premise that through industry, economy, education, and moral improvements, blacks would ultimately convince whites to concede genuine freedom and equality.[41] By subscribing to moral suasion, blacks somehow seemed to acknowledge and validate the pro-slavery contention that race had nothing to do with the negative and dehumanizing experiences blacks were subjected to. According to this reasoning, blacks were subordinated and denied equality not because of their race but due largely to their wretched condition. Presumably, improving the condition would eradicate discrimination. Motivated by moral suasion, blacks embarked upon the early convention movement, focusing on efforts that would enhance their social, economic, educational, and moral developments.

Delany's active involvement in abolitionist activities began in 1843. Two key developments underscored both his growing maturity and commitment to the black struggle. The first was his marriage in 1843 to Catherine A. Richards, the mulatto daughter of Charles Richards and granddaughter of the wealthy realtor and butcher Ben Richards. This union secured for Delany a connection to the economic elite of black Pittsburgh.[42] He and Catherine had eleven children, seven of whom survived. Second, that same year, perhaps in response to John Russwurm's call for blacks to "plead our cause," Delany began publishing his own newspaper, the *Pittsburgh Mystery*, giving clear indication that he understood and appreciated the power of the media and its potential as a tool in the abolitionist struggle.[43] Subscription sold for $1.50 annually, and more than a thousand initial copies sold in Pittsburgh alone. Delany had agents in towns and cities in Pennsylvania, Ohio, Indiana, Massachusetts, New York, Virginia, Iowa, and Illinois.[44] During its brief existence, the *Mystery* lit the fires of antislavery and kept the flames alive and burning with its scathing editorials and criticisms of slavery. Despite its short lifespan, the paper profoundly impacted the antislavery cause and garnered accolades and commendations from the black community. At a meeting in Shiloh Baptist Church in Philadelphia in July 1846, delegates acknowledged the *Mystery* as "a powerful instrument in effecting the social and political disenthralment and elevation of blacks."[45] In Pittsburgh the black community rallied around the paper. Each winter ladies held fundraising soirees, and in the summer they organized picnics and festivals, with the proceeds going to the *Mystery*. Praises for the paper also came from the White press. Papers such as the *Pennsylvania Freeman*, the *Chronicle*, and *the Annual Business Directory* acknowledged Delany's ability and the noble deeds of his paper for the black community.[46] In 1847 the African Methodist Episcopal Church bought the paper and renamed it the *Christian Herald*. In 1852 the paper's operations were moved to Philadelphia, and it was renamed the *Christian Recorder*.[47]

In 1847 Frederick Douglass visited Pittsburgh and solicited Delany's services to help start, coedit, and lecture for the *North Star*. Delany agreed, and thus his career took on a much more expansive scope. He relocated to Rochester, New York, and spent the next two years as a roving lecturer, propagating antislavery and moral suasion ideas to free black communities in the West, Midwest, and North. His tours brought him face-to-face with some of the critical problems and challenges of blacks which he highlighted in his periodic reports in the *North Star*.[48] His moral suasionist crusade entailed exposing the evils of slavery and educating blacks on strategies for self-improvement, education, and moral reform.

Delany was bitterly critical of slavery and discrimination in his antislavery meetings and lectures. His lectures highlighted strategies for social, economic, and moral improvements. He was convinced that the more blacks improved themselves, the more likely it was that white society would concede their rights and privileges. His activities, however, provoked conflicting reactions both within black communities and among whites. Many blacks appreciated and commended his efforts. Others, particularly within the religious community, objected strongly to the this-worldly emphasis of his antislavery activities.[49] Among whites, Delany earned some support and sympathy but also strong opposition, even hostility. But he would not be deterred. He developed a reputation as a conscientious black leader focused on the advancement of his race.

By the late 1840s, it was clear that moral suasion was not sufficient to change white society's view of blacks. Although Delany discovered ample evidence of black industry, self-development, and moral improvement, the dominant society responded negatively and violently. In fact, Philadelphia in the 1840s has been referred to as the race riot capital of the country. Industrious and economically successful blacks and institutional manifestations of black industry and progress such as churches and cooperative and fraternal societies became targets of racial violence.[50] This reality and subsequent political developments in the early 1850s, specifically the Compromise of 1850 and the Fugitive Slave Act, convinced Delany of the depth and pervasiveness of racism. These developments undermined his faith in moral suasion and the malleability of American society.[51] But Delany was not alone in reaching this conclusion. There was a growing concern among blacks in the late 1840s that no amount of moral reform would change America. As the "Colored Citizens" of Pennsylvania underlined in their 1848 "Appeal" to the Commonwealth,

> The barrier that deprives us of the rights which you enjoy finds no palliative in merit—no consolation in piety—no hope in intellectual and moral pursuits—no reward in industry and enterprise . . . we may exhaust our midnight lamps in the prosecution of study, and be denied the privileges of the forum—we may be embellishing the nation's literature by our pursuits in science—the preceptors of a Newton in astronomy—the dictators of Philosophy to Locke or a Bacon—the masters of a Montesquieu or a Blackstone on Civil and international law—or could we equal the founder of Christianity in the purity of our lives . . . yet with all these exalted virtues we could not possess the privileges you enjoy in Pennsylvania, because we are not "white."[52]

Delany fully concurred. With the apparent failure of moral suasion and what he discerned as a pervasive and seemingly indestructible culture of racism, he gave up on the country and began to advocate emigration. For other blacks, however (including such prominent figures as Frederick Douglass), the best strategic response called for intensified integrative initiatives and efforts. With the passage of the Fugitive Slave Act in 1850, Delany assumed leadership of the emigration movement. He became convinced that America was irredeemably racist and that blacks would never secure justice. He embarked upon a course that soon became the defining essence of his life and struggles: emigration.[53] Delany saw no viable alternative to an externally situated and independent black nationality. Due to his emigration ideas and activities, Delany quickly developed an enduring reputation as a separatist.

Delany expatiated his emigration and nationalist arguments in two key publications: *The Condition, Elevation, Emigration, and Destiny of the Colored People of the United States* (1852) and "Political Destiny of the Colored Race on the American Continent" (1854). In these publications, he addressed the anguish, disappointments, and frustrations of blacks who had become disillusioned and were desperately searching for an alternative nationality.[54] In 1854 Delany helped convene and organize a National Emigration Convention in Cleveland, Ohio. Delegates from different parts of the country assembled to brainstorm on the challenges confronting blacks and discuss prospects for emigration. It was before this gathering that Delany delivered his four-hour address titled "Political Destiny," in which he argued passionately and fervently for an independent black nationality. The convention set up a National Board of Commissioners to function as a coordinating body, with subcommittees on foreign, financial, and domestic relations. Delany was appointed the board's first president, in which capacity he began corresponding with foreign governments in Central and South America. In two subsequent presidential reports, Delany reaffirmed the imperative of emigration. He discerned a nationwide consensus on black inferiority, and on the basis of that consensus he predicted the imminent nationalization of slavery. He opined that slavery would cease to be sectional. All political indicators, he believed (referencing the Fugitive Slave Act), portended this gloomy future for blacks. Emigration was the path to a viable future.[55]

In 1856 Delany moved to Chatham, Canada West. Two years later, under the auspices of the National Board of Commissioners, he embarked upon an investigatory and exploratory journey to Africa. He traveled extensively in the Niger Valley of West Africa, visiting such countries as Liberia and Nigeria, to investigate prospects for the projected black nationality. He discovered a hospitable and welcoming environment and people. Africa, he quickly concluded, possessed all the requisites for a black nationality in the forms of abundant land, resources, and manpower.[56] He was highly impressed and elated. He returned to the United States late in 1860; his emigration convictions strengthened and reinforced. Delany publicly declared his determination to relocate to Africa and launched a nationwide lecture to publicize his findings and galvanize support for emigration.[57] But the seductive force of the gathering storms of the Civil War proved irresistible and compelling. Like other leading blacks, Delany could not ignore the fact that slavery had become a divisive force among whites. The prospect for genuine freedom and equality for blacks had never seemed brighter. Given this development, emigration now seemed ill-advised. Delany promptly abandoned emigration and joined Frederick Douglass, Henry H. Garnet, and other black leaders in pursuit of integration. He thrust himself to the forefront, urging blacks to embrace the Civil War as the path to genuine freedom and equality.

The Civil War became for Delany and other black leaders a means to the elusive American Dream. The war marked a turning point in Delany's career. It transformed him from a pessimist who had once lost all hope in the malleability of America to an optimist whose enthusiasm and faith in America's future seemed boundless. The war, in fact, inaugurated arguably the most significant and accomplished phase of his public life. As had Douglass and Garnet, Delany sought and secured an audience with President Abraham Lincoln, during which he argued fervently for black enlistment and for the adoption of emancipation as a war strategy. He insisted that such a policy would result in a speedy defeat of the rebellion. In recognition of Delany's efforts, Lincoln recommended his commissioning into the Union Army as the first black combat major. Delany gladly accepted the honor and moved his family from Canada to the United States, settling his wife, Catherine, and the children in Xenia, Ohio. He became actively engaged in recruiting several Colored regiments, including the Fifty-Fourth Massachusetts Regiment, the Rhode Island Heavy Artillery, and the 104th and 105th US Colored Troops. In his recruitment posters, Delany urged blacks to enlist, once again demonstrate their patriotism and loyalty to the nation, and contribute to securing their long-elusive freedom.[58]

Delany's combat abilities were never tested because the Civil War ended shortly after his commissioning. In fact, his military service lasted less than six months. After the war, he was assigned to the newly established Freedmen's Bureau as sub-assistant commissioner and posted to Hilton Head, South Carolina, where he was charged with the supervision and management of twenty-one government owned plantations that were acquired back in 1863 when they were auctioned for nonpayment of US direct tax. He was also responsible for the welfare of the freedmen on the plantations, overseeing issues such as health, education, labor, contracts, and productive activities.[59] Delany served as a Freedmen's Bureau agent from 1865 to the demise of the institution in 1868. His performance as bureau agent was most exemplary, considering the comments and commendations of his peers and superior officers. After the termination of his bureau agency, Delany became actively involved in politics in South Carolina.

Delany's political activities in South Carolina bore the imprints of the paradox of his earlier career, resulting in some of the greatest political challenges and trials of his life. As did most other blacks, he began his political career within the Republican Party: the party of Abraham Lincoln, the emancipator! But his loyalty to the party was not unconditional and absolute. Delany adduced a utilitarian conception of politics that tied political loyalty and affiliation to utilitarian factors, as opposed to ideological, doctrinal, or racial considerations. As he once declared, "Politics are intended for the benefit of the people."[60] Political loyalty, he insinuated, should be determined by the degree to which a party satisfied the needs of its membership for sustenance and survival.[61] In Delany's judgment, regardless of ideological or racial considerations, a party that failed to provide its members access to the means of sustenance and proved incapable of guaranteeing their physical and economic survival did not deserve their unswerving loyalty. With this conviction, Delany constantly challenged what he saw as the corrupt, exploitative, and divisive policies of the ruling Republican Party.

Delany introduced into South Carolina politics a pragmatism that complicated what he characterized as the ideologically and racially driven platform and politics of the Republican Party and its black leadership supporters. He believed that the reforms of the Civil War and early Reconstruction era had fundamentally transformed American society. The Thirteenth Amendment had abolished slavery. The Fourteenth and Fifteenth Amendments had granted blacks citizenship and equal protection of the law, and the franchise, respectively. Delany concluded that these changes, along with other Reconstruction reforms, had significantly revolutionized race relations by integrating blacks into the mainstream and transforming them from marginalized and subordinated to "an integral and essential part of the ruling elements of the nation."[62] What was most urgently needed, he stressed, was a reciprocal policy of reconciliation and appeasement toward the defeated and bitter southern whites (ex-slaveholders). To accomplish this, Delany urged the Republican Party to grant unconditional pardon and amnesty to former rebels and implored blacks also to seek the friendship and goodwill of southern whites.[63]

In fact, had death struck Delany in 1868, he most certainly would have died a happy man. After all, just under a decade and half before, he had predicted the imminent nationalization of slavery and had given up all hope, condemning America as irredeemably racist. These national concessions to black demands convinced Delany of the necessity for reciprocal concessions on the part of blacks, concessions that he defined in terms of political conservatism and appeasement of southern whites. For Delany, Reconstruction politics called essentially for a policy that would reconcile blacks with their erstwhile masters, who still controlled the economic levers of the state. Instead of reconciliation, Delany lamented that Radical Reconstruction had propelled blacks on a confrontational course by focusing on and encouraging black political rights and power. Radical Reconstruction was, in his view, a misguided and misdirected program. Delany believed that to empower blacks politically would alienate them from the state conservatives, whose goodwill and support were indispensable to blacks' gaining access to the more critical economic resources and power.

Delany therefore proposed a pragmatic approach which entailed surrender of political power to whites in return for concessions of economic benefit. At a time when South Carolina conservatives were politically weakened, humbled, and in desperate search for a political power base, Delany's ideas offered them a much-needed existential corroboration and validation. It was reassuring for South Carolina conservatives to hear such ideas voiced by a black man! Thus, Delany gave conservatism a voice and respectability that had been both subdued and discredited by Radical Reconstruction. His ideas gave conservatism poignancy, substance, and credibility, at least in the judgment of Democrats and ex-Confederate defenders of the old order. Enthused and energized, they responded by trumpeting and referencing Delany's ideas to corroborate their discredited and racist worldview. Delany would soon become a major force in the political rejuvenation of the conservative movement in South Carolina. Needless to say, the Republican Party and other black leaders rejected Delany's policy of appeasement.

Delany's persistent opposition to Radical Reconstruction alienated many within the Republican Party. Radical Republicans (black and white) became deeply suspicious of his motives, as his ideas reflected more the conservative themes of the erstwhile slave owners and the Democratic Party. He soon attained a pariah status within the Republican Party, and by the mid-1870s, his membership in the party had become untenable. Despised and distrusted, Delany found himself denied access to positions of political responsibility. Unlike other blacks who held positions of power, influence, and responsibility and, therefore, had access to the spoils of office, Delany was largely confined to the status of an outside agitator. In 1874 he joined a coalition of conservatives, ex-Confederates, and "liberal" Republicans to launch the Independent Republican Movement aimed at toppling Radical Republicans from political power and redirecting state politics along a conciliatory and conservative course. The IRM challenge however failed as the Radical Republicans won the election.[64] The movement fizzled shortly after the election, and with no viable political base, Delany had no choice but to return, like the biblical prodigal son, to the fold of a party he had rejected and disparaged: the Republican Party.

His relationship with the Republican Party remained strained and fragile. However, one unanticipated occurrence was Republican governor Daniel Chamberlain's appointment of Delany as trial justice for Ward 3 of the City of Charleston.[65] As counterintuitive as it seemed, Chamberlain's decision was consistent with his campaign pledge to fight corruption by appointing to office only those he deemed honest and efficient. Delany's appointment, however, did not receive the blessing of Radical Republican stalwarts, who had grown bitterly resentful of his conservative ideas and strategies. Neither did the appointment mellow Delany. He remained adamantly and bitterly critical of and opposed to black political power. He accused black politicians of ignorance and corruption. In the ensuing 1875 municipal election in Charleston, Delany vigorously opposed a proposal to field a black candidate for mayor because, according to him, the corruption and excesses of black politicians statewide had tainted and tarnished the reputation of South Carolina. He urged Charlestonians to continue their tradition of white mayors and campaigned vigorously against radical candidates.[66] Delany's anti-radical tirades and activities created such a deep resentment within the Republican Party that he began to anticipate retaliatory conspiracy. In 1875 this conspiracy came in the form of a grand larceny lawsuit. He went through a trial that he characterized as a charade contrived primarily to punish him for his persistent opposition to radical policies. He was found guilty and sentenced to twelve months in the penitentiary. Pending decision on his appeal, Delany was set free but relieved of his trial justice post.[67]

Although Chamberlain eventually pardoned Delany, the trial and conviction irreversibly tarnished his reputation. He remained essentially alienated and isolated from the orbit of political power and felt victimized and constantly dodged by radical conspirators, whom he accused of attempting to impose the ultimate punishment upon him: death. As he reported to his friend Frederick Douglass, "Crush me to earth, they were determined upon, and all because I could not be used, was above their influence, and would as I ever shall, oppose dishonesty, corruption and imposition upon the people's rights."[68] Continued membership in the Republican Party therefore seemed once again untenable. By 1876 Delany had formally declared for the Democratic Party and assumed a pivotal role in the political resurgence of the party.[69] The conservative media hailed this development and quickly absorbed Delany into its campaign apparatus. The Democrats had adopted a "liberal" platform that included a pledge to respect the political rights of blacks and to protect them in the exercise of those rights. This was certainly not the old antebellum proslavery party! Or was it?

Delany stormed the campaign trail on behalf of the Democrats and their gubernatorial candidate, Wade Hampton. There was a familiar ring to his campaign speeches. He urged blacks to abandon the Republican Party and seek reconciliation with their former slave masters. Delany opined that the Democratic Party platform offered everything blacks demanded. Consequently, he advocated giving the Democrats a chance. He was convinced that Democrats had changed and would uphold the liberal promises of their platform. He accused Radical Republicans of exploiting blacks to advance their narrow political agenda. He insisted that the platform of the Democratic Party held greater prospect for the economic development and empowerment of blacks.[70] His campaign activities and speeches further infuriated and alienated blacks. Many wondered if this was the same Delany of the antebellum era who had inspired fear in whites and the proslavery establishment, if this was indeed the same individual who once unfurled the banner of militant Black Nationalism and separatism. Blacks reacted with frustration and anger, resulting in a violent and deadly attack that left six whites dead and one black injured at a campaign rally in Cainhoy, South Carolina, in October 1876. Delany narrowly escaped death.[71] Democrats won the epochal 1876 election, effectively terminating Radical Reconstruction, and restored the ancien régime to political power in South Carolina. Would the Democrats keep their campaign promise and pledge? Or would their return to political power portend reversal and circumscription of black political and civil rights?

Delany's precise role in and contributions to the restoration of Democratic Party rule in South Carolina remain the subject of speculation. Whatever the case, Delany undoubtedly benefited from the Democratic victory. He was among a few notable black Democrats that Governor Wade Hampton rewarded with political appointments after the election: he was restored to his trial justice post in Charleston.[72] Unfortunately, Delany's rapprochement with the state conservatives was short-lived. The romance lost its steam just as quickly as it had begun. It became clear that the Democrats had not been sincere in their liberal promises. It dawned on many that the "liberal" platform of the Democrats was just a campaign ploy and that they never intended to respect the political rights of blacks. Under pressure from the triumphant ultraconservative wing of the party, Hampton soon relieved Delany of his trial justice post.[73] The ultraconservatives, or Redeemers as they fondly called themselves, unleashed a reign of terror on blacks, especially prominent and ambitious blacks whose actions seemed to be challenging, directly or indirectly, the status quo of white supremacy.[74]

Betrayed by the Democrats and distrusted by the Republicans, Delany seemed caught between the devil and the deep blue sea. For a brief period he donned his old emigration robes and became actively involved in the new Liberian exodus movement that developed among blacks in South Carolina.[75] His emigration aspirations reignited, by the early 1880s Delany began corresponding with key officials of the American Colonization Society, soliciting their assistance for emigration.[76] There are no indications that he received any tangible supports from the society. This latter phase of his nationality dream quickly fizzled. Broken, frustrated, chronically unemployed, helpless, and shadowed by what he termed "the chicanery of wily politicians" determined to destroy him due to his anti-radical political views, Delany turned to the one and only place left where he felt he could receive the comfort, consolation, and reassurance he so desperately needed: Xenia, Ohio, his wife Catherine, and the children. Unfortunately, the struggles had been both emotionally and physically taxing. According to a local Xenia newspaper, the Delany that returned in late 1884 was emotionally and psychologically a broken man.[77] He died on January 24, 1885.

Notes

1. August Meier, "Afterword: New Perspectives on the Nature of Black Political Leadership during Reconstruction," in Rabinowitz, *Southern Black Leaders of the Reconstruction Era*, 393–406.
2. Ullman, *Martin R. Delany*, ix.
3. *North Star*, June 16, 1848, emphasis added.
4. *North Star*, June 2, 1848.
5. Rollin, *Life and Public Services*, 19.
6. Payne, *Recollections of Seventy Years*, 160–61.
7. *Liberator*, May 7, 1852.
8. Nelson T. Grant to F. L. LeMoyne, June 4, 1847, Margaret C. McCulloch Papers, 1822–1875, box 4, folder 2, Amistad Research Center, Tulane University, New Orleans, Louisiana.
9. William H. Burleigh to F. L. LeMoyne, June 29, 1841, McCulloch Papers.
10. William M. Shim to Rev. Geo. Whipper, June 26, 1858, American Missionary Association Papers, Amistad Research Center, Tulane University, New Orleans, Louisiana.
11. Edward M. Stoeber to Brevt. Major S. M. Taylor, July 28, 1865, Record Group 105, Letters Received, Assistant Commissioner, South Carolina, National Archives and Records Administration, Washington, DC.
12. *News and Courier* (Charleston), October 5, 1874.
13. *News and Courier* (Charleston), October 24, 1874.
14. Theodore Draper, "The Father of Black American Nationalism," *New York Times Review of Books*, March 12, 1970. See also his *The Rediscovery of Black Nationalism*.
15. Litwack and Meier, *Black Leaders*; and Rabinowitz, *Southern Black Leaders*.
16. Meier, "Afterword," 402.
17. Harding, "Beyond Chaos"; Stuckey, "Twilight of Our Past"; Harding, *There Is a River*.
18. Peter Walker, *Moral Choices: Memory, Desire and Imagination in Nineteenth Century American Abolitionism* (Baton Rouge: Louisiana State University Press, 1978).
19. Walker, 222. This practice is also reflected in some of the early biographies of Frederick Douglass. See Foner, *Frederick Douglass*; and Benjamin Quarles, *Frederick Douglass* (New York: Atheneum, 1967).
20. Rollin, *Life and Public Services*, 23, emphasis added.
21. Holly, "In Memoriam," 119–20, emphasis added.
22. McAdoo, "Pre-Civil War Black Nationalism." See also his full-length study *Pre-Civil War Black Nationalism*.
23. Ullman, *Martin R. Delany*; Sterling, *Making of an Afro-American*; Miller, *Search for a Black Nationality*; Griffith, *African Dream*.
24. Hill, *Walter Rodney Speaks*, 69.
25. Foner, *Life and Writings of Frederick Douglass*; Washington, *Booker T. Washington Papers*; Du Bois, *W. E. B. Du Bois Reader*; Sundquist, *Oxford W. E. B. Du Bois Reader*; Crummell, *Africa and America*; Crummell, *Future of Africa*; Redkey, *Respect Black*; Johnson, *Forgotten Prophet*.
26. Levine, *Martin R. Delany: A Documentary Reader*.
27. Sterling, *Making of an Afro-American*, 251.
28. See these reports in *North Star*, March 3, April 14, May 26, April 7 and 28, June 9, June 16, August 4, 1848, and February 16, June 15, July 6, 1849.
29. Martin R. Delany, "A Political Review," *Daily Republican* (Charleston), August 15, 1871, emphasis added.
30. Davis, *Shenandoah*.

31. Davis.
32. Bushong, *History of Jefferson County*.
33. Sterling, *Making of an Afro-American*, 33–34; Rollin, *Life and Public Services*, 37–38.
34. Rollin, *Life and Public Services*, 38–42.
35. Adeleke, "Afro-Americans and Moral Suasion"; McCormick, "William Whipper"; Bell, "American Moral Reform Society."
36. Rollin, *Life and Public Services*, 40.
37. Reed, *Platform for Change*.
38. Lincoln and Mamiya, *Black Church*, 20–76; Mitchell, *Black Church Beginnings*, 46–71.
39. Dann, *Black Press*, 34, 11–30.
40. Bell, *Survey of the Negro Convention Movement*; Pease and Pease, "Negro Convention Movement," 191–205.
41. Bell, "American Moral Reform Society"; McCormick, "William Whipper," 23–46.
42. Rollin, *Life and Public Services*, 28.
43. Dann, *Black Press*, 34.
44. Sterling, *Making of an Afro-American*, 82; Ullman, *Martin R. Delany*, 49.
45. *Pennsylvania Freeman*, August 20, 1846, 3.
46. Sterling, *Making of an Afro-American*, 82–83.
47. See "Introduction," in *Christian Recorder* (microfilm), Mother Bethel African Methodist Episcopal Church Prints, July 13, 1854–June 29, 1865, Garrett-Evangelical Theological Seminary Library, Evanston, IL.
48. See these reports in *North Star*, March 3, April 14, May 26, April 7, 28, June 9, June 16, August 4, 1848, and February 16, June 15, July 6, 1849.
49. Adeleke, "Religion in Martin R. Delany's Liberation Thought."
50. Simmons, "Ideologies and Programs," chapter 1. See also Elizabeth Geffen, "Violence in Philadelphia."
51. Martin R. Delany, "National Disfranchisement of Colored People," in his *Condition, Elevation, Emigration, and Destiny*, 147–58.
52. "Minutes of the State Convention of the Colored Citizens of Pennsylvania Convened At Harrisburg, December 13th and 14th, 1848," in *Proceedings of the Black State Conventions, 1840–1865*, vol. 1, ed. Philip S. Foner and George E. Walker (Philadelphia: Temple University Press, 1979), 124.
53. Miller, *Search for a Black Nationality*; Griffith, *African Dream*.
54. Delany, *Condition, Elevation, Emigration, and Destiny*. See also his "Political Destiny of the Colored Race on the American Continent," in Rollin, *Life and Public Services*, 327–67.
55. Martin R. Delany, "Political Aspect of the Colored People in the United States," *Provincial Freeman*, October 13, 1855; Martin R. Delany, "Political Events," *Provincial Freeman*, July 5, 1856.
56. Delany, *Official Report of the Niger Valley Exploring Party*.
57. S. N. Geers, "Brooklyn Affairs," *Weekly Anglo-African*, November 2, 1861; "Dr. M. R. Delany," *Douglass' Monthly*, August 1862; Delany, "Moral and Social Aspect."
58. Rollin, *Life and Public Services*, chapters 18, 19, 25.
59. Rollin, chapter 28; Martin, *"Dear Sister,"* 43, 101; Elizabeth A. Summers (1844–1900) 11, mss., 24 April–15 June 1867, South Caroliniana Research Library, University of South Carolina, Columbia.
60. *News and Courier* (Charleston), October 16, 1874.
61. *Daily Republican* (Charleston), July 5, 1870, July 15, 1870; *News and Courier* (Charleston), October 7, 1874.
62. Martin Delany to Rev. Henry H. Garnet, Hilton Head Island, July 27, 1867, in Delany, *Trial and Conviction*, 4–5.

63. Delany, *Trial and Conviction*, 9.

64. Simkins and Woody, *South Carolina during Reconstruction*, 470–73.

65. Ullman, *Martin R. Delany*, 465.

66. Martin Delany, "Seventh Offense," in his *Trial and Conviction*, 10.

67. Delany, 15–16; *News and Courier (Charleston)*, March 23, 1876, 2.

68. Delany, *Trial and Conviction*, 10.

69. Ullman, *Martin R. Delany*, 477.

70. *Daily Register* (Columbia), September 28, 1876; *News and Courier* (Charleston), September 19, 1876, 4; October 4, 1876, 4; October 13, 1876, 4; October 14, 1876, 4.

71. *News and Courier* (Charleston), October 1, 1876, 3; October 17 and 18, 1876; Henry T. Thompson, *Ousting the Carpetbaggers from South Carolina* (New York: Negro University Press, 1926), 120.

72. Holt, *Black over White*, 211.

73. Sterling, *Making of an Afro-American*, 318–23.

74. Belton O. Townsend, "The Result in South Carolina," *Atlantic Monthly* 41 (January 1878); 2–3.

75. Sterling, *Making of an Afro-American*, chapter 25; *News and Courier* (Charleston), July 16, 1877, July 16, 1878.

76. Martin Delany to H. R. Latrobe, President, American Colonization Society, Charleston, South Carolina, July 8, 1878; Delany to William Coppinger, Charleston, South Carolina, August 18, 1880; Delany to William Coppinger, Charleston, South Carolina, December 18, 1880, American Colonization Society Papers, Library of Congress, Washington, DC.

77. *Xenia (OH) Gazette*, January 7, 1885.

CHAPTER 1
THE BLACK MAJOR

Introduction

The outbreak of the Civil War marked a turning point in Martin Delany's career. He had spent much of the 1850s spearheading emigration and the quest for a black nationality. In fact, by 1852 Delany had concluded that political developments, especially the passage of the Fugitive Slave Act, foreshadowed an ominous future for blacks. Slavery was, he argued, slowly but steadily becoming a national institution. Now distrustful of white liberals and abolitionists, Delany denounced America as irredeemably racist. He saw only one viable path for blacks: emigration and the creation of an independent nationality. He aggressively pursued this goal from 1850 through the early 1860s, traveling to the Niger Valley of West Africa. He visited Liberia and Nigeria. In Abeokuta, a town in southwestern Nigeria, Delany convinced the local chiefs to grant a plot of land upon which he hoped to resettle black emigrants from the United States. However, the outbreak of the Civil War changed everything. Upon his return to the United States, Delany saw the developing conflict as an opportunity for blacks to advance and achieve their full potential in America. Abandoning his emigration platform, he joined Frederick Douglass, Henry H. Garnet, and other leading blacks to advocate black enlistment. He immersed himself in efforts to ensure that blacks contributed actively to the Union cause. For Delany and other leading blacks, the Civil War involved two opposing forces: freedom and slavery. The choice for blacks couldn't be clearer. He sought and secured an audience with President Abraham Lincoln during the first week of February 1865, at which he convinced Lincoln of the imperative of making black freedom a war strategy and authorizing the enlistment of blacks.

Delany deemed the subject of black enlistment and participation crucial to Union war efforts. In fact, he believed that the war meant much more for blacks than for whites. This war would determine blacks' ultimate redemption from centuries of bondage. Given this reality, Delany argued against denying blacks the opportunity of fully and actively participating. His activities reflected the importance he attached to the war, and the documents in this chapter highlight those activities. Despite his initial reluctance and opposition to conceiving the Civil War as a struggle against slavery, President Lincoln was ultimately compelled by several factors, including pressure from leading blacks such as Delany, Douglass, and Garnet and early defeats of Union forces on the battlefield, to reconsider his position. He would thereafter recommend Delany's commission into the Union Army as the first black combat major. He subsequently referred Delany to the secretary of war, Edward M. Stanton, who referred him to the assistant adjutant general of volunteers, Colonel C. W. Foster for muster into the army. This launched Delany's brief but epochal military career.

In document 1 Delany appealed to the government to consider the benefits of enlisting blacks and particularly stressed how his unique role and experiences would enhance black recruitment. He spoke to his ability and effectiveness in recruiting blacks, especially in the South. Delany stressed his and other black leaders' readiness to rally behind and advance the Union war efforts by helping to raise black volunteers and recruits. Document 2 is a proclamation by Secretary of War Edwin M. Stanton announcing Delany's commissioning as a combat major in the Union Army. Delany functioned essentially as a recruiting agent, assisting to create several black regiments. In addition to recruiting, he also often advised freedmen on how to adapt to the new dispensation. Such advice was often viewed negatively by government officials who deemed Delany's activities provocative and destabilizing. Document 3 is a letter from C. W. Foster, the assistant adjutant general of volunteers, to Captain Henry Keteltas, Fifteenth US Infantry Commissary of Musters, authorizing Delany's muster into the army and specifying his duration of service. Document 4 is the official letter of muster from C. W. Foster, assistant adjutant general of volunteers, to Delany. The next selection, document 5, is Delany's acceptance letter and pledge never to betray or dishonor the position, and document 6 is correspondence from C. W. Foster to General Rufus Saxton confirming Delany's appointment as a recruiting agent for the government. He was assigned to Charleston, South Carolina.

Document 7 is a letter Delany wrote to Adjutant General Colonel Foster, in which he mentioned a strategic meeting he held with blacks in Ohio on how best to counteract Confederate attempts to recruit black soldiers for combat. Delany also requested transportation funds for two men whose services he deemed crucial to the Union efforts. In response (doc. 8), Colonel Foster maintained that the two men could not be funded unless they were formally recruited into the army. Documents 9 and 10 highlight Delany's recruitment efforts and strategies and provide information about pay, pensions, and disability benefits and other remunerations. In both documents, Delany stressed the importance of the war to the future of blacks. He urged blacks to come forward and vindicate their manhood by actively contributing to the War. Their future and destiny depended on its outcome.

The next selection (doc. 11) is a report on an address Delany delivered to freedmen of Saint Helena Island, South Carolina. His scathing critique of slavery and racism and admonitions to freedmen to resist future attempts at enslavement or exploitation of any sort ruffled the feathers of white listeners. He reiterated that slavery was over and assured blacks that they had the capacity to resist its reintroduction in any form or shape. He rejected the notion of black inferiority and reminded the audience that black labor had built Western civilization. He portrayed Africans as an industrious people, contrary to European views. He described whites as parasitic and exploitative; people who built their affluence and wealth on the backs of others, including blacks. He explained how black labor and industry had built the wealth of the South. He warned the freedmen to be wary and suspicious of dubious and fraudulent government and missionary agents who would attempt to exploit their ignorance and gullibility. Though some of these agents had good intentions, Delany observed that many were of questionable and dubious intentions. He advised freedmen to pool their resources and strive for the means that would solidify their freedom: land with which to cultivate not just subsistence crops but also exportable ones such as cotton and tobacco.

His speech elicited both excitement and anger among his listeners. The pervasive militant mood scared several whites in attendance, prompting one Edward Stoeber, a first lieutenant with Delany's regiment, the 104th US Colored Troops, to accuse Delany of peddling "falsehood" and "misrepresentation" and to characterize his speech as designed to incite blacks against the government. Stoeber concluded that, in his opinion, Delany was anti–US government and "a thorough hater of the white race." Document 12 is one such reaction to this same lecture. H. J. Hawkins, a captain in the Sixth US Infantry, reported that Delany had created dissatisfaction and disaffection among freedmen and that many were becoming indignant and uncooperative. In the last two documents (docs. 13 and 14), Delany requested for and acknowledged receipt of replacement for his damaged US Army Commission.

DOCUMENT 1
Delany to Secretary of War

P.O. Box 764, P.S.
172 Clark Street
Chicago, Ill.,
Dec. 15, 1863

Hon. Secy. War,

Sir:

The subject and policy of Black Troops have become of much interest in our country, and the effective means and method of raising them is a matter of much importance.

In consequence of this, Sir, I embrace the earliest opportunity of asking the privilege of calling the attention of your Department to the fact, that as a policy in perfect harmony with the cause of the President and your own enlightened views, that the agency of intelligent competent black men adapted to the work must be the most effective means of obtaining black troops, because knowing and being of that people as a race, they can command such influence as is required to accomplish the object.

I have been successfully engaged as a Recruiting Agent of Black Troops, first as a Recruiting Agent for Massachusetts 54th Regt., and from the commencement as the Managing Agent in the West and South-West for Rhode Island Heavy Artillery, which is now nearly full, and now have the contract from the State Authorities of Connecticut for the entire West and South-West, in raising Colored Troops to fill her quota.

During these engagements, I have had associated with me Mr. John Jones, a very respectable business colored man of this city, and we have associated ourselves permanently together in an Agency for raising Black Troops for all parts of the country.

We are able, Sir, to command all of the effective black men as Agent in the United States, and in the event of an order from your department giving us authority to recruit colored troops in any of the southern or seceded states, we will be ready and able to raise a Regiment, or Brigade if required, in a shorter time than can be otherwise effected.

With the belief, Sir, that this is one of the measures in which the claim of the Black man may be officially recognized, without seemingly infringing upon those of other citizens, I confidently ask, Sir, that this humble request may engage your early notice.

All satisfactory references will be given by both of us. I have the honor to be, Sir,

    Your most obt., very humble servt.
    M. R. Delany.

SOURCE: Martin R. Delany Correspondence, War Records Office, National Archives and Records Administration, Washington, DC.

DOCUMENT 2
THE SECRETARY OF WAR OF THE UNITED STATES OF AMERICA

TO ALL WHO SHALL SEE THESE PRESENTS, GREETINGS:

Know ye, that, reposing special trust and confidence in the patriotism, valor, fidelity, and abilities of MARTIN R. DELANY, the President does hereby appoint him Major, in the One Hundred and Fourth Regiment of United States Colored Troops, in the service of the United States, to rank as such from the day of his muster into service, by the duly appointed commissary of musters, for the command to which said regiment belongs.

He is therefore carefully and diligently to discharge the duty of Major, by doing and performing all manner of things thereunto belonging. And I do strictly charge, and require, all officers and soldiers under his command to be obedient to his orders as Major. And he is to observe and follow such orders and directions, from time to time, as he shall receive from me or the future Secretary of War, or other superior officers set over him, according to the rules and discipline of war. This appointment to continue in force during the pleasure of the President for the time being.

Given under my hand at the War Department, in the City of Washington, D.C., this twenty-sixth day of February, in the year of our Lord one thousand eight hundred and sixty-five.

By the Secretary of War

EDWIN M. STANTON

C. W. Foster, Assistant Adjutant General Volunteers.

(Indorsement)

Mustered into the United States Service, February 27, 1865
HENRY KETELTAS, Captain 15th Infantry,
Chief Muster and District Officer

SOURCE: Frank (Frances) Rollin, *Life and Public Services of Martin R. Delany* (Boston: Lee and Shepard, 1868), 178–79.

DOCUMENT 3
C. W. FOSTER TO CAPT. HENRY KETELTAS

War Department
Adjutant General's Office
Washington, D.C.
February 27, 1865.

Captain Henry Keteltas
15th U.S. Infantry
Commissary of Musters
Washington, D.C.

Captain,

I am directed by the Secretary of War to instruct you to muster Major Martin R. Delany U.S. Colored Troops, blank regiments, into the service of the United States, for the period of three years or during the war, as of this date.

Very Respectfully
Your obdt., Servant
(signed) C. W. Foster.
Official copy respectfully furnished for the information of Captain F. W. Taggard A.A. Genl. Vols. Bureau for Colored Troops.
C. W. Foster,
Asst. Adjt. Genl. Vols.

SOURCE: Martin R. Delany Correspondence, War Records Office, National Archives and Records Administration, Washington, DC.

DOCUMENT 4
C. W. Foster to M. R. Delany

ADJUTANT GENERAL'S OFFICE,
WASHINGTON, Feb. 27, 1865

Sir:
I forward herewith your appointment of Major in the U.S. Colored Troops; your receipt and acceptance of which you will please acknowledge without delay, reporting at the same time your *age* and *residence*, when appointed, the *state* where *born*, and your full *name* and correctly *written. Fill up, subscribe,* and return as soon as possible, the accompanying *oath*, duly and carefully *executed*.

You will report in person to Brevet Major General R. Saxton, Beaufort, South Carolina.
I am, sir, very respectfully,
Your obedient servant
C. W. Foster
Assistant Adjutant General Volunteers
Major Martin R. Delany, *U.S. Colored Troops.*

SOURCE: Frank (Frances) Rollin, *Life and Public Services of Martin R. Delany* (Boston: Lee and Shepard, 1868), 179.

DOCUMENT 5
Delany to C. W. Foster

Col. C. W. Foster,

Sir: I have the honor to accept the appointment of Major in the U.S. Colored Troops to which the Honorable Secretary of War has been pleased to commission me on the 26th instant, and give to him my heartfelt thanks for the honor conferred, with the assurance that my trust shall never be betrayed, nor position dishonored.

Please, Colonel, convey to the Honorable Secretary of War, the assurance with which I have the honor to be, Sir,
Your most obedient, very humble servt

M. R. Delany
Major U.S.C.T.
Col. C. W. Foster, Asst. A.G.V.

SOURCE: Martin R. Delany Correspondence, War Records Office, National Archives and Records Administration, Washington, DC .

DOCUMENT 6
C. W. FOSTER TO RUFUS SAXTON

War Department A.G.O.
Washington, D.C.
February 27, 1865.

Brevet Major General R. Saxton
Supt. Recruiting Organization of Colored Troops
Dept., of the South, Beaufort, S.C.

General:

I am directed by the Secretary of War to inform you that the bearer, Major M. R. Delany, U.S. Colored Troops, has been appointed for the purpose of aiding and assisting you in recruiting and organizing colored troops, and to carry out this object you will assign him duty in the city of Charleston, S.C.

You will observe that the regiment to which Major Delany is appointed is not designated, although he has been mustered into service. You will cause Major Delany to be assigned to, and his mane placed upon the rolls of the first regiment of colored troops you may organize, with his proper rank. Now however with a view to his doing duty with such regiment.

I am directed to say that Major Delany has the entire confidence of the Department.
I have the honor to be, General
Very Respectfully
Your Obedient Servant,
C. W. Foster.
Copy for Major Delany
Endorsement on this: Saxton, Genel. R.
February 27, 1865.

SOURCE: Martin R. Delany Correspondence, War Records Office, National Archives and Records Administration, Washington, DC.

DOCUMENT 7
Delany to C. W. Foster

24th March, 1865

Colonel C. W. Foster
A.A. Genl. Vol.

Sir:

I have the honor to state that while waiting for the making of my clothes, I held several important meetings among the blacks in Cleveland and Xenia, Green Cos., Ohio, setting on foot important measures looking to the Rebel organization of Black troops, some of the effects of which are already showing themselves in and around Richmond.

Remaining with my family five days to arrange their finances, I left Xenia (the place of residence) Wednesday 15th and by bad railway arrangement, missing connections, and water bound by the late freshet, I only reached New York yesterday noon; and the next transport sails on next Thursday—one week from yesterday—by the statement of Capt. Stinson, Quartermaster.

I have with me, Colonel, two persons, one an excellent scout, just such a person as I want for certain purposes South, who was born and raised in and about Charleston, and belonged to and served and traveled with Major Rhett, a rebel officer acting as his confidant, until the Major, leaving him a certain place, he escaped and came North about nine months ago, since when he has heard of the death of Rhett. The other is an intelligent young man, of fair education, who has been an officer and drillmaster of a colored volunteer company in Detroit, Mich., for several years. I wish to take them both, and present them to Brev. Major Gen. Saxton, as I know them to be just such persons as we shall want.

The Quartermaster says that it is necessary for me to obtain an order for transportation for them both before they can go.

The name of the Scout is Barnwell, and that of the young drill officer Charles Henry Webb. Colonel, would you be pleased to present these facts to the Honorable Secretary of War, and obtain the necessary transportation, sending it on immediately, as it has time to reach here against Thursday? And obliged, very respectfully, Sir,
Your most obt., Servt.
M. R. Delany
Major U.S.C.T.

SOURCE: Martin R. Delany Correspondence, War Records Office, National Archives and Records Administration, Washington, DC.

DOCUMENT 8
C. W. Foster to Delany

War Dept.
27th March, 1865

Major M. R. Delany
104th U.S. Colored Troops
541 Broome Street
New York City, N.Y.

Major:

In reply to your letter of the 24th inst., asking for transportation for two colored men to the Department of the South, I am directed to say that it is not considered expedient to furnish such transportation as the men could not be paid for services as "scouts" from the fund for "collecting, drilling and organizing volunteers," nor from any fund pertaining to the voluntary recruiting service. It is only entering the military service that they can be employed and paid services in connection with the recruitment of colored troops.

Very Respectfully,
Your Obedient Servt.
C. W. Foster
[title illegible]

SOURCE: Martin R. Delany Correspondence, War Records Office, National Archives and Records Administration, Washington, DC.

DOCUMENT 9
Attention, Charlestonians! Rally Round the Flag!

Charleston, S.C.
April 28, 1865.

To the Free Colored Men of Charleston,

The free colored men in this city, between the ages of eighteen and forty-five, are hereby earnestly called upon to come forward to join the
    CHARLESTON REGIMENT
Now to be organized. It is the duty of every colored man to vindicate his manhood by becoming a soldier, and with his own stout arm battle for the

emancipation of his race. I urge you by every free inspiration which a sense of liberty has kindled in your hearts, to be soldiers, until the freedom of your race is secured. The prospect of your future destiny should be enough to call every man to the ranks. But in addition, you are to have the
PAY, RATIONS AND CLOTHING,

Let a full regiment of the Colored Freedmen of Charleston be under arms, to protect the heritage which has been promised to your race in this department.

PAY OF ARTILLERY, INFANTRY, AND CAVALRY SOLDIERS

GRADE	PAY PER MONTH	PAY PER YEAR
Sergeant Major of Cavalry Artillery, and Infantry	$26.00	$312.00
Quartermaster Sergeant, Cavalry, Artillery and Infantry	$22.00	$264.00
Commissary Sergeant	$22.00	$264.00
Orderly Sergeant	$24.00	$288.00
Sergeants	$20.00	$240.00
Corporals	$18.00	$216.00
Privates	$16.00	$192.00
Musicians	$16.00	$192.00
Principal Musicians	$22.00	$264.00

In addition to the pay as above, one ration per day and an abundant supply of good clothing are allowed to each soldier. Quarters, fuel, and medical attendance are always provided by the government, without deduction from the soldier's pay. If a soldier should become disabled in the line of his duties, the laws provide for him a pension; or he may, if he prefers it, obtain admission into the soldier Home, "which will afford him a comfortable home so long as he may wish to receive its benefits." It is the intention to make this an excelsior regiment. All desired information given at Recruiting Office, No. 64 St. Philip Street Corner, Calhoun.
Major M. R. Delany
104th United States Colored Troops.
R. P. Hutchings, Colonel
Office No. 123 Calhoun Street.

SOURCE: Frank (Frances) Rollin, *Life and Public Services of Martin R. Delany* (Boston: Lee and Shepard, 1868), 211–12.

DOCUMENT 10
Black National Defenders

The state of Connecticut is authorized to raise Colored Troops; and any number of her quotas of 5000 may be colored men. 29th Regiment Connecticut Volunteers, is now being formed at camp Buckingham, composed entirely of colored men, located at the beautiful city of New Haven, the seat of Yale University.

STATE BOUNTY
$200.00 CASH!
ON BEING SWORN IN

By an old law of the state, 30 dollars a year are allowed to each soldier for clothing, 10 dollars of which is paid down at the time of entering their service, the other 20 dollars being paid in four month payments each, making 210 dollars Bounty-Cash, on joining the regiment and 20 dollars more during the year.

An important fact connected with this recruiting is, that the contract for raising the troops has been given to a colored man; and Connecticut is the first State, since the war commenced, which has been thus liberal and considerate.

This fact alone should be an inducement for COLORED MEN to rally to her standard: all the Recruiting Agents in the West being Colored: and this principle should prevail everywhere. Colored men should recruit colored men, as best adapted to it.

The most liberal compensation will be given to Good Agents, about 50 such being now wanted, and to whom will be paid cash so soon as service is rendered.

APPLY WITHOUT DELAY TO
M. R. DELANY:

State Contractor, Headquarters of the West and South-Western States and Territories, 172 Clark Street, Top Storey, Chicago, Ill.

Source: Delany Recruitment Posters, War Records Office, National Archives and Records Administration, Washington, DC.

DOCUMENT 11
Martin R. Delany Counsels Freedmen:
Address to freedmen on St. Helena Island, July 28, 1865

Brevt Maj. S. M. Taylor
Asst. Adjt. General

Major:

In obedience to your request, I proceeded to St. Helena Island yesterday morning, for the purpose of listening to the public delivery of a lecture by Major Delany 104th U.S. Col. Troops.

I was accompanied by Lieut. A. Whyte Jr. 128th U.S.C.T., under orders of Col. C. H. Howard 128th U.S.C.T. Comd. Post.

The meeting was held near the Brick Church. The congregation numbering from 500 to 600.

As introduction, Maj. Delany made them acquainted with the fact that slavery is absolutely abolished, throwing thunders of damnations and maledictions on all the former slaveholders and people of the South, and almost condemned their souls to hell.

He says "It was only a War policy of the Government, to declare the slaves of the South free, knowing that the whole power of the South laid in the possession of the slaves. But I want you to understand that we would not have become free, had we not armed ourselves and fought out our independence" (this he repeated twice).

He further says "If I had been a slave, I would have been most troublesome and not to be conquered by any threat or punishment. I would not have worked, and no one would have dared to come near me, I would have struggled for life or death: and would have thrown fire and sword between them. I know you have been good, only too good. I was told by a friend of mine, that when owned by a man and put to work on the field, he laid quietly down, and just looked out for the overseer to come along, when he pretended to work very hard. But he confessed to me, that he never has done a fair days work for his master. And so he was right, so I would have done the same, and all of you ought to have done the same."

People say that you are too lazy to work, that you have not the intelligence to get on for yourselves without being guided and driven to the work by overseers. I say it is a lie, and a blasphemous lie, and I will prove it to be so.

I am going to tell you now, what you are worth. As you know, Christopher Columbus landed here in 1492. They came here only for the purpose to dig gold, gather precious pearls, diamonds and all sorts of jewels, only for the proud Aristocracy of the White Spaniards and Portuguese, to adorn their persons; to have brooches for their breasts, earrings for their ears, bracelets for their ankles and rings for their limbs and fingers.

They found here (red man) Indians, whom they obliged to dig and work and slave for them but they found out that they died away too fast and cannot stand the work. So the whites could not stand the work. In course of time, they had taken some blacks (Africans) along with them, and put them to work, they could stand it, And yet they (the whites) say they are superior to our race, though they could not stand it. At the present day in some of the Eastern parts of Spain, the Spaniard there (having been once conquered by the black race) have black eyes, black hair, black complexion. They have Negro blood in them!!! The work was so profitable which those poor blacks did, that in the year 1502, Charles the V gave permission to import into America yearly 4000 blacks. The profit of those sales was so immense, that afterwards even the virgin Queen of England and James the 1st took part in the slave trade and were accumulating great wealth for the treasury of the Government. And so you always have been the means of riches.

I tell you I have been all over Africa (I was born there)[1] and I tell you (as I told to the Geographical Faculty in London)[2] that those people there, are a well driving class of cultivators, and I never saw or heard of one of our brethren there, to travel without taking seeds with him as much as he can carry and to sow it where ever he goes to, or to exchange it with his brethren.

So you ought further to know that all the spices, cotton, rice and coffee has only been brought over by you, from the land of our brothers.

Your masters who lived in opulence, kept you to hard work, by some most contemptible being called overseer who chastised and beat you whenever he pleased while your master lived in some Northern town or in Europe to squander away the wealth only you acquired for him. He never earned a singled dollar in his life. You men and women, everyone of you around me, made thousands and thousands of dollars, only you were the means for masters to lead the idle and inglorious life, and to give his children the education, which he denied to you, for fear you may awake to

---

1. This was not meant to be taken literally. Delany was not born in Africa; he was just underlining his deep African roots. He was born in Charles Town Virginia (now West Virginia). His maternal grandparents were born in Africa.
2. This was a reference to Delany's participation in the International Statistical Congress in London during his brief stopover there while returning to the United States from his Niger Valley exploration trip in 1861.

conscience. If I look around me, I tell you, all the houses on this island and in Beaufort, they are all familiar to my eye, they are the same structures which I have met in Africa. They have all been made by the Negroes, you can see it by their rude exteriors. I tell you they (white men) cannot teach you anything, and they could not make them because they have not the brain to do it. (After a pause) At least, I mean the Southern people: "Oh the Yankees they are smart." Now tell me from all you have heard from me, are you not worth anything? Are you those men whom they think, God only created as curse and for slave? Whom they do not consider their equal? As I said before, the Yankees are smart there are good ones and bad ones. The good ones, if they are good they are very good, if they are bad, they are very bad. But the worst and the most contemptible, and even worse than even your masters were, are those Yankees, who hired themselves as overseers.

Believe not in these school teachers, emissaries, ministers and agents, because they never tell you the truth, and I particularly warn you against those cotton agents, who come honey mouthed unto you, their only intent being to make profit by your inexperience.

If there is a man comes to you, who will meddle with your affairs, send him to one of your more enlightened brothers, who shall ask him, who he is, what business he seeks with you etc.

Believe none but those Agents who are sent out by the Government, to enlighten and guide you. I am an officer in the U.S. Government and ordered to aid Genl. Saxton, who has only been lately appointed Asst. Commissioner for South Carolina, so is Genl. Wild, Asst. Comm. For Georgia. When Chief Justice Chase was down here to speak to you, some of those malicious and abominable New York papers derived from it that he only seeks to be elected by you as President, a white or a black one. I don't care who it be, it may be who has a mind to. I shall not be intimidated whether by threats or imprisonment, and no power will keep me from telling you the truth. So I expressed myself even at Charleston, the hotbed of those scoundrels, your old masters, without fear or reluctance.

Now I will come to the main purpose for which I have come to see you. As before the whole South depended upon you, now the whole country will depend upon you. I give you advice how to get along. Get up a community and get all the lands you can if you cannot get any singly.

Grow as much vegetables etc. as you want for your families, on the other part of land you cultivate rice and cotton. Now for instance, one acre will grow a crop of cotton of $90, now a land with 10 acres will bring $900 every year, if you cannot get the land all yourself, the community can, and so you can divide the profit. There is tobacco for instance (Virginia is the great place for tobacco). There are whole squares at Dublin and Liverpool named after some places of Tobacco notoriety, so you see what enormous value your labor was to the benefit of your masters. Now you understand that I want you to be the producers of this country. It is the wish of the Government for you to be so.

We will send friends to you, who will further instruct you how to come to the end of our wishes. You see that by so adhering to our views, you will become a wealthy and powerful population.

Now I look around me and notice a man, bare footed covered with rags and dirt. Now I ask, what is that man doing, for whom is he working? I hear that he works for that and that farmer "for 30 cents a day." I tell you that must not be. That would be cursed slavery over again. I will not have it, the Government will not have it, and the Government shall hear about it. I will tell the Government.

I tell you slavery is over, and shall never return again. We have now 200,000 of our men well drilled in arms and used to warfare, and I tell you, it is with you and them that slavery shall not come back again, and if you are determined it will not return again.

Now go to work and in a short time I will see you again, and other friends will come to show you how to begin.

Have your fields in good order and well tilled and planted and when I pass the fields and see a land well planted and well cared for, then I may be sure from the look of it that it belongs to a free negro, and when I see a field thinly planted and little cared for, then I may think it belongs to some man who work it with slaves. The Government decided that you shall have one third of the produce of the crops from your employer, so if he makes $3, you will have to get $1 out of it for your labor. The other day some plantation owners in Virginia and Maryland offered $5 a month for your labor, but it was indignantly rejected by Genl. Howard, the commissioner for the Government.

These are the expressions, as far as I can remember, without having made notice at the time.

The excitement with the congregation was immense, groups were formed talking over what they have heard, and ever and more cheers were given to some particular sentences of the speech.

I afterwards mingled with the several groups, to hear their opinions. Some used violent language, "saying they would get rid of the Yankee employer." "That is the only man who ever told them the truth." "That now those men have to work themselves or starve or leave the country, we will not work for them anymore."

Some whites were present, and listened with horror depicted in their faces, to the whole performance. Some said "what shall become of us now" and if such a speech should be again given to those men, there will be open rebellion. Major Delany was afterwards corrected by Mr. Town, the Superintendent at that place, to the effect that the pay of laborers on this island is not 30 cents a day. But 30 cents for a task, and that a man can easily make from 75 to 90 cents a day. Major Delany then corrected himself accordingly, saying that he must have been misinformed.

My opinion of the whole affair is that Major Delany is a thorough hater of the white race, and tries the colored people unnecessarily. He even tries to injure the magnanimous conduct of the Government towards them, either intentionally or through want of knowledge. He tells them to remember, "That they would not have become free, had they not armed themselves and fought for their independence." This is a falsehood and misrepresentation. Our President Abraham Lincoln declared the colored race free, before there was even an idea of arming colored men. This is decidedly calculated to create bad feeling against the Government.

By giving some historical facts and telling them that neither Indians nor whites could stand the work in his country, he wants to impress not the colored man with the idea that, he in fact, is superior not only in a physical view but also in intelligence. He says, "believe none of the ministers, school teachers, emissaries, because they never tell you the truth." It is only to bring distrust against all, and gives them to understand, that they shall believe men of their own race. He openly acts and speaks contrary to the policy of this government, advising them not to work for any man, but for themselves.

The intention of our Government is, that all the men should be employed by their former masters as far as possible, and contracts made between them, superintended by some officer empowered by the Government.

He says it would be the old slavery over again, if a man should work for an employer, and that it must not be. Does he not give a hint of what they shall do, by the uttering, "That if he had been a slave etc." Or by giving the narrative for the slaves who did not work for his master? Further as he says: that a field should show by its appearance by whom and for whom it is worked?

The mention of having two hundred thousand men well drilled in arms: Does he not hint to them what to do? If they should be compelled to work for employers?

In my opinion by this discourse, he was trying to encourage them, to break the peace of society and force their way by insurrection to a position he is ambitious they should attain.

I am, Major,
Very Respectfully
Your obedient servant
Edward M. Stoeber
1st Lieut. 104th U.S.C.T.

SOURCE: Record Group 105, Letters Received, Assistant Commissioner, South Carolina, National Archives and Records Administration, Washington, DC.

DOCUMENT 12
H. J. HAWKINS ON DELANY

Hilton Head, S.C.
August 13, 1865.

1st. Lieut. J. H. Clons,
A.A.A.G District of Port Royal.

Sir:

I have the honor to entrust the following report of a special inspection made throughout this District for which I was detailed.

The system of contract seems to be working well in the Islands, but upon the main few if any have been entered into, in this regard I regret that it is my duty to report that a Major Delany of the 104th U.S.C.T has created great dissatisfaction among the evil-disposed towards the whites; in a late public address in which he cautioned the colored people to beware of all whites, Northerners and Southerners, telling them that they owed their liberty to their own strong arms alone; that they should disregard all contracts made with the whites, that they are entitled to their share of the crops, and that he would see they obtained it.

Many Negroes disposed of their cotton crop of 1864 at one dollar per pound and were to have secured an additional fund provided the New York market remained at this their rate. The capture of Savanna cotton caused an immediate rapid fall and the additional price could not.

This the Negroes cannot understand and Major Delany's remarks have only heightened their discontent at a supposed breach of contract and increased their jealousy of the whites.
(signed)

H. J. Hawkins
Capt. 6th U.S. Infantry

SOURCE: Records of the Assistant Commissioner of the State of South Carolina, Bureau of Refugees, Freedmen, and Abandoned Lands, 1865–1870, Microcopy 869, Roll 34, 202–3, National Archives and Records Administration, Washington, DC.

DOCUMENT 13
DELANY TO C. W. FOSTER

Headquarters, Bureau District, Hilton Head
Port Royal, S.C.
February 5th 1867

Col. C. W. Foster
Asst. Adjt. Genl.
War Dept.
Washington, D.C.
Colonel:

    I have the honor to ask as a special favor if it be not objectionable to you—a duplicate of my commission in the Army, as by an accident of water by leakage, the parchment has become much soiled and partially defaced, so as to quite spoil it.
    As I desire to preserve it quite unsullied, and have now a proper tin tube for my documents, I do not expect a like accident to happen, and shall deem it a great favor should you honor my request.
I have the honor to be, Colonel,
Your most obt., servt.
M. R. Delany
Major; S.A. Comm.

SOURCE: Martin R. Delany Correspondence, War Records Office, National Archives and Records Administration, Washington, DC.

DOCUMENT 14
DELANY TO C. W. FOSTER

Head Quarters Sub. Dist.
Port Royal, S.C.
April 4, 1867.

Col. C. W. Foster
Asst. Adj. Genl. Vol.,
War Dept.,
Washington, D.C.
(Through Head Quarters, Dept. South Charleston, S.C.)
Colonel:

    I have the honor to acknowledge the receipt of your communication of Feb. 16th and a copy of my appointment in the Army as Major of 104th U.S.C. Troops, to supply the original parchment, damaged and somewhat defaced by leakage of water in my Quarters.
For which favor, Colonel,
I have the honor to be,
Your most obedient servant
M. R. Delany
Major S.A. Comm.

SOURCE: Martin R. Delany Correspondence, War Records Office, National Archives and Records Administration, Washington, DC.

CHAPTER 2

FREEDMEN'S BUREAU SUB-ASSISTANT COMMISSIONER

INTRODUCTION

At the end of the Civil War, Delany was assigned as a sub-assistant commissioner of the Freedmen's Bureau and posted at Hilton Head Island, South Carolina.[1] He was given responsibility over some twenty government plantations seized as abandoned lands or for the nonpayment of taxes. He conceived his prime responsibility as one of developing a framework that would enable planters (former slave owners) and freedmen (former slaves) to function amicably in a postslavery environment. He wanted to create the kind of harmony that would facilitate mutual benefits and advancement. Although his underlying vision was for an independent black yeomanry whereby every black family would acquire economic self-sufficiency through land redistribution and ownership, Delany was also cognizant of the challenges of such a goal, especially after President Andrew Johnson pardoned ex-Confederates and

---

1. The Bureau of Refugees, Freedmen, and Abandoned Lands (Freedmen's Bureau) was established by the US Department of War in 1865 to help freed slaves, refugees, and destitute families obtain reliefs, lands, jobs, fair treatment, and education.

ordered restoration of their lands. Delany, therefore, realized early that land redistribution would be a difficult and potentially destabilizing solution. In the absence of land ownership, blacks had no choice but to work for white planters, albeit under a completely new dispensation. They were no longer slaves, so they expected to be compensated for their labor. Delany assumed the responsibility of framing a system that would prevent the previously unrestricted practice of labor exploitation that defined the slavery era.

As a Freedmen's Bureau agent, his work on behalf of blacks in his district entailed helping them attain some measure of economic independence through land acquisition and efficiency in the production and marketing of cotton. The strategy he developed is represented by his triple alliance doctrine, premised on the imperative of aligning three factors of production and economic growth in a relationship of fairness and mutuality: land, labor, and capital. The one fundamental change his triple alliance underscored was the insistence that black labor (previously exploited and uncompensated) would be considered an equal partner of the triple alliance (land, labor, capital), and fairly and adequately compensated. The first five selections of this chapter (docs. 1–5) are parts of a series of seven articles Delany published in the Hilton Head Island *New South* titled "Prospects of the Freedmen on Hilton Head." In this series, Delany made a strong case for prioritizing the economic development of blacks. He contended that becoming self-sufficient was crucial to solidifying their freedom and that such self-sufficiency should be a matter of national priority. He argued that blacks had already proven their capacity for industry and resourcefulness and ability for higher attainments. Slave labor had built the country, and that same labor would be crucial to continued national development, if properly and adequately harnessed and compensated in freedom. For this to happen, however, Delany insisted that blacks should be encouraged and assisted to obtain land. Each black family should be able to own a small plot. This called for land redistribution. Such a policy would broaden and diversify land ownership as opposed to the existing situation where a few monopolized the land. This policy, in turn, would tremendously enhance national development, while providing blacks the resources with which to become self-sufficient and to care for their families.

Delany urged the government to redistribute the land and then sell it in small plots at affordable prices to blacks. Such redistribution would have ripple economic effects beneficial to the entire nation. He considered blacks' landownership vital to overall national development. Land redistribution would enhance not only the South's but the entire nation's economy. Delany also advocated the adoption of political economy as the basis for equitable redistribution of the nation's wealth. He had introduced this concept in the 1840s as he sought to convince blacks to embrace the philosophy of moral suasion and wealth accumulation.[2] Now, in the early Reconstruction period, Delany broadened the concept to include a controversial political strategy: deemphasizing political rights. In Delany's view, blacks needed economic status most in postslavery America, not political rights. He believed that the quest for political rights would provoke resentment in a society in which whites seemed reluctant to relate to blacks in ways other than those dictated by the old slavery system. His call to deemphasize political rights and power also derived from his optimistic belief in the progressive character of American political culture. He opined that equality of political rights which he characterized as "the genius of the American Government" would materialize as the broader political culture evolved. Thus, he urged blacks to prioritize the quest for economic development, which led him to attempt to discourage blacks from contesting for positions of political responsibilities. He maintained that blacks would someday achieve political equality, whether they fought for it or not. Therefore, they should concentrate efforts on improving their economic condition.

Linked to political economy, Delany's triple alliance system (doc. 6) tied the interests of blacks closely to that of northern capitalists and southern landowners. According to this paradigm, the economic regeneration of the entire nation depended on an alliance for mutual progress involving three agents: land (available in the South), labor (provided by blacks), and capital (from northern investors). The triple alliance system Delany developed and implemented in his bureau district on Hilton Head Island was a microcosm of what he envisaged for the entire South. His vision entailed not only that blacks would provide labor and be fairly and adequately compensated but also that they be afforded the opportunity of becoming landowners as well. Documents 7, 8, and 9 are letters Delany wrote to Senator Henry Wilson and Colonel D. L. Eaton, titled "Homes for Freedmen," in which he argued the necessity of assisting blacks to acquire lands in the South. Through these essays, he appealed to philanthropists in the North to come South and help finance blacks' purchases of land from southern landowners. He argued that freedmen needed homes that would enhance and solidify their freedom and enable them to sustain themselves and their families. He emphasized to the philanthropists and capitalists that helping blacks obtain lands would benefit everyone and enhance the economic prosperity of the South and the entire nation. The formula he proposed was for each black family to obtain ten acres.

Delany urged northern capitalists to invest in purchasing the South's abundant surplus lands and reinvest by making them affordable to blacks.

---

2. Martin R. Delany, "Domestic Economy," *North Star*, March 23, 1849, April 13, 1849, April 20, 1849.

He assured these capitalists and potential investors that blacks were willing to purchase lands and could be trusted to use them for profitable and productive endeavors that would accrue profits to all. Furthermore, he believed that such development would also be a means of making taxes less burdensome and equitably distributed. According to him, the more widespread land was redistributed and owned, the broader the tax base. He attributed the existing high and burdensome tax system to its narrow base: only a few were taxed. Enabling blacks acquire and own land would expand the tax base and would bring stability to labor supply. Affording blacks stable and permanent residence also meant a steady and ready supply of labor. The broader impact would be felt beyond the realm of economics and politics. It would impact education, religion, and social services. As blacks became more economically self-sufficient and stable, there would be increased demands for schools, growth of churches, and improved social services. Consistent with his political economy and triple alliance doctrines, Delany opined that the economic impacts and benefits of blacks' owning lands would be felt by everyone across the South and the nation.

Document 10 is War Department Special Orders No. 372, relieving Delany of his war duties and reassigning him to the Freedmen's Bureau. The next four documents (docs. 11, 12, 13, 14) are Delany's annual reports to bureau headquarters on the state of the plantations and the conditions of freedmen in his district. It is important to note Delany's attempts to help freedmen deal with the ever-present challenge posed by land speculators who bought up land and resold it to blacks at exorbitant rates, as well as the exploits of the cotton industry's second brokers and middlemen, who siphoned off much of the profits, leaving freedmen with next to nothing. To alleviate these challenges, Delany established a cotton agency, a kind of cooperative institution to enable freedmen to pool their efforts and resources for better management of their economic activities. He developed a strategy that enabled freedmen to obtain land at a low rate of a dollar per acre. He was thus able to make more lands available to black families. His vision was for every black family to own at least twenty acres which would enable them to care for their families, especially the aged and indigent.[3] His periodic reports show marked improvement in the lives of the freedmen. He also urged diversification of agriculture, instead of concentrating on capital intensive crops such as cotton and tobacco, and suggested some attention to subsistence farming. His reports touched upon

---

3. The twenty acres recommendation came earlier in his Freemen's Bureaus reports (1865–68). However, in his 1871 letter to US Senator Henry Wilson (doc. 7 in this chapter), Delany, perhaps now cognizant of the difficulty of land procurement, revised down his recommendation to ten acres.

crucial issues such as morals, health condition, policing, family life, and education facilities and reforms.

Delany also advanced a progressive philosophy of education, arguing for the creation of school environments conducive to learning. He condemned the widespread use of corporal punishment and urged the hiring of teachers able to instruct and nurture children without resorting to the whip. He wanted schools to be "pleasurable" places. He emphasized to the school district the importance of encouraging and supporting the education of freedmen. He called for appropriations for more schools and educational supplies to provide more black children with access to learning. Overall, his reports underscore Delany's commitment to the welfare of the freedmen. No longer slaves, yet not completely free, these freedmen often appeared confused and overwhelmed by the complexities of the changes around them and, therefore, were left vulnerable. Delany assumed the responsibility of making life more bearable and meaningful for them. His underlying motivation was to ensure that blacks were not exploited and victimized as they had been under slavery. Document 15 is a generic contract that Delany developed for his district. What is particularly unique to this contract is its attempt to foster awareness of mutual responsibility and fairness, obligations, and indebtedness on the part of both planters and freedmen, such that neither was left feeling disadvantaged. The contract inculcates Delany's vision of mutuality, fairness, and shared responsibility as enshrined in the triple alliance.

Delany's function as a bureau agent was a success, in terms of his impact both on the freedmen in his district and generally on the overall developments throughout that district. Freedmen and planters found his efforts rewarding and acceptable. He succeeded in creating peace and harmony, a condition that was lacking in other bureau districts. Documents 16 and 17 are testimonies to Delany's success and impact on Hilton Head Island. The first is an excerpt from a report by one Major Roy of the Sixth US Infantry, commending Delany's performance as a bureau agent. The second is an editorial of the Hilton Head Island *New South*, praising Delany as a fair and just agent, someone highly appreciated by planters and freedmen alike. His performance established peace in the community. Finally, document 18 is a letter from R. K. Scott, assistant commissioner to General O. O. Howard, commissioner of the Freedmen's Bureau, recommending Delany's reassignment, as his services were no longer needed. This effectively terminated his bureau agency.

DOCUMENT 1
Prospects of the Freedmen of Hilton Head Island 1

Every true friend of the Union, residing on the island must feel an interest in the above subject, regardless of any other consideration than that of national polity. Have the blacks become self-sustaining? And will they ever, in a state of freedom, resupply the products which comprised the staples formerly of the old planters? These are questions of importance, and not unworthy of the consideration of grave political economists.

That the blacks of the island have not been self-sustaining will not be pretended, neither can it be denied that they have been generally industrious and inclined to work. But industry alone is not sufficient, nor work available, except these command adequate compensation.

Have the blacks innately the elements of industry and enterprise? Compare them with any other people, and note their adaptation. Do they not make good "day laborers"? Are they not good field hands? Do they not make good domestics? Are they not house servants? Do they not readily "turn their hands" to anything or kind of work they may find to do? Trained, they make good body servants, house servants, or laundresses, waiters, chamber and dining-room servants, cooks, nurses, drivers, horse "tenders", and indeed, fill as well, and better, many of the domestic occupations than any other race. And with unrestricted facilities for training, will not be denied that they are as susceptible of the mechanical occupations or trades as they are of the domestic? Will it be denied that a people easily domesticated are susceptible of the higher attainments? The slaveholder, long since, cautioned against "giving a nigger an inch, lest he should take ell."

If permitted, I will continue this subject in a series of equally short articles, so as not to intrude on your columns.

Source: Frank (Frances) Rollin, *Life and Public Services of Martin R. Delany* (Boston: Lee and Shepard, 1868), 230–41.

DOCUMENT 2
Prospects of the Freedmen of Hilton Head Island 2

This subject must now be examined in the light of political economy, and for reasons stated in a previous article, treated tersely in every sentence, and therefore, will not be condemned by the absence of elaboration and extensive proof.

America was discovered in 1492—then peopled only by the original inhabitants, or Indians, as afterwards called. No part of the country was found in a state of cultivation, and no industrial enterprise was carried on, either foreign or domestic. Not even in the West Indies—prolific with spices, gums, dye-woods, and fruits; was there any trade carried on among or by the natives. These people were put to labor by the foreigners; but, owing to their former habits of hunting, fishing, and want of physical exercise, they sank beneath the weight of toil, fast dying off, till their mortality, in time, from this cause alone, reached the frightful figure of two and a half million (see Ramsay's History).[4]

The whites were put to labor, and their fate was not better—which requires no figures, as all are familiar with the history and career of Thomas Gate and associate at one time; John Smith and associates, as colonists in the South, at another; how, not farther than Virginia,—at most, North Carolina,—they "died like sheep," to the destruction of the settlements, in attempting to do the work required to improve for civilized life. Neither whites, as foreigners, nor Indians, as natives, were adequate to the task of performing the labor necessary to their advent in the New World.

So early as 1502—but ten years after Columbus landed—"the Spaniards commenced bringing a few negroes from Africa to work the soil." (See Ramsay's History). In 1515, but thirteen years afterwards, and twenty-three from the discovery of America, Carolus V. King of Spain, granted letters patent to import annually into the colonies of Cuba, Ispaniola (Hayti), Jamaica, and Puerto Rico, four thousand Africans as slaves: people contracted with to "emigrate" to these new colonies, as the French, under Louis Napoleon, attempted, in 1858, to decoy native Africans, under the pretext of emigration to the colonies, into French slavery, then reject international interference, on the ground that they obtained them by "voluntary emigration."

Such was the success of this new industrial element, that not only did Spaniards and Portuguese employ them in all their American colonies, but so great was the demand for these laborers, that Elizabeth, the Virgin Queen of England, became a partner in the slave trade with the infamous Captain Hawkins; and, in 1618, her successor to the throne, and royal relative, James 1, King of England, negotiated for and obtained the entire carrying trade, thus securing by international patent, the exclusive right for British vessels alone to "traffic in blood and souls of men," to reap the profit arising from their importation.

Was it the policy of political economists, such as were then the rulers and statesmen of Europe, to employ a people in preference to all others for

---

4. Delany is referring to David Ramsay's *History of South Carolina* (1858).

the development of wealth, if such people were not adapted to the labor designed for them? Would the civilized and highly polished, such as were then the Spanish, French, and Portuguese nations, together with the English, still have continued the use of these people as laborers and domestics in every social relation among them, if they had not found them a most desirable element? Would, after the lapse of one hundred and sixteen years rigid trial and experience from their first importation, the King of England have been able—whatever his avarice as an individual—to have effected so great a diplomatic treaty, as the consent from all civilized nations having interest here to people their colonies with a race if that race had been worthless as laborers, and deficient as an industrial element? Would, in the years of the grace of Jesus Christ, and the light of the highest civilization, after the lapse of two hundred and twenty years from James's treaty, the most powerful and enlightened monarchy have come near the crisis of its political career in its determination to continue the system, and for two hundred and forty-seven years the most powerful and enlightened republic that ever the world saw have distracted the harmony of the nations of the earth, and driven itself to the verge of destruction by the mad determination of one half of the people and leading states, to perpetuate the service of this race as essential to the development of the agricultural wealth of the land? After these centuries of trial and experience, would these people have been continually sought after, had they not proven to be superior to all others as laborers in the kind of work assigned them? Let political economists answer.

SOURCE: Frank (Frances) Rollin, *Life and Public Services of Martin R. Delany* (Boston: Lee and Shepard, 1868), 230–41.

DOCUMENT 3

PROSPECTS OF THE FREEDMEN OF HILTON HEAD ISLAND 5

As shown in my last article, these people are the lineal descendants of an industrious, hardy race of men—those whom the most powerful and accomplished statesmen and political economists of the great states of Europe, after years of trial and rigid experience, decided upon and selected as the element best adapted to develop in a strange and foreign clime—a new industry and labor necessary to the new life. This cannot and will not be attempted to be denied without ignoring all historical authority, though presented in a different light—and may I not say motives?—From that in which history has ever given it.

These people are of those to retain whom in her power the great British nation was agitated to the point, at as late a period as 1837–8, of shattering the basis of its political foundation; and, within the last four years, the genius of the American government was spurned, assaulted and trampled upon, and had come well-nigh its final dissolution by full one half of the states, people, and statesmen inaugurating a civil war, the most stupendous on record, for no other purpose than retaining them as laborers. Does any intelligent person doubt the utility of such a people? Can such a people now be worthless in the country? Does any enlightened, reflecting person believes it? I think not.

But this is an experiment. Have we no precedent, no example? What of the British colonies of the West Indies and South America? Let imperial history and dispassionate, intelligent investigation answer. The land in the colonies was owned by wealthy capitalists and gentlemen who resided in Europe. The "proprietors", or planters, were occupants of the land, who owned the slaves that worked it, having borrowed the capital with which to purchase them at the Cuba markets or barracoons and supply the plantations. In security for this, mortgages were held by those in Europe on "all estates, real and personal," belonging to the planters who paid a liberal interest on the loans.

When the opposition in the British Parliament, led by Tories, who were the representatives of the capitalists, yielded to the Emancipation Bill, it was only on condition of an appropriation of twenty million pounds sterling, or one hundred million dollars, as remuneration to the planters for their slaves set free. This proposition was so moderate as to surprise and astonish the intelligent in state affairs on both sides of the ocean, as the sum proposed only amounted to the penurious price of about one hundred and twenty dollars apiece, when men and women were then bringing at the barracoons in Cuba from five to six hundred dollars apiece in cash; and the average of men, women, and children, according to their estimate of black mankind, were "worth" four hundred and fifty dollars. Of course the tutored colonial laborer would be worth still more.

After the passage of the Act of Emancipation by The Imperial Parliament, the complaint was wafted back by the breeze of every passing wind, that the planters in the colonies were impoverished by emancipation, and dishonest politicians and defeated, morose statesmen seize the opportunity to display their duplicity. "What will become of the far colonial possessions? The lands will go back into a wilderness waste. The negroes are idle, lazy, and will not work. They are unfit for freedom, and ought to have masters. Where they do work, not half the crop is produced on the same quantity of land. What will the whites do if they don't get servants to work for them? They and their posterity must starve. The lands are lying waste for the want of occupants, and the negroes are idling their time away, and will not have them when offered to them. The social system in the West Indies has been ruined by the emancipation of the negroes." These, and a thousand such complaints, tingled upon the sensitive ear in every word that came from the British colonies, as the key-note of the pro-slavery British party, till caught up and reechoed from the swift currents of Southern extremity of Brazil to the banks of the Potomac, the Northern extremity of the slave territory of the United States. But alive to passing events, and true to their great trust, the philanthropist and people soon discovered, through their eminent representatives and statesmen in Parliament, that the whites in the colonies had never owned the lands nor the blacks which they lost by the Act of Emancipation. And when the appropriation was made by Parliament, the money remained in the vaults of the banks in Europe, being precisely the amount required to liquidate the claims of the capitalists and to satisfy the mortgages by those gentlemen against "all estates" of the borrowers in the colonies, both "real and personal."

The cause of the cry and clamor must be seen at a glance. The money supposed to be intended for the colonists, small as it was, instead of being appropriated to them, simply went to satisfy the claims of the capitalists who resided in Great Britain, not one of a hundred of whom have ever seen the colonies. And the land being owned in Europe, and the laborers free, what was to save the white colonists from poverty? All this was well known to leading pro-slavery politicians and statesmen in Europe as well as America; but a determination to perpetuate the bondage of a people as laborers—a people so valuable as to cause them, rather than lose their grasp upon them, to boldly hazard their national integrity, and set at defiance the morality of the civilized world in holding them—caused this reprehensible imposition and moral outrage in misleading to distraction their common constituency.

SOURCE: Frank (Frances) Rollin, *Life and Public Services of Martin R. Delany* (Boston: Lee and Shepard, 1868), 230–41.

DOCUMENT 4
PROSPECTS OF THE FREEDMEN OF HILTON HEAD ISLAND 6

Mr. Editor: This is my sixth article on the subject of the "Prospect of the Freedmen of Hilton Head Island," which you have so generously admitted into the columns of *The New South*, and for which liberality towards a recently liberated people, I most heartily thank you. The time may come when they, for themselves, may be able to thank you. I hope to conclude with my next.

After what has been adduced in proof of their susceptibility, adaptation, and propensity for the vocations of the domestic and social relations of our civilization, what are their PROSPECTS? For that now must be the leading question, and give more concern to the philanthropist, true statesmen, and Christians, than relating to their fitness or innate adaptation, since that I hold to be admitted, and no longer a question—at least with the intelligent inquirer.

What should be the prospect? Will not the same labor that was performed by the slave be in requisition still? Cannot he do the same work as a freeman that he once did as a slave? Are the products of slave labor preferable to free? Or are the products of free labor less valuable than slave? Will not rice and cotton be in as great demand after emancipation as before it? Or will these commodities cease to be used, because they cease to be produced by the labor of slaves? All these are questions pertinent, if not potent, to the important inquiry under consideration: the prospect of the freedmen of Hilton Head.

Certainly these things will be required, in demand, and labor quite as plentiful; but not one half of the negroes can be induced to work, as was proven in the West Indies, and is apparent from the comparative number who now seek their old vocations to those who formerly did the same work.

Grant this,—which is true, and is it an objectionable feature, or does it impair the prospect of the freedmen? By no means; but, on the contrary, it enhances his prospects and elevates his manhood. Here, as in the case of West Indian emancipation, before emancipation took place every available person—male and female—from seven years of age to decrepit old age (as field hands) was put into the field to labor.

For example, take one case to illustrate the whole. Before liberated, Juba had a wife and eight children, from seven to thirty years of age, every one of whom was a labor in the field as a slave. When set free, the mother and all of the younger children (consisting of five) quit the field, leaving the father and three older sons, from twenty-five to thirty years of age, who preferred field labor; the five children being sent to school. The mother, now the bride of the recently-elevated freedman, stays in her own house, to take charge, as a housewife, in her new domestic relations—thus permanently withdrawing from the field six-tenths of the service of this family; while the husband and three sons (but four-tenths) are all who remain to do the work formerly performed by ten-tenths, or the whole. Here are more than one half who will not work in the field. Will anyone say they should? And this one example may suffice for the most querulous on this subject. Human nature is all the same under like circumstances. The immutable, unalterable law which governed or controlled the instincts or impulse of a Hannibal, Alexander, or Napoleon, are the same implanted in the brain and breast of page or footman, be he black or white, circumstances alone making the difference in development according to the individual propensity.

As slaves, people have no choice of pursuit or vocation, but must follow that which is chosen by the master. Slaves, like freemen, have different tastes and desires—many doing that which is repugnant to their choice. As slaves, they were compelled to sub-serve the interests of the master regardless of themselves; as freemen, as should be expected and be understood, many changes would take place in the labor and pursuits of the people. Some who were field hands, among young men and women of mature age, seek employment at other pursuits, and choose for themselves various trades—vocations adapted to their tastes.

Will this be charged to the worthlessness of the negro and made an argument against his elevation? Truth stands defiant in the pathway of error.

SOURCE: Frank (Frances) Rollin, *Life and Public Services of Martin R. Delany* (Boston: Lee and Shepard, 1868), 230–41.

DOCUMENT 5
Prospects of the Freedmen of Hilton Head Island 7

I propose to conclude the subject of "THE PROSPECTS OF THE FREEDMEN OF HILTON HEAD" with this article, and believe that the prospects of the one are the prospects of the whole population of freedmen throughout the South.

Political economy must stand most prominent as the leading feature of this great question of the elevation of the negro—and it is a great question—in this country, because, however, humane and philanthropic, however Christian and philanthropic we may be, except we can be made to see that there is a prospective enhancement of the general wealth of the country,—pecuniary benefit to accrue by it to society,—the best of us, whatever our pretensions, could scarcely be willing to see him elevated in the United States.

Equality of political rights being the genius of the American government, I shall not spend time with this, as great principles will take care of themselves, and must eventually prevail.

Will the negroes be able to obtain land by which to earn a livelihood? Why should they not? It is a well-known fact to the statisticians of the South that two thirds of the land have never been cultivated. These lands being mainly owned by but three hundred and twelve thousand persons (according to Helper)—one third of which was worked by four millions of slaves, who are now freemen—what better can be done with these lands to make them available and unburdensome to the proprietors, than let them out in small tracts to the freedmen, as well as to employ a portion of the same people, who prefer it, to cultivate lands for themselves.

It is a fact—probably not so well known as it should be—in political economy, that a given amount of means divided among a greater number of persons, makes a wealthier community than the same amount held or possessed by a few.

For example, there is a community of a small country village of twenty families, the (cash) wealth of the community being fifty thousand dollars, and but one family the possessor of it; certainly the community would not be regarded as in good circumstances, much less having available means. But let this amount be possessed by ten families in sums of five thousand dollars each, would not this enhance the wealth of the community? And again, let the whole twenty families be in possession of two thousand five hundred dollars each of the fifty thousand, would not this be still a wealthier community, by placing each family in easier circumstances, and making these means much more available? Certainly it would. And as to a community or village so to a state; and as to a state, so to a nation.

This is the solution to the great problem of the difference between the strength of the North and the South in the late rebellion—the North possessing the means within itself without requiring outside help, almost every man being able to aid the national treasury; everybody commanding means, whether earned by a white-wash brush in black hands, or wooden nutmegs in white; all had something to sustain the integrity of the Union. It must be seen by this that the strength of the country, internationally considered, depends greatly upon its wealth; the wealth consisting not in the greatest amount possessed, but the greatest available amount.

Let, then, such lands as belong to the government, by sale from direct taxation, be let or sold to these freedmen, and other poor loyal men of the South, in small tracts of from twenty or forty acres to each head of a family, and large landholders do the same,—the rental and sales of which amply rewarding them,—and there will be no difficulty in the solution of the problem of the future, or prospects of the freedmen, not only on Hilton Head, but of the whole United States.

This increase of the wealth of the country by the greater division of its means is not new to New England, nor to the economists of the North generally. As in Pennsylvania, many years ago, the old farmers commenced dividing their one hundred and one hundred and fifty acre tracts of lands into twenty-five acres each among their sons and daughters, who are known to have realized more available means always among them—though by far greater in numbers—than their parents did, who were comparatively few. And it is now patent as an historic fact, that, leaving behind them the extensive evergreen, fertile plains, and savannas of the South, the rebel armies and raiders continually sought the limited farms of the North to replenish their worn-out cavalry stock and exhausted commissary department—impoverished in cattle for food, and forage for horses.

In the Path Valley of Pennsylvania, on a single march of a radius of twenty-five miles of Chambersburg, Lee's army, besides all the breadstuffs that his three thousand five hundred wagons (as they went empty for the purpose) were able to carry, captured and carried off more than six thousand head of stock, four thousands of which were horses. The wealth of that valley alone, they reported, was more than India fiction, and equal to all of the South put together. And whence this mighty available wealth of Pennsylvania? Simply by its division and possession among the many.

The Rothschilds are said to have once controlled the exchequer of England, compelling (by implication) the Premier to comply with their requisition at a time of great peril to the nation, simply because it depended upon them for means; and the same functionaries are reported, during our recent struggle, to have greatly annoyed the Bank of England, by a menace of some kind, which immediately brought the institution to their terms. Whether true of false, the points are sufficiently acute to serve for illustration.

In the apportionment of small farms to the freedmen, an immense amount of means is placed at their command, and thereby a great market opened, a new source of consumption of every commodity in demand in free civilized communities. The blacks are great consumers, and four million of a population, before barefooted, would here make a demand for the single article of shoes. The money heretofore spent in Europe by the old slaveholders would be all disbursed by these new people in their own country. Where but one cotton gin and a limited number of farming utensils were formerly required to the plantation of a thousand acres, every small farm will want a gin and farming implements, the actual valuation of which on the same tract of land would be several fold greater than the other. Huts would give place to beautiful, comfortable cottages, with all their appurtenances, fixtures, and furniture; osnaburgs and rags would give place to genteel apparel becoming a free and industrious people; and even the luxuries, as well as the general comforts, of the table would take the place of black-eye peas and fresh fish, hominy and salt pork, all of which have been mainly the products of their own labor when slaves. They would quickly prove that arduous and faithfully fawning, miserable volunteer advocate of the rebellion and slaveholder's rule in the United States,—*The London Times*,—an errant falsifier, when it gratuitously and unbidden came to the aid of its kith and kin, declaring that the great and good President Lincoln's Emancipation Proclamation would not be accepted by the negroes; "that all Cuffee wanted and cared for to make him happy was his hog and his hominy;" but they will neither get land, nor will the old slaveholders give them employment. Don't fear any such absurdity. There are too many political economists among the old leading slaveholders to fear the adoption of any such policy. Neither will the leading statesmen of the country, of any part, North or South, favor any such policy.

We have on record but one instance of such a course in history of modern states. The silly-brained, foolhardy King of France, Louis V, taking umbrage at the political course of the artisans and laborers against him, by royal decree expelled them from the country, when they flocked into England, which readily opened her doors to them, transplanting from France to England their arts and industry; ever since which, England, for fabrics, has become the "workshop of the world," to the poverty of France, the government of which is sustained by borrowed capital.

No fears of our country driving into neighboring countries such immense resources as emanate from the peculiar labor of these people; but when worst comes to worst, they have among them educated freemen of their own color North, fully, competent to lead the way, by making negotiations with foreign states on this continent, which would only be too ready to receive them and theirs.

Place no impediment in the way of the freedmen; let his rights be equally protected and his chances be equally regarded, and with the facts presented to you in this series of seven articles as the basis, he will stand and thrive, as firmly rooted, not only on the soil of Hilton Head, but in all the South,—though a black,—as any white, or "Live Oak", as ever was grown in South Carolina, or transplanted to Columbia.

SOURCE: Frank (Frances) Rollin, *Life and Public Services of Martin R. Delany* (Boston: Lee and Shepard, 1868), 237–41. Numbers 3 and 4 of the series are missing.

DOCUMENT 6
Triple Alliance: The Restoration of the South —Salvation of Its Political Economy

The restoration of the industrial prosperity of the South is CERTAIN, if fixed upon the basis of a domestic triple alliance, which the new order of things requires, invites and demands.

Capital, land, and labor require a co-partnership. The capital can be obtained in the North; the land is in the South, owned by the old planters; and the blacks have the labor. Let, then, the North supply the capital (which no doubt it will do on demand, when known to be desired on this basis), the South the land (which is ready and waiting), and the blacks will readily bring the labor, if only being assured that their services are wanted in so desirable an association of business relations, the net profits being equally shared between the three,—capital, land, and labor,—each receiving one third, of course. The NET has reference to the expenses incurred after gathering the crop, such as transportation, storage, and commission on sales.

Upon this basis I propose to act, and make contracts between the capitalist, landholder, and laborer, and earnestly invite and call upon all colored people,—the recent freedmen,—also capitalists and landholder within the limits of my district, to enter at once into a measure the most reasonable and just to all parties concerned, and the very best that can be adopted to meet the demands of the new order and State of Society, as nothing can pay better where the blacks cannot get land for themselves.

I am at liberty to name Rev. Dr. Stoney (Episcopal Clergyman), Joseph J. Stoney, Esq., Dr. Crowell, Colonel Colcock (late of the Southern army)—all the first gentlemen formerly of wealth and affluence in the State; and Major Roy, of the United States Regular Army, Inspector General of the department; Colonel Green, commanding district, and Lieutenant Colonel Clitz, commanding post, also of the regular army, each having friends interested in planting, who readily endorse this new partnership arrangement. Of course it receives the approval of Major General Saxton.
I am, sir, very respectfully
Your most obedient servant
M. R. Delany
Major and A.S.A. Commissioner
Bureau R.F.A.L. HILTON HEAD,
December 7, 1865

Source: Frank (Frances) Rollin, *Life and Public Services of Martin R. Delany* (Boston: Lee and Shepard, 1868), 242–43.

DOCUMENT 7
HOMES FOR THE FREEDMEN 1

Charleston, S.C.
March 7, 1871

To Hon. Henry Wilson,
U.S. Senator.
SIR:

As one of the early friends of equal rights, I take the liberty of calling your attention to an important subject.

The thing now most required for the freedman is a home—one that he can call his own, and possess in fee simple, to insure the subsistence of himself and family. This is very desirable and, without it, the life of these poor people is a miserable burden, to be relieved of which, death will soon become a welcome messenger to the most of them, and liberty itself an evil.

I would call the attention of the philanthropic capitalists to this suggestion, which would benefit both black and white, and amply secure themselves in the capital invested.

Estimating the population of freedmen at four hundred thousand (400,000), with the usual allowance of five persons to a family, will give eighty thousand (80,000) families. Ten acres in this climate will be ample as a means of sustenance for all necessary family comforts to a rural population; more than this would not be asked as a start in life for them.

Allowing ten acres to each family (this would be the average, as some would require more and some less); it would amount to eight hundred thousand (800,000) acres.

There is at present an abundance of surplus lands in this state, which could be purchased at such a figure as to enable the purchaser to dispose of them to the freedmen at an average advance of fifty per cent on the original purchase money, and then be fully within their reach to meet with all their contingencies, such as improving and stocking their little farms.

What the freedman wants is land of his own, with time to pay for it. What the land owner wants is cash for his surplus lands. He has been impoverished by the late civil war, having nothing left but these surplus lands, and when not living by their products, he can only afford to part with them for cash. This cash the poor, industrious, hard-laboring freedmen has not got, nor can he get while only receiving the wages of labor, or paying such rentals as he must, and is generally paying, either in cash or portion of the crop.

There are cases of rentals in which the occupants of the land, whether in cash or produce, do pay more per acre for the use of the land (and in many cases two and three hundred per cent more) than what the same land could be bought for in cash if sold. It will be seen at a glance that this is ruinous to the laborer, who never will be able to make more than his bread; for in thousands of cases, indeed the majority of the rural population, the men and women are in rags, and the smaller children of both sexes either stark naked, or cover with but a single shirt.

Nor would this securing of homes to the rural population impoverish the State by depriving the land holders of labor; but, to the contrary, it would be a lasting benefit, by securing an industrious and fixed laboring element, the surplus of whose labor would always be ample for all the demands of the large land owners and planters, with advanced wages; as both land and the wages of labor would enhance in value, just in proportion to the general permanent improvement of these numerous little farming neighborhoods.

I am continually being called upon by gentlemen who are willing to sell lands at the lowest figure, to secure such homes to the freedmen, because they knew that it would be mutually beneficial to themselves, the freedmen, and the commonwealth at large.

Sir, will you call the attention of philanthropists to this important subject?
I am sir, very respectfully
Your most obedient servant
M. R. Delany
Late Major 104th U.S.C.T., and Sub-Asst. Com. Bureau R.F. and A.L.
Charleston, S.C.

SOURCE: *Daily Republican* (Charleston), March 7, 1871.

DOCUMENT 8
HOMES FOR THE FREEDMEN 2

Charleston, S.C.
March 23, 1871

Col. D. L. Eaton, Washington, D.C.
Sir,

On the 7th inst., I addressed a communication through the Charleston DAILY REPUBLICAN to Senator Wilson, on the subject of "Homes for the Freedmen".

In that, I showed how small farms of an average of ten (10) acres could be secured to each of the eighty thousand families of freedmen, at the present low price of lands, giving them ample time to pay, and yet be a profitable investment to the philanthropic capitalists, and a cheap home to the people.

In addition to the importance of securing cheap homes on easy terms to four hundred thousand people, there is another feature of this, scarcely less important, to which I would especially invite your attention.

At the present the taxes in this State are very heavy and burdensome, not perhaps because they are so very high, but mainly because of the disproportion in the estimates, and nearly the whole coming off the few.

This could not be a point of objection if the property taxed were generally available, producing an income adequate to the expenses. But this far from the reality, as there are numerous cases in which property (especially lands) when sold, could not bring half, no, not one-fourth, of the assessment estimate for taxes. This is a matter worthy of note.

Land in South Carolina is greatly depreciated, while taxes have become proportionably higher. These taxes are mainly paid by a very few of the citizens, as the great majority own little or no real estate, paying little else than the simple capitation tax.

By securing home for the homeless, it must be affected by the much desirable division of lands, and by this division of lands, a division of the taxes, the source of the public revenue.

When the expenses of government are proportionately borne by the people generally, whatever excesses there may be committed by those to whom they have entrusted the duties and functions of State affairs, then, and not till then, will they be sufficiently interested to hold them accountable for their doings.

Let the people, then—those now homeless—generally become freeholders, possessors of the land, with improved real estate, and they at once become proportionably interested in all the affairs of the State, and they, who are the principal voters, will see to it that reckless and incompetent men will not be sent a second time to misrepresent them and the interests of the State.

But let the freedmen have homes of their own, fixed and established interests in the soil and State that others have, and that never—failing natural desire for each other's welfare and the protection of each other's interests, will establish that neighborly friendship throughout the entire State, without which, freedom would be a curse alike to black and white, and republican liberty a mockery and lie.

Sir, I renew the invitation of your attention to my letter of the 7th instant on "Homes for the Freedmen," above referred to, and hope that so desirable an object may engage the attention of the philanthropic capitalists.

I am, sir, in behalf of a suffering people of a State of both races almost distracted.

Your most obedient servant
M. R. Delany
Charleston, S.C.

SOURCE: *Daily Republican* (Charleston), April 5, 1871.

DOCUMENT 9
HOMES FOR THE FREEDMEN 3

Charleston, S.C.
May 1, 1871

COL. D. L. Eaton, Washington, D.C.
Sir,

This is my third letter on the subject of "Homes for the Freedmen," the second, which you kindly gave a place, being written on the 23rd of March.

This subject is of much importance, and becomes even imminent as time passed, because, so soon as emigration turns its tide in this direction; which is now being earnestly solicited by organizations of prominent and popular gentlemen—the golden opportunity now offered of obtaining lands at the lowest cash price will have passed forever.

Nothing can add more to the permanent peace and pecuniary interests of this State than the possession of fixed homes, owned in fee simple by the laboring classes once slaves.

Capital will not be invested without labor, and labor will neither remain nor go where there is no choice of employment. Consequently, capitalists are fearful to invest in planting, because there is no certainty that labor will be secure, as the laborer is continually changing places in search of permanent employment.

Besides this, the more intelligent the laborer, the more productive the labor. This is demonstrated in the German, who by odds is the best agriculturalist to be found. This is simply because the German is intelligent; he must be educated. Every child must go to school and learn to read, write and cipher, compelled by law; hence his intelligence.

The freedmen, too, must be educated, but it will be impossible to establish facilities for education till they become settled and fixed in neighborhoods. It would be a waste of time and money to build school houses and make other outlays for such purposes where there is no certainty of the people remaining beyond one planting season. And to expect the same development from the freed people as other citizens, without the same kind of facilities for moral, intellectual and religious culture, is to expect an impossibility.

And what will these people be as a social and political element to the Society or State at large without this moral, intellectual and religious culture? Simply a curse instead of a blessing. The Church and the school must stand side by side, projecting their gable peaks or belfry spires in silent eloquence toward the skies in every district, settlement among these people.

But before either the Church or school house can be erected, the people themselves must be settled in HOMES OF THEIR OWN. This can be the only indemnity or security against all investments for permanent improvements in the social and industrial condition of the people, black and white, in the rural or agricultural districts.

The surplus lands are abundant, and the people waiting and ready to settle them. The owners are willing and anxious to sell them, on terms for cash entirely satisfactory and advantageous to the purchasers. But the purchases must be special, through agencies for this object, and not by speculation to put money in the pockets of persons disinterested in a philanthropic enterprise which would only defeat the intention by increasing the required investment too great to make it practicable and profitable.

The lands purchased for this enterprise must be secured at first and not second hand prices, and the only cost in doing so, must simply be that of the commission of the agent, which, in this arrangement, is made to come off the seller, and not those who purchase for the freedmen, so that there will be actually no expense incurred in the agency, leaving the entire margin clear to the philanthropists who sell to the freedmen.

I am sure that this will justify the investment even if the terms be in five annual payments (with interest, of course).

There can be no safer nor surer investment of any kind than this—being in land, which must continually enhance in value—and in four years it will reimburse the funds with an advance of two-fifths or forty percent, on the whole amount expended, with an addition of seven per cent interest, the legal rate of the State. In this there can be no losing risk.

If the friends of humanity and progress of the South will accept of this and act at once, in less than one year every family of freedmen in South Carolina will be in full possession of a house of TEN ACRES, held in fee simple, forever.

I think, sir, that I have now placed all before you necessary on this important subject, consequently this will close my series.

All other required information will be carried in through private correspondence.

In conclusion, if there be not prompt and decisive action, all may be lost by permitting the golden opportunity of obtaining lands at so low a figure to pass by forever.

I am, sir, very respectfully
M. R. Delany
Charleston, S.C.

Source: *Daily Republican* (Charleston), May 2, 1871.

DOCUMENT 10
Special Orders No. 372

WAR DEPARTMENT, ADJUTANT GENERAL'S OFFICE,
WASHINGTON, D.C., JULY 15, 1865.

Special Orders, No. 372.

Extract.

46. The following named officers of the 104th United States Colored Troops are hereby relieved from duty with that regiment, and assigned to duty in the Bureau of Refugees, Freedmen, and Abandoned Lands.

They will report in person without delay, to Brevet Major General R. Saxton, Assistant Commissioner for the States of South Carolina and Georgia.

Major MARTIN R. DELANY

By order of the Secretary of War,
E. D. Townsend,
Asst. Adjt. Gen.

Source: Frank (Frances) Rollin, *Life and Public Services of Martin R. Delany* (Boston: Lee and Shepard, 1868), 225–26.

DOCUMENT 11
Delany's Freedmen's Bureau Report, December 1865

Bureau R.F.A.L.
Hilton Head, S.C.
Dec. 19, 1865

Major C. D. Newman
Asst. Adjt. General
Head of U.S. Asst. Comm'r Bu. R.F.A.L. and Ga.,

Major:

I have the honor to report for the month of December, the proximate quantity of lands and houses. I can only give a proximate statement because there as yet has been no proper survey of lands, no census of population or number of houses taken.

I would respectfully call your attention to Pinckney, Bale's Lemonaire and other Islands in the neighborhood, by nature seeming to be adjuncts of Hilton Head, none of which have an agency of the Bureau over there, but all of which apply to the Bureau at Port Royal, Hilton Head, to have their affairs adjusted. I have generally assumed tacitly in such cases official action over their affairs on these ... act of which have been accepted by the people both black and white.

But I would respectfully suggest to the Major General, Asst., Commissioner, the importance of including these islands under the jurisdiction of Hilton Head.

I have the honor to be, Major.
Your most obedient servant
M. R. Delany
Major, A.S.A.C.

Source: Records of the Assistant Commissioner of the State of South Carolina, Bureau of Refugees, Freedmen, and Abandoned Lands, 1865–1870, Microcopy 849, Roll 33, 102–4, National Archives and Records Administration, Washington, DC.

DOCUMENT 12
Delany's Freedmen's Bureau Report, March 1867

Headquarters Bureau Department,
Hilton Head, Port Royal, S.C.
March 1st 1867.

Brevet Major Gaton I. Drane
A.A.A. General,
Headquarters, Charleston, S.C.

Major:

I have the honor to report to the Major General Commanding Military District of South Carolina, the operations of the Bureau in this District, since my last official report, ending with the year 1866.

It was apparent from observation and experience, that the custom of renting the lands to speculators, who sub-let them to, or employed, the freedmen to work for them at disadvantageous rates, that these same people at the end of the planting year, habitually come out with nothing, absolutely nothing generally, nay worse than nothing, as those working the lands shares, having rations supplied from the stores of the speculators, or renting the lands and obtaining rations on credit from such stores, when the crops are realized, paid them all away to these stores for the scanty mouthful they received on credit, finding themselves with nothing—in rags and in search for a "balance diet", on the books of these first hand leasers and supply speculators. This most reprehensible custom, continued from the coming of the U.S. direct tax Commissioners into Office, till the end of the past calendar year.

But how could the Commissioners do better, as those very excellent gentlemen—especially Judge Nording—have repeatedly informed me that their orders and instructions from the Department at Washington, were to rent the lands at the highest cash offer regardless of domestic surrounding, which they did. This of course threw out the freemen and Refugees/poor whites, placing them entirely dependent upon and at the mercy of theses speculators. To these, there were some excellent exceptions, of whom may be named that excellent gentleman (with an equally excellent lady), Henry C. Vail, Esqr, planter of Pinckney Island, leasee of Elliott and Seabrook Plantations, and of the plantation firms of Whitmell and Vail, whoever advised the people against unnecessary and extravagant expenditures, letting them have lands on the most reasonable terms, and provision and clothing supplies according.

And those who had a little chance of raising crops for themselves to advantage were equally the victims of the brokers and petty cotton traders (from their superior knowledge and intelligence), and the almost entire want of these qualifications on the part of the freedmen, their cotton being sacrificed in the market.

It was evident from these facts, that there could be little or no chance for the Freemen of Refugees, to compete with the bidders or leases of the lands, let at the highest cash price, frequently far above their value in this District, except by the adoption of some measure for their protection, whereby a fraction of their scanty earnings could be saved, and the lands let to them at prices suited to their means, in preference to speculators and capitalists.

To this end, I recommend the establishment of a Freedmen' s Cotton Agency, to be attended to by a competent Agent, where all who desired it, could have their cotton deposited on consignment, cutted, (assorted), ginned, packed (bagged) and sold at the highest cash market value in Charleston, they realized the net profit themselves, instead of the speculators.

To make such establishment profitable to the freedmen, the expenses should be as moderate as possible, and less than the usual rates of charges in such establishments. Hence to accomplish which, a suitable building not required for use at the time, was obtained from Quarter Master's department (free of rent, of course) and all or any Freedmen owning foot gins were invited to put them up in this establishment, where they might be run in ginning the cotton brought by freedmen for market, charging twenty percent, or one fifth less than the market price for ginning, and receiving when not run by themselves, one fourth of the proceeds of the gin, the freedmen who run it receiving the other three fourths as his share, thus making them self-sustaining, as well as self-reliant.

The agent supplied the bagging, and received as compensation for the advances thus made, the pay for the weight of the bag, deducted from the price of the bag of cotton. This will be understood in mercantile trade, as bagging is always worth in weight the price of cotton pound.

By this means, a percentage could be charged, so as to cover actual expenses, and give the agent a reasonable living compensation, such as his services were worth under the circumstances, whereby at least thirty per cent, or one third of the price of the cotton could be saved to the freedmen.

The whole arrangement being devised and recommended by the Bureau here as previously reported to Headquarters, Charleston, and approved, was carried on under the official protection of these Headquarters, to which everything done was frequently reported, according to instructions given.

The Freedmen generally in this Bureau District, availed themselves of the advantage of this establishment.

The next effort officially, was to secure to them the advantages of the lands at a firsthand low rate, as they now were able to raise the means among themselves, by which to secure the leases. To this end, interviews and correspondence were had with the Tax commissioners, who being without instructions and awaiting the action of Congress and the Government in relation to the division and assignment of land on the tenure of Lieut. General Sherman's great Field Order, No. 15, after mature consideration, as the season for planting was rapidly approaching and the people clamorously anxious to go to work to prepare for cultivation; concluded to divide the responsibility with the Bureau (at its earnest solicitation, suggestion and representations) and let the lands to the freedmen at <u>one dollar an acre</u>, for the next year 1867.

They had been advised to prepare to obtain the lands at the dollar an acre, the leases to be made to one man on each Island, who would receive and pay over their money, and see the lands properly divided.

In less than three weeks from the time notice was given to this effect, upwards of three-thousand ($3000.00) dollars in cash and cotton vouchers were deposited in the Bureau to secure the leases, and fourteen plantations were thus broken, with the extreme satisfaction, of paying back to each individual, one half of his money, or one dollar for every acre of land taken by him. This last act of the Commissioners Crowns their Official doings with discretion and liberality, which should entitle them to at least the thanks of the friends of humanity, if not respectful consideration of Congress.

By care, frugality and proper management with the required protection in their operations, at the end of the planting season, I anticipate for the freedmen in the Bureau District of Hilton Head, better prospects than any preceding year since their emancipation.

I should have mentioned in this connection, that the official High Agent of the Bureau in the District is William H. Calvert, Esqr, (white) and the faithful conductor of the Freedmen's Cotton Agency, is Robert L. Houston, Esqr., (Colored) later Purser on the Steamer <u>Planter</u>.

Contracting for planting the current year has been very general, and lands easily obtained, as a year experience has made them understand the problem much better than at first, the excellent form of contract recommended by the Major General Asst. Commissioner, being acceptable to both cultivators and planters. Many planters from the Main and other parts come to this district for the approval of their contracts, all of whom without exception accept the form recommended by the General, whatever the modifications of terms.

Misdemeanors are less frequent among the people, as they comprehend their relation to society in their new life, and they are much improving in their social relations.

There are still old people indigent or destitute, and helpless orphans, who have not relatives to care for them, and are quite burdensome to others, who scarcely able to support themselves. For this class, now comparatively few in this District, some provisions for subsistence or ration on the part of the Government—for at least one part of the year—would be commendable.

All the plantations in the Bureau District of Hilton Head, have been let solely for the benefit of the freedmen at first-hand, and with but one exception (the Elliott Place) leased directly to Blacks now through the Actg. Asst. Commissioner of the Bureau—the latter by mutual understanding being taken by H. C. Vail, Esqr., to obtain the privileges of but eleven (11) acres of potato land, and the mansion, all the rest with buildings going to the freedmen.

The past military administration at this post, especially the Provost Department, was very unsatisfactory, and frequently unjust and injurious to the freedmen; but now under Brevet Lieut. Col. John Hamilton, very different. The Colonel is a high-minded, just and impartial officer, and generous hearted gentleman in his dealings.

I avail myself of this occasion to again bring before the attention of the Major General, the fact, that all of the contingent expenses of the office of the Bureau at these Headquarters, as lights, brooms, and all other office allowance, are borne by me from my private funds; and have been ever since my appointment to the office on the seventh (7th) day of August, 1865, under Major General R. Saxton, there never having been a requisition for anything excepting stationery, firewood, and forage accepted. If there be any provisions by which these supplies are to be made, and expenses covered by the government, I ask the favor of being officially informed.

James H. Tonking Esqr., late captain in the 33rd, U.S. Colored Troops, is still doing duty a portion of his time as *staff* at these Headquarters, there being no provisions made for such duties, the business of this office being quite important, and could give constant employment to a clerk under proper directions.

The Police system among the freedmen still works well, and is doing much good toward regulating their domestic and social affairs.

I have the honor to be Major.

Your most obedient servant,
M. R. Delany
Major and A.A. Commissioner

SOURCE: Records of Assistant Commissioner of the State of South Carolina, Bureau of Refugees, Freedmen, and Abandoned Lands, 1865–1870, Microcopy 849, Roll 35, 9–15, National Archives and Records Administration, Washington, DC.

DOCUMENT 13
Delany's Freedmen's Bureau Report, September 1867

Headquarters, Field District
Hilton Head, S.C.
September 27th 1867

Brevet. Major Edward L. Diane
A.D.C. and A.A.A. General
Bureau R.F. and A.L.,
Charleston, S.C.

Major:

I have the honor herewith to transmit to the Brevt, Major General Asst. Commissioner in obedience to instruction of the 16th Inst; my annual report for the current year.

There is apparent among the freedmen, a marked improvement in their domestic relations each succeeding years since the establishment of the Bureau; their manners, habits, and customs, having materially changed.

Industry and thrift, self-reliance and providence, being better understood, the land is eagerly sought, that they may depend upon their own labor for subsistence.

At the beginning of the year, as given in a general report in May sent to Headquarter, the land were obtained directly from the Tax Commissioners, at the cost of one ($1) dollar per acre.

The number of plantation tracts thus taken in whole or part, are: Drayton, 100 acres; Seabrook, 127 acres; Pope, 133 acres; Stoney, 100 acres; Jenkins Island, 82 acres; Spanish Hills, 133 acres; Marshland, 58 acres; Cherry Hill, 44 acres; Cane Hill, 60 acres; Grassland, 250 acres; Chaplin, 55 acres; Folly Reid, 100 acres; Point Comfort, 50 acres; Lawton, 100 acres; Bradlock's Point, 100 acres; besides a number of acres rented on land of the U.S. Cotton

Company; Pinckney, Dawfuskie and Savage Islands, making an aggregate of probably 200 acres more.

This course gave a decided advantage to the people over the former system of obtaining the lands at second hand, at an average of fifteen ($15) dollars per acre; the manner in which they had to pay for it, invariably took their entire crop leaving them in debt to the leaser and supplier, without anything, except rags, squalid poverty, and a bad name.

Even to make this an effective and self-sustaining measures, the local habits of the occupant must be essentially changed. Instead of the former old plantation people remaining in the places as a local preference, which generally allows but an average of five (5) acres to the family, the lands must be let in portions of twenty acres, and from that, to forty acres to each family, before they can be made available to their support. This would necessitate a general scattering, or greater division of the people, causing at first quite a change of places with many. To do justice to the people as an available social or domestic element, no one hundred acres of farming land should be occupied by more than five (5) families, thus allowing (20) acres to the family, which in the light of domestic or political economy, is little enough. Less than this, is to place them in a position of hazardous uncertainty and anxiety, and encourage idleness and improvidence, by inducing the thriftless to settle under circumstances, which must make them burdensome to the thrifty and provident. By this course the aged and otherwise needy and deserving helpless, could be easily aided by their neighbors, without, as now, being over burdensome.

It is very evident that the entire system of cultivation will have to be changed, both in the method of doing it, and, more especially, the produce raised, to suit and meet the change in the social system, the demands and status of the new possessors and permanent residents of small farms and gardens. Every month in the year but one (December) may be made productive of some vegetable for provisions or family use, whereby the people may be independent in subsistence. It is a settled matter, that in this country, cotton can only be profitably produced, by extensive cultivation and large capital under favorable circumstances; consequently, it is a loss of time and labor, for the freedmen to plant cotton with their limited means of land and materials, as the ground to them, can be put to a much more useful purpose.

I am preparing the people in this District to this end, and believe that against the approaching leasing year, they would be quite ready and willing to enter into the new system of habitation and occupancy.

Among the arrangements made for the benefit of the Freedmen, was the establishment of a cotton agency (which has previously been formally reported to Headquarters, Bureau, Charleston) where it was intended and arranged for the people to prepare their own cotton, and have it bagged, and sold for them by the agent at Charleston market price, the cash to be paid here at Hilton Head on delivery. This arrangement was working well, and enabled the people to husband sufficient means, to lease and pay cash for the lands as herein before stated.

Gen. Order No. 18, Department S.C., prohibiting Military Officers in commission, having anything to do directly with trade in planting staples or other commodities, placed entire control of the establishment under the agent, who taking advantage of the inducements presented by the business, became a defaulter to the Freedmen and Merchants who credited him, to the amount of about $3,000. So soon as the fraud was discovered, accompanied by R. C. McIntyre Esqr., Merchant, and principle creditor, I repaired in May last directly to Charleston, his former residence, where the agent was detected, and by Order issued by the Adjt. General, Headquarters Assistant Commissioner, had him arrested by a Military guard, and held in custody, till he executed a Bond and Mortgage to the full amount of his liabilities to the Freedmen, which I placed in the hands of eminent counsel (Messrs. Whaby & Co., agent in trust, of the property of the defaulter), who executed the papers.

This cotton agent was Mr. R. L. Houston Jr., formerly purser on the Government Transport Steamer Planter, commanded by Capt. Robert Smalls. This whole case, has been officially reported to Headquarters, Bureau, Charleston. It should have been stated, that the agency after thorough inspection and investigation by Brig. Gen'l Faust, was approved by order of Major General Scott, by Gen'l Faust, bearing date October 29th 1866.

During the current year, there have been no rations issued in this sub-District, except two hundred (200) bushels of corn for the Southern Relief Association, and five hundred (500) bushels, and one thousand (1000) lbs of beacon, in the Congressional appropriation, assigned through the commissary of subsistence, Bureau, Charleston.

The schools, three (3) in Mitcheville, one (1) Seabrook, two (2) in Stoney, one (1) at Marshland, one (1) at Lawton, and one (1) on Dawfuskie Island, nine (9) in all, under patronage of the American Missionary Association, New York, have been well kept up during the school term with an average attendance in the aggregate of one hundred children daily.

In this sub-District there has been no expenditure for school House by the sub. Asst. comm., for the reason that materials for building are so scarce, that no person could be found to undertake the contracts, except at such prices as entirely included an entertainment and report of them to Headquarters. The continuance of these schools I would most earnestly recommend to the favorable consideration of the Bureau. The examples and precepts of the teachers have been such, as to merit my most hearty approval. But there is one custom as yet common to schools, and almost regarded as an essential part of training, and which I most heartily desire should be done away with. I refer to whipping children as a correction in school. It is simply a relic of ignorance, and should not be tolerated by intelligence. And while this will be tolerated, teachers will resort to it, as the easiest and to them, least troublesome mode of correction.

A teacher is, or is not adapted to teaching. If properly adapted, they could and should teach without whipping. If they cannot control and correct their pupils without whipping, then it only proves that such are not adapted to teaching, and all such should seek some other employment. This is not a reflection on any particular teacher or teachers, but a condemnation of the general custom of schools. A school should be made a place of the most pleasurable resort and agreeable associations to children; but certain it is that in nowhere can this be the case, where the great hickory, long, leather strap, or bridle rein meets, as it enters the school house, the child's, as it does the eye of the visitor, reminding one, as it must them, of entering the presence of the old plantation overseer, in wait for his victim.

There has been an expenditure of $150 in repairing buildings of Headquarters, in this sub-District, officially reported to Headquarters, Bureau, Charleston.

The Police system on the plantations and in village settlements, as Mitchellville, still continues with beneficial results to the community at large, also to the Freedmen themselves in particular, by shielding their status and self-respect as citizens.

Registration progressed orderly and satisfactorily to the entire community in this sub-District, the freedmen seeming fully to comprehend and appreciate it.

In the matter of cotton speculation, but little will be done the approaching season, little comparatively having been raised, the people having been advised from these Headquarters to turn their attention more to breadstuffs, which would be the most available appropriation of the land to them.

A series of successful Temperance meetings in accordance with instructions form Headquarters, Bureau, Charleston, May 21st Circular, H'qrs., Bureau, Washington May 15th; are being held under auspices of the Bureau every Sabbath afternoon, in one of the three churches among the freedmen in Mitchellville. These meetings are well attended, with increased interest and promise much for the morals of the freedmen in this sub-District if they can be continued through the plantation settlements contemplated.

The case of the claim Division of my Office as previously reported, has been attended to by ex-Capt. J. H. Tonking, whom I engaged especially for that purpose. He had in addition rendered faithful service in special official duties assigned him as clerk of the clothing division, and making out of other reports and special papers and document, without compensation form the Bureau, as previously reported.

Of the claimants, four have been paid, two of whom deposited their money in Beaufort Bank (the other two being Northerners), and three more claims are granted and the funds in the hands of the Chief Debt Officer, Washington D.C.

... Five parents claims for arears of Pay and Bounty about ... soldiers claims for Bounty have been forwarded to the Department at Washington form this office, besides numerous unfinished business of the old Sanitary Commission which usually voluntarily come, besides being forwarded by Messr Brown of Leaton, Successor to the U.S.S. Commission, all of which, besides the arduous work of making out each paper of the claimants, an average of three different times, according to the requirements of the rulings of the Dept., Washington; there has been as yet the writing of six hundred letter required.

Since the relief of Brevt Lt. Col. Hamilton, and his immediate subordinate officers, the Bureau has met with little aid from the new administration; and I think; the freedmen, little favor. But the functions of the office at these Headquarters, have by no means been deterred, nor permitted to be illegitimately interfered with, but all have gone on regularly and well.

I have the honor to be Major,
Yours most obedient servant
M. R. Delany
Major and S.A.C.

Source: Records of the Assistant Commissioner of the State of South Carolina, Bureau of Refugees, Freedmen, and Abandoned Lands, 1865–1870, Microcopy 849, Roll 35, 354–62, National Archives and Records Administration, Washington, DC.

DOCUMENT 14
Delany's Freedmen's Bureau Report, May 1868

Brevet Major A. Neide, A.A.A. Gen.,
Bu. R.F. and A. Lands
Charleston, So.Ca.
Major:

I have the honor to submit for the consideration of the Major General, Assistant Commissioner, the following cursory official report.

First—The lands occupied by the freedmen last year, were generally well cultivated, and the crops goods, the tracks being small, and the season favorable for bread stuff, to which they principally confirmed their planting.

The yields of corn and sweet potatoes were very good, the latter being greater in quantity, and the vegetable large, than had been grown probably ever before by them; the people reported.

Health—The health of the district was very good, there being tittle sickness which may be attributed mainly to the ability, professional skill, and commendable attentions of the excellent young gentleman and medical officer, Stephen Van Duyer, M.D., A.A. Surgeon, Department of the Bureau. I cannot but attribute the absence of much of the diseases and morality common to these localities, to his professional skill and attention, because in many other neighboring parts, disease and mortality prevailed.

Second—On leasing for the current year, I restricted families ten (10) acres of lands minimum, and as much more as they were able to obtain and work, allowing none others but old less industrious men and women with small children, to ... thus compelling all able bodied single men and women, to hire out or contract with those able to employ and subsist them instead of idling about on the different places, pretending to plant one acre or a fraction, and at the end of the planting season only have nothing, being thrown upon those who had lend aid to them up to that period, or the government for support, till next planting season. Old and sickly people, or invalids, were given the lands without charge, such not being reported to the U.S. Tax Commissioners, as leased deciding it much better policy to let such people occupy the very land subject to reclaim and thereby become self-supporting, than refuse them ... and supply them with rations.

Population—In consequence of this ten acre arrangement, the population in this sub-District—especially on Hilton Island—have become much reduced, compared with the last year out thereby, an undesirable part retained.

Social Relations—There is evidently an advancing improvement in the general social relations of the people in this island, a higher sense of their social status, a better conception of their moral obligations, with a higher sense of their religious aims, consequently a more general knowledge of their duties as members of the body social and politic.

Schools—There have been schools in but four localities during the current year in this District; those of the Post known as the "Mitchellville Schools"—one at Seabrook, one at Stoney, and one at Marshland plantation or settlement, Scarbon and the Dawfuskie Island schools have not been opened.

The attendance of the children has not been equal to that of last farming season in consequent of an increased demands for their services at home, by the excess of lands obtained this year.

School Houses—Good and suitable houses are very much needed, there not been good or suitable school house in the whole sub District of Hilton Head; at present the teachers being obliged to make use of temporary ill-constructed little "Shanties" in such churches as they may be permitted to occupy for the times, either of which is ill adapted to the purpose of a school—master. At present the post school is being kept in the old park military-chapel,—the teachers residing also in a government building, but all this is merely temporary, and quite inconvenient, the teachers and school having had to move once during the season, the building being required for government use.

As stated in a former report to the Major General; a school-house should be a desirable place of resort to the pupils; consequently can only be made so by associations of pleasurable remembrance,—among which are, besides good and agreeable teachers, pleasant rooms, comfortable seats and desks, with equal playground and scenery. Throughout this entire sub-District, every plantation has a spot upon it, the greater part of which plantation belong to the government, and there is not apparent any good reason why there have not been school appropriations made in this District, as well as the sub-district of Beaufort and others, as the people and children here in point of merit, will compare favorably with those of any rural district in the Bureau District of South Carolina. The attention of the Major General, Assistant Commissioner, is respectfully invited to the plight of the schools in the sub-district of Hilton Head, the American Missionary Association, New York, alone having kept up and sustained the schools here, no appropriation of the school—funds of the Bureau, ever as yet having been obtained, though requisitions have been several times made from this office; the last application having been reported against by the sub-intending officer of schools, under the Bureau for this District as "unnecessary".

Self-Reliance—Our debts comparatively have been contracted during the last year, and those for the most part very small, and contingent, if not necessary. The people are decidedly self-sustaining, and—with the exception of two hundred bushels of corn sent by the Southern Relief Association, New York, 1866, and five hundred bushels of corn, and one thousand pounds of bacon; quota from the Congressional appropriation of five hundred thousand dollars, to prevent starvation in the South, 1867,—neither of which was solicited.—There have been no rations in record either to Refugees or Freedmen; for two years. There are some <u>three score</u> or more of old men and women worn out by the <u>formidable ills</u> of life, and superannuated under the old slave system, and some orphans and invalids, who might justly be candidates for any appropriation which may exist for such purpose. It is somewhat burdensome to the people among whom they reside, who are poor, to support them. Yet they actually do in a commendable manner, willingly without stint to the best of their ability. For the most part, these indigents, are thrown upon those not their relations, whom they have lost.

Police—The Rural Police System still continues, having been approved by Brevet Brig. Gen. H. B. Clitz, Commanding Post Charleston, South Carolina. But it is to be regretted, that although this Police is the main dependence of the citizens for such duties under the Bureau, there is no appropriation or means whatever, of paying them for services which are constant and many; except what those who call upon them, may choose to give. Indeed they are almost as frequently doing duty for the military as for the citizens. I respectfully invite the attention of the General to this fact, as the Rural or special police here, is almost a necessity.

Conjugal Relations—I respectfully invite the attention of the General to the suggestion, that the Commissioner of marriages be sent through this District, who should make it obligatory for all who are living together as husband and wife, to assemble on fixed occasions at some church or stated place, and there in his presence, either by himself or the Pastor of their respectful church, receive the marriage ceremony and obligation, with a certificate. This would do much towards correcting an existing evil among many, and raise in estimation, by adding to it the importance of government sanctions.

Election—In this District of Hilton Head, Registration has been general, and very highly appreciated by the freedmen, who have readily embraced the opportunity of manifesting their privilege of the great boon of freedom by depositing the ballot in the box. But in consequence of a loss of the "original book" of registration at Headquarters, 2nd Military District, Charleston, South Carolina, a large number of those who had registered and voted at the first election for Delegates to Constitutional Conventions—lost their vote at the last—for state affairs. The error is expected to be corrected in the last releases of the Registrars to take place. On each occasion of voting, the elections passed off with most commendable propriety, the suffrages deporting themselves like old exemplary citizens.

Soldier Claims—of the five hundred and odd claims at the Department, the following figures show the entry taken thus far in relation to them.

Audited	48 amounting to $7104.40	
Paid	+ $6424.06	
Not Paid	498.74	
Dead	181.60	7104.40
Deposited in Bank		$3634.31
Paid in Cash		$2789.75
	Total Paid	$6424.06
No. of those disallowed for Desertion	16	
No. of those disallowed for Military	4	
No. of those allowed	48	68
No. of those disallowed for other causes	150	150
Total		218

In this connection, I may be permitted to state, that in the payment of claims of the 21st Regt. U.S.C.T., the Department has decided on allowing them the old one hundred dollars Bounty, because their names are born on the Muster Rolls as slaves. I especially invite the attention of the Major General to this important fact, that he may give it his serious consideration.

I have the honor to be General.
Yours most obedient servant
(signed)
M. R. Delany
Major & A.S.A. Commissioner
B.R.F.A. Lands

SOURCE: Records of the Assistant Commissioner of the State of South Carolina, Bureau of Refugees, Freedmen, and Abandoned Lands, 1865–1870, Microcopy 849, Roll 35, 773–79, National Archives and Records Administration, Washington, DC.

DOCUMENT 15
A Typical Contract between Freedmen and Planters in Delany's District

Article 1: This contract between Justice Goodman and the freedmen, whose names are hereinto affixed, is on the basis of an equal partnership between Capital, Land and Labor—each receiving one third of the proceeds of the productions of the cultivated plantation or homestead farm, Beaufort District, South Carolina, and to continue till January 1, 1867.

Article 2: Each laborer is to receive (besides the privilege of firewood, with team and vehicle to haul it, and <u>one acre</u> of land to each family) one third of all that he or she is able to produce by cultivation, clear of all expenses except those incurred in the transportation and sale of the staple, as freight and commission on storage and sales, they supporting themselves and families, the proprietor making all advances of provisions or rations on credit (if required), finding all dwellings for the contractors, supporting all farming utensils, vehicles, machinery, sufficient working stock; and no labor is to be performed by hand or by a person that can better be done by animal labor or machinery.

Article 3: All restrictions and obligations legally binding contracting parties in the fulfillment of their articles of agreement are implied in this article, and all damage for injury or loss of property by carelessness is to be paid by fair and legal assessment.

Article 4: Negligence of duty in cultivation, so as to become injurious to the proprietor or other contracting parties, either by loss in the production of staples, or example in conduct or precedent, may, by investigation, cause a forfeiture of the interest of such person in their share of the crop. Any contractor taking the place of the dismissed shall succeed to all of their rights and claims on the part of the crop left by them; otherwise it shall be equally divided between those who work it.

Article 5: All Thanksgiving Days, Fast Days, "Holidays" and national celebration days are to be enjoyed in all cases by contractors, without being regarded as a neglect of duty or violation of contract.

Article 6: Good conduct and good behavior of the freedmen towards the proprietor, good treatment of animals, and good care of tools, utensils, etc., and good and kind treatment by the proprietor to the freedmen, will be strictly required by the authorities, and all dwellings and immediate premises of freedmen must be kept neat and clean, subject to inspection and fine for neglect by such sanitary arrangements as government may make.

Article 7: No sutler store will be permitted on the place, and nothing sold on account except the necessaries of life, such as good, substantial food and working clothes, conducive to health and comfort, at cost, that no inducements may be given for spending earnings improperly. Spirituous liquor will not be permitted.

Article 8: All accounts must be entered in a passbook, to be kept by each family or individual for the purpose, that no advantage be taken by incorrect charges; and no account against them will be recognized except such entry be made. No tobacco charge above fifty cents a month will be recognized by the Bureau. In all cases of the loss of their account books, then the account in the proprietor's books must be taken to date of loss, when another passbook must be obtained, and entries of accounts made as before.

Article 9: In all cases where an accusation is made against a person, the proprietor or his agent, one of the contractors or freedmen selected by themselves, and a third person chosen by the two,—provided neither of these three is biased or prejudiced against the accuser,—shall be a competent council to investigate and acquit the accused; but in all cases where a decision is to be made to dismiss or forfeit a share of the crop, the officer of the Bureau, or some other competent officer of the government, must preside in the council of trial, and make decision in the case. When the proprietor is biased or prejudiced against an accused person, he must name a person to take his place in the council who shall neither be biased nor prejudiced against the accused.

Witness our hands and signs this 17th day of February, 1866.

SOURCE: Frank (Frances) Rollin, *Life and Public Services of Martin R. Delany* (Boston: Lee and Shepard, 1868), 260–62.

DOCUMENT 16
D. E. Sickles to Gen. E. D. Townsend on Delany

Headquarters, Dept. S.C.
Charleston, S.C.
January 30, 1866.

General:

I have the honor to invite your attention to the following extract from a recent report of Major J. P. Roy, 6th United States Infantry, and Acting Inspector General of this department, regarding the service of Major M. R. Delany, 104th United States Colored Troops:

> Before closing this report, I desire to bear testimony to the efficient and able manner in which Major Delany, 104th United States Colored Troops, and agent of the Freedmen's Bureau, is performing his duties. I took occasion several times during my stay to go to his office, and hear him talk and explain matters to the freedmen. Being of their own color, they naturally reposed confidence in him. Upon the labor question he entirely reflected the views of the major general commanding, and seemed in all things to give them good and sensible advice. He is doing much good, and in the event of his regiment being mustered out, I hope he may be retained as an agent of the freedmen's Bureau

I have also received the same satisfactory reports from other sources, and concurring in the foregoing suggestions of Major J. P. Roy, I must respectfully recommend that Major M. R. Delany be, for the present, retained in the services of the United States. I have ordered his muster out to be postponed until a reply is received to this communication.
I have the honor to remain, general,
Very respectfully
Your obedient servant
D. E. Sickles
Major General Commanding
To Brig. Gen. E. D. Townsend
A.A.G., War Dept.

Source: Frank (Frances) Rollin, *Life and Public Services of Martin R. Delany* (Boston: Lee and Shepard, 1868), 265–66.

DOCUMENT 17
Excerpts from an Editorial of the *New South*

Major M. R. Delany, the "black major" of the Freedmen's Bureau, is now on the right tract. Comprehending the situation of affairs, he has seized at once upon its difficulties, and is doing a noble work for his race. His sympathies are, of course, with those of his own color, but, being a man of large experience, highly educated, and eminently conscientious, he does not allow prejudice to sway him one way or the other, and consequently, he has a wonderful influence for good over the freedmen. He tells them to go to work at once; that labor surely brings its own reward; and that after one more good crop is gathered, they will find their condition much better than at present. And he tells the planters they must be kind and just to their laborers, if they would quickly bring order out of chaos, and establish prosperity far beyond what they ever dreamed of in the dark and dreadful era of slavery.

Our whole community here is taking heart. One obstacle after another, to thorough regeneration, is being removed. As the planters succeed in procuring laborers, their credit is improved, and the merchants of this place come forward to assist the onward movement. Agriculture implements, seeds, subsistence, and the various wants of a plantation, are being much more liberally supplied than they were a month ago. We all look forward to a large measure of success the present season.

SOURCE: *New South* (Hilton Head Island, SC), February 3, 1866.

DOCUMENT 18
R. K. SCOTT TO GEN. O. O. HOWARD

Headquarters, Assistant Commissioner
Bureau Refugees, F. and A. Lands
District of South Carolina
Charleston, S.C.
July 22, 1868.

Major General O. O. Howard
Commissioner, Bureau R.R. & A.L.
Washington, D.C.
General:

I have the honor to inform you that after the 1st proximo, the services of Major M. R. Delany U.S.C.T. (now on duty as Asst. Sub. Asst. Comm. at Hilton Head) will not be required in this District, and would recommend that he be ordered to report elsewhere for duty.

I make this recommendation not because of any fault to be found with Maj. Delany whose services have always been characterized by zeal, and efficiency, and have resulted in great good to the people of the islands, but after the 1st prox. I do not think that occasion for his presence there will longer exist.

I am, General
Very Respectfully,
Your obedient servant
R. K. Scott
Assistant Commissioner, South Carolina.

SOURCE: Records of the Assistant Commissioner of the State of South Carolina, Bureau of Refugees, Freedmen, and Abandoned Lands, 1865–1870, National Archives and Records Administration, Washington, DC.

CHAPTER 3
THE CONSERVATIVE REPUBLICAN

INTRODUCTION

Delany's commission into the Union Army and subsequent appointment as a Freemen's Bureau sub-assistant commissioner finally secured for him the acceptance and recognition that long eluded him. Based on his personal experience, Delany saw (at least thought he saw) the dawn of a new age in America. The Civil War, he argued, had transformed blacks from passive objects and property to "an integral and essential element in the body politic of the nation" (chapter 5, document 1, "Delany to Frederick Douglass"). There was, he opined, no more cause for racial animosity. Everything he saw around him seemed to portend the emergence of a new social and political order. This new establishment, in his judgment, held great prospects for the future of both races, particularly blacks, if unobstructed by what he deemed premature, radical, and irresponsible political demands. Delany thus developed a more conciliatory and accommodating view of white conservatives, the group he had spent decades castigating and challenging. Where other black leaders sensed danger, he saw hope; when they advocated radical solutions and choices, he cautioned and counseled moderation and compromise. His ideas were, therefore, controversial and provocative, especially since not every other black leader shared the same degree of optimism. The controversies Delany's ideas generated first emerged in the area of black political demands.

In early February 1866, a delegation of black leaders, including Delany's one-time coeditor and friend Frederick Douglass and ideological mentor William Whipper, called on President Andrew Johnson to demand complete enfranchisement for blacks. In response, President Johnson not only rejected their demand but in fact also lamented that blacks had benefited from the Civil War at the expense of poor whites. In a letter to the delegation (doc. 1), Delany advised these leaders not to be discouraged or disheartened by Johnson's reply. Delany reassured them that he shared their concerns and aspirations. Nonetheless, he urged caution, respect, and deferential attitudes vis-à-vis the president. He reminded the delegates that blacks already had cause for celebration: the Civil War had ended slavery, and blacks were free. More importantly, he implored the leaders to make allowance for racial differences and, therefore, not demand or expect too much from the president. Above all else, he counseled moderation and advised them to trust in the ultimate wisdom and power of God, the same God who saw them through the Civil War and the destruction of slavery. However, in a follow-up letter to President Johnson (doc. 2) Delany made a strong case for the enfranchisement of blacks. He reasoned that since blacks had helped in preventing the defeat and dissolution of the Union during the War, their enfranchisement would further strengthen the nation. He drew a compelling and persuasive link between the nation's destiny and blacks' political rights. Not only had blacks "saved the nation from destruction" in previous times of "imminent perils" (Revolution and the Civil War); their "enfranchisement" would "secure and perpetuate the integrity of the Union." From documents 1 and 2, it would appear that Delany shared the aspirations of the black leadership. He was probably apprehensive of their strategy.

The Freedmen's Bureau barred its agents from active political engagements. They were expected to devote their efforts to ensuring the efficient and effective supervision and management of their plantations. Despite this restriction, Delany refused to be apolitical. There was so much at stake in Reconstruction, and he was unwilling to leave everything to the hands of black leaders he perceived as politically immature. The new dispensation demanded political prudence and caution, so he did not shy away from offering and voicing political opinions even while serving as a bureau agent. He never hesitated to criticize what he saw as blacks' political immaturity and youthful exuberance and the misguided nature of their political demands. Reconstruction, in Delany's view, had made blacks now "an integral part and essential element in the body politic of the nation." Having attained this level of political integration, he believed that blacks had to be cautious in their demands and aspirations as they progressed, especially on the controversial and provocative subject of political equality. To ensure peace and harmony conducive to an atmosphere that would enable blacks to enhance their new freedom, Delany advocated a policy of appeasement and reconciliation. In pursuit of this, he called for amnesty and universal and unconditional pardon for former slaveholders and ex-Confederates. His preference was for blacks to seek reconciliation and cooperation with their former oppressors. He believed this was necessary in order for blacks to have a chance to advance in postslavery South.

Document 3 is a letter Delany wrote while still a Bureau agent to a prominent black leader, Reverend Henry H. Garnet, strongly objecting to what he perceived as the premature, militant, and provocative nature of black political demands and aspirations.[1] He harshly condemned a call by Wendell Phillips, a white abolitionist, for a black vice president for the country.[2] Delany characterized Phillips's suggestion as "nonsense" and premature, a demand that could create more problems for blacks. A black vice president was, Delany contended, too high a position for blacks to aspire to at this time. He urged blacks to adopt gradualism instead, seeking only local offices, until they were *ready* and *qualified* for higher ones.

In an unsigned article (doc. 4), published in *the New York Times* and titled "Colored Officials," an editorialist applauded Delany's critique of black political aspirations and Wendell Phillips's suggestion. The author was critical of black political aspirations, described blacks as corrupt and unfit for office, and, furthermore, opined that the political emancipation of blacks had been premature. Blacks were not yet ready for governing positions and should not be misled into thinking otherwise. The author further argued that the fact that blacks had the vote did not necessarily translate into qualification for holding office. Blacks lacked intelligence, a crucial qualification for office, and until they acquired it, the writer insisted, they should adopt gradualism, and seek only lower-level positions that required little intelligence—certainly not the vice presidency of the country. Blacks, the writer continued, were of the "lower race" and lacked the "requisite training" for public office. The writer praised Delany and referenced the letter to Henry Garnet in which Delany advised blacks to "be satisfied to take things in their natural course and time" focusing on lower

---

1. Henry Highland Garnet was a Black Nationalist and a leading advocate of the African civilization and emigration movement Delany had worked with during mid- to late 1850s.
2. The reference to Wendell Phillips as "a young man of 27 or 28 . . . without any political experience" is simply wrong. Born in 1811 in Boston, he was a leading abolitionist and advocate and defender of black rights during Reconstruction. When Delany wrote this letter to Henry Garnet, Phillips was sixty-six years old, in fact one year older than Delany.

level positions. The writer further described the call for social equality at the core of the black struggle as "unnatural and impossible state." It is clear that this writer was more concerned about the social implication of black political office-holding. Social inequality was, in the writer's view, the natural order and could not be undone by political radicalism.

In document 5, a letter addressed to another prominent black leader, L. S. Langley, a member of the South Carolina State Constitutional Convention, Delany declined nomination for a congressional position on the grounds that it was premature for blacks to seek such representations and that the nation was not ready for black visibility at such a level. He reaffirmed his earlier call for prudence and caution on the part of blacks. A black representation in Congress was, in Delany's words, "not necessary to our claims as American citizens." He again condemned Wendell Phillips's call for a black vice president as unrealistic, premature, and ill advised. Document 6 is a case, written under the pseudonym Fides, against black political aspirations. Fides argued that the entire nation was not ready for black political enfranchisement and condemned the Republican Party for being selective in its promotion of black political empowerment. Fides further observed that such support was limited to the South and did not extend to the North. The author warned blacks against being seduced by the promises of Radical Republicans. Such promises would only lead to disaster. The writer called on blacks to abandon the Republican Party and seek immediate reconciliation with their former master, local whites. Fides also accused the Republican Party of hypocrisy for advancing social equality in the South while maintaining social inequality in the North. He warned blacks that the Radical Republicans were only exploiting them for political benefits and urged blacks to abandon that relationship and seek alliance and reconciliation with southern whites.

Fides also referenced Delany to corroborate the view that blacks were not ready and qualified for political responsibilities. The writer questioned whether the nation was ready for "universal suffrage" and quoted copiously from Delany's letter to Langley to bolster the claim that blacks were not ready for such political roles. The appointment of blacks to higher positions of politics, Fides opined, would only incite racial animosity. Fides cautioned blacks against being misled and seduced by radical leaders and "pretended friends" who really did not care for them and were primarily advocating black political rights in the South. Their desire to empower blacks politically did not extend to the North. In essence, Fides noted that the Radical Republican crusade for black political rights and empowerment did not apply nationwide. Fides, therefore, urged blacks to resist the temptations of these northern adventurers and false friends whose only objective, he insisted, was to drive a wedge between blacks and the "southern friends" with whom they shared a destiny.

It is clear that the climate and culture of South Carolina was not in favor of black political empowerment. Despite Radical Republican rule, the state was overwhelmingly opposed to black political power and authority. There were seething resentments and widespread opposition to blacks' occupying positions of political responsibility. Paradoxically, less than two years after the end of his bureau functions, Delany's views had changed. He was no longer opposed to black political visibility. He began agitating for more black political roles within the Republican administration. It is important to contextualize the sudden change in Delany's political orientation, which was largely in response to the changing political dynamics and landscape of the country. By June of 1870, both the Fourteenth and Fifteenth Amendments to the US Constitution had been ratified. Blacks gained citizenship and the promise of equal protection of the law as well as the right to vote and be voted for in elections. Delany perceived these developments as suggestive of a fundamental shift in how the nation viewed blacks. They were no longer slaves but free and now, in Delany's words, "an essential part of the *ruling element* of the nation." In other words, blacks had become "a new political element." The future seemed bright and promising. However, it was a future also fraught with challenges and uncertainties, one that required adequate knowledge and preparation on the part of the newly emancipated and enfranchised black population. To address this contingency, Delany wrote a series of tracts titled "On National Polity," which were published in the Washington, DC, *New National Era* from January to March 1870.

He would subsequently reproduce the tract in an address he would deliver to the faculty, students, and trustees of Wilberforce University in Xenia, Ohio. Delany wrote this address (doc. 7) primarily to serve as a critical reference resource on politics for the emerging leadership of the newly enfranchised black population. He argued that America had evolved and established "an impartial and truly national government" in contrast to the previous system of segregation, racial privilege, and hierarchy that excluded and subordinated blacks. His optimism about the prospects of the new political order compelled Delany to write and offer this "elementary instruction in the principle of national polity" as a guide for blacks as they attempted to exercise the rights and privileges deriving from their enfranchised status. The piece was also meant to provide informed understanding of "these elementary lessons" on political principles and theories and the nature and functions of the national governments and key political documents such as the Constitution.

The article is divided into four broad themes: citizenship, civil rights, the Constitution, and secession. On the topic of citizenship, Delany derived his definition of a citizen from the Roman legal tradition, which defined a "citizen" as someone without any restraint, one who possessed the inviolable power of political representation. Based on this definition, he argued that blacks in the United States had long been denied citizenship. However, he conceded that in some states, such as New York and Ohio, blacks had restricted freedom. They could only vote for others to represent their interests. In other words, under the old system, blacks could not exercise suffrage free and independent of whites, which limited and curtailed their freedom. In essence, they were not part of the *ruling element* of the nation. This would change with emancipation and the constitutional amendments and other reforms of Reconstruction. In Delany's view, these reforms eradicated "all legal disabilities and repeal all unjust laws," transforming the black American into "a citizen by nature, with claims and rights as inviolable, inherent and everlasting." With this transformation, Delany was hopeful that blacks would now have the opportunity to exercise unhindered all the rights and privileges of citizenship. However, this political transformation had to be matched by adequate knowledge and preparation, so Delany offered blacks this piece of political education that he felt they lacked but desperately needed.

Discussing civil rights, Delany referred to the French political tradition that combined civil and political rights as one and inseparable. He contrasted this tradition with the British and American systems, in which such rights were separate and distinct; one could have one and not the other. Although everyone was supposedly equal before the law, political restrictions were imposed on some people due to property or race. In essence, national governments in both the United States and Great Britain were built on foundations of privilege and hierarchy. But post–Civil War reforms changed the American political landscape. Slavery ended, and blacks were enfranchised, their civil and political rights acknowledged. Given this development, Delany argued that blacks, who previously had "few or no obligations," now had the "responsibilities" of being part of the nation. These responsibilities required "possessing such information and having such qualifications," adequate for and enhancing their new roles. Delany hoped that this "new political element" (blacks) would benefit from his "elementary lessons" on national polity.

On the theme of the Constitution: Delany described a constitution as a legal guarantee of the rights and privileges of the people. He compared the British constitution, which he said was derived from the Magna Carta, a progressive document that affirmed and safeguarded the rights of the people to that of the United States which he described as conservative. He argued that before the Civil War, the US Constitution did not protect the rights of all the people. It was an ambiguous document that was easily manipulated and subverted and did little to protect the people's human rights. It most certainly violated the "natural rights" of a segment of the population (blacks). But that was then, according to Delany. Post–Civil War political reforms fundamentally changed the status of blacks. With the changed political status came new responsibilities and obligations which required appropriate political education and orientation.

Finally, on secession, Delany engaged ongoing debates among national politicians on whether or not the rebellious confederate states had physically withdrawn from the Union. President Lincoln had argued that they were never physically out of the Union. Delany contended that these states had only politically, not geographically, severed their relationship to the Union, and thus it was imperative that the relationship be restored by the national government's prescribing "terms and conditions" for their political reabsorption.

The overall thrust of Delany's pamphlets "On National Polity" was to underscore the fundamental transformation that had occurred in the political status of blacks and, therefore, the need for political education on how best to function under the new political dispensation. The article is both a critique and comparative analysis of the nation's political history, showing the changes blacks experienced in the transition from slavery and dependency to citizens with rights and obligations. Delany does not provide much of a prescription for the newly enfranchised blacks, besides emphasizing that their newly acquired political status and roles came with immense obligations and responsibilities. Delany was convinced that the nation had shifted from a conservative political tradition built on race, privilege, and hierarchy to one in which all the people, including blacks, enjoyed equal rights and privileges. This assumption forms the basis for his call for increased black political participation. Some observers, particularly within Republican Party leadership, deemed this about-face disturbing and potentially destabilizing. Document 8 is a commentary on the calls by Delany and two other black leaders (Richard H. Cain and Robert DeLarge) for more black political representation. The Republican Party condemned and rejected the demand as uncalled for and racially divisive. Document 9 is a report on a meeting of Ward 4, Charleston, where Delany, perhaps responding to growing criticisms, reaffirmed his dedication to the Republican Party. He criticized and rejected the Reformer platform and urged unity within the Republican Party.

Document 10 is an excerpt of a speech Delany delivered at a mass meeting where he seemed to concede that blacks were inferior and less intelligent. At the same time, he demanded more black representation on the basis of justice and equality but also appeared to be appeasing white anxiety by denouncing social equality. He emphasized the need for justice within the Republican Party, which called for giving blacks, who constituted the majority in South Carolina, a proportionate share of political positions, including congressional representation. He also called for more black leadership representation within the government. Delany wanted blacks represented by "our own people." He denounced the rumor that he and other blacks were trying to start a "Black Man's Party," reassuring everyone that blacks were not in a position to pursue such a goal. However, since blacks were the majority in South Carolina, Delany argued that it was only fair that they be given fair representation in state politics, though not necessarily at the top leadership echelons. Delany's ideas undoubtedly generated animosity within a party hierarchy still very much opposed to black political representation.

Document 11 is a report from a meeting of Republicans in Charleston, during which party stalwarts rejected and condemned the call for more black representation as racially motivated and divisive. Suddenly, Delany's ideas on race now seemed "extreme and impracticable." In document 12, a group of Republicans denounced Delany's advocacy of more black leaders as a self-serving effort designed to secure a position for himself. Document 13 reports on a meeting of Ward 6 Republicans where Delany, DeLarge, and others again came under harsh criticisms. A key speaker, L. J. Taylor, described Delany's ideas as designed to enhance his chances for a senatorial position and accused Delany of failure to advance the interest of blacks during his bureau agency. Perhaps reacting to the criticisms, Delany delivered a speech at a mass meeting in Edgefield (doc. 14) reiterating his devotion and commitment to the Republican Party and repudiating any intention to form a third party. He called for universal suffrage and more equitable distribution of resources between the races.

At a Fourth of July celebration in Charleston, Delany spoke (doc. 15) of his responsibility as a black man to offer sound political advice to his race without being intimidated or misconstrued. Blacks, he argued, needed informed advice from one of theirs. Once again he reaffirmed his dedication to the Republican Party. In document 16, Delany refuted a report alleging that he was prevented from speaking at a political rally. Document 17 is a report on a meeting organized to discuss the principles of Republicanism. In this piece, Delany observed that the principles had been neglected and urged the party to embrace and practice true Republicanism, which he characterized as colorblind. Delany's conception of Republicanism was a disguised criticism of what he characterized as the racially biased and divisive policies of the Radical Republican administration in the state.

By 1871 Delany's appeals and calls for moderation and color-blind policy seemed to have fallen on deaf ears. In frustration, he wrote a scathing critique and review of Radical Reconstruction. Document 18 is a letter Delany wrote to Frederick Douglass cataloging the challenges of radical rule in South Carolina. This "Political Review" focused on South Carolina, but Delany suggested that it was applicable nationwide. He denounced Republicans for abandoning the true spirit of Republicanism: equal rights. Instead, they had nurtured divisive consciousness and racial discord and introduced and implemented policies that established a reign of terror and social unrest across the South. To solidify their narrow and selfish political agenda, the Republicans, Delany maintained, exploited black ignorance and gullibility. They misled blacks into endorsing and associating with a government from whose policies they derived little, if any, benefits. More significantly, these policies had only bolstered racial discord and prevented blacks from reconciling with the state's critical elements, such as local whites and former slaveholders, whose goodwill and supports were crucial to their development. He also faulted the Republican administration for ignoring competent and educated blacks. The government, according to Delany, deliberately sowed seeds of corruption and inculcated in blacks a color-phobic and divisive consciousness. He was particularly harsh on those blacks whom he described as ignorant people with a penchant for violence, and he blamed them for the violence and unrest in the state. Delany particularly loathed Radical Republicans, who he denounced for misrepresenting Republicanism and failing to pursue equal rights for everyone.

Delany was especially distraught by the negative and corruptive effects of Radical Republicanism on what he characterized as a largely ignorant and gullible black population. In consequence, blacks corrupted other blacks and misled them into supporting and backing an administration and programs that only further destabilized the domestic peace and harmony they needed to survive and succeed in post–Civil War South. He accused blacks of aping the racial consciousness that defined the larger society by developing "Brown" societies that drove a wedge between lighter skin and darker skin blacks. Delany accused the Republican administration of a reluctance to acknowledge and reward black merit while fostering instead a culture of black mediocrity by appointing blacks only to menial positions. He also discerned a deep-rooted anti-black culture in the national Republican administration, reflected in the failure to appoint "pure blacks" in official positions, and thus their nonrepresentation in the political arena. The few blacks appointed to offices were mostly light skinned. He found only two exceptions to this widespread color bias: the appointment of a black postmaster (which he attributed to the influence of the Democratic community) and a black consul general and minister to Liberia. With the exception of these two, Delany insisted that there were no "pure black" appointees in the national government beyond menial positions. Generally, he lamented that the government seemed reluctant to acknowledge, showcase, and reward black merit. For respectable offices, the government, Delany observed, seemed to prefer corrupt and incompetent blacks whose predictably dismal performances were then used as justification to further malign the entire race. Delany closed his letter with a list of recommendations for dealing with the myriad problems and challenges he highlighted, including the appointment of more intelligent and qualified blacks, the adoption of proportional representation to enable blacks fair and adequate representation in government commensurate with their population size, and an end to racial profiling and discrimination. He also urged blacks to reconcile with one another and end color-phobic divisions. Finally, he advocated for strict adherence to true "Republicanism" by pursuing equality for everyone and for the appointment of intelligent and qualified members of both races to government positions.

In his response (doc. 19) Douglass agreed with several of Delany's concerns but took serious exception to his disparaging of blacks and blaming them for social discord in the South. Though Douglass conceded they were not perfect, he thought they deserved more credit than Delany acknowledged. Given their slavery background and the challenges they confronted, ignorance should be expected. The violence in the South was not solely caused by blacks, and they certainly did not start it. Violence had been part of southern culture. For Douglass, the violence was much broader and deeper. He also saw the violence on the part of blacks as reactive. He disagreed with Delany's harsh criticisms of black character. Douglass believed it was unfair to expect blacks to remain peaceful and civil in a context in which they were constantly experiencing violence or to expect them to continue the differential culture of slavery, which, Douglass believed, was at the root of some of the violence that whites perpetrated against blacks. Though he condemned the existence of color-phobia among blacks in South Carolina as identified by Delany, Douglass disagreed with Delany's criticism of the national administration for discrimination against blacks. He also cautioned against the application of proportional representation, which he characterized as an absurd strategy that was both impractical and unlikely to benefit blacks.

In another reaction to Delany's letter (doc. 20), a South Carolina black senator, S. N. Gailliard, denounced Delany as selfishly motivated to advance himself as someone deserving of government appointment. Though he agreed that there were social divisions among blacks in South Carolina, he accused Delany of overstating those divisions to create discord between darker skin and lighter skin blacks. He accused Delany of sowing seeds of racial division and thus undermining the Republican Party and Republicanism. A significant aspect of the exchange between Delany and Douglass was that the state conservatives, politically humbled and marginalized by Radical Reconstruction, saw Delany's letter as a welcome and much-needed corroboration of their largely unpopular ideas and platforms. They promptly ran a three-part series of commentaries on Delany's letter (docs. 21, 22, 23), citing copiously from it, to support their claims of black inferiority and their negative portraits of radical rule. In their view, the decline in black character Delany highlighted would not have happened had blacks been left alone to the care of "those who had been their best friends all their lives" (that is, former slaveholders). They cited Delany to corroborate their own claims that blacks had since emancipation perpetrated violence, thievery, lawlessness, and so on. They agreed with Delany that black character had degenerated due to Radical Republican false promises.

They also agreed with Delany's social and political criticisms and used his letter to buttress their claim that color-phobia among blacks was tantamount to reverse discrimination against whites. However, they disagreed with Delany on the ethnological argument. They rejected his call for racial equality and proportional representation, insisting that blacks were innately inferior and that given their African background slavery was in fact a beneficial and uplifting experience. They presented Delany himself as prime example for the essential goodness of slavery. Had his ancestors not been taken from Africa, he would not be the educated and intelligent black he became. They urged blacks in the South to resist utopian dreams and unrealistic goals such as equality. While agreeing that there were few blacks in offices in the national administration, the paper argued that this had nothing to do with racism but the absence of qualified blacks.

One of the examples of Republican discrimination against pure blacks Delany cited in his letter to Douglass was the appointment of a postmaster in Richmond, Virginia, which Delany had attributed to Democratic influence. Document 24 is a refutation of Delany's attribution of this appointment to Democratic influence. There was evidence in the form of a letter of one Charles H. Porter of Richmond, Virginia, a Republican sympathizer and supporter suggesting that the postmaster in question, James H. Cunningham of Manchester Virginia, was a staunch Republican who got the appointment at the solicitation of one Charles H. Porter.

Delany's letter to Douglass does not appear to have affected political developments within South Carolina. Nor did it reverse the course of radical politics. Delany remained a political outsider, disgruntled and vehement in his attacks on political radicalism and the corruption which he associated with it. His anticorruption campaign and the prevalence of corruption in South Carolina politics led him to oppose Franklin J. Moses, Republican gubernatorial candidate for the ensuing 1874 election. But Moses's promise to fight corruption if elected changed Delany's mind. On the basis of this promise Delany campaigned for Moses and traveled to New York to reassure South Carolina bondholders and potential bondholders. There were indications that Moses may in fact have promised Delany a political office if elected.

The next two documents (25 and 26) are letters Delany wrote and published in New York appealing to South Carolina bondholders and potential bondholders and vouching for Moses's anticorruption pledges. If elected, Delany reassured the audience, Moses would honor all financial obligations and restore confidence in the finances of the state. Franklin Moses won the election and became South Carolina governor. However, no job offer was extended to Delany. Document 27 is a letter from Reverend Richard H. Cain to Moses imploring him to keep his promise and provide a job for Delany. Cain made it clear that Delany had abandoned his initial opposition to Moses's candidacy at his (Cain's) assurance that Moses had been unfairly misrepresented and that he would, if elected, fight corruption. There was also the hint that Delany could be rewarded with an appointment. Cain was particularly emphatic about Delany's desperate economic situation and thus his need for a job. Delany was apparently at this time, in Cain's words, a person "without money, without friends, without a position, with pressing necessities." As hinted above, Moses did not appoint Delany to office. This letter offers a glimpse into Delany's desperate financial and economic condition.

Being unemployed did not deter Delany from his crusade against radical politics. He wrote a letter (doc. 28) to the black State Supreme Court Justice Jonathan J. Wright in which he reiterated his call for minority representation and urged blacks to accommodate and make concession to the political needs of the minority white population. This was crucial, since he believed that whites would soon assume preponderance due to increased immigration. He believed that the adoption of minority representation would accord whites representation in proportion to their numbers in the hope that they too would reciprocate when they inevitably became the majority. He repeated his earlier suggestion that blacks had been misled by political radicalism into equating political emancipation with political power and equality. Delany painted a gloomy future for black political empowerment. He described the expectation that blacks would ascend to positions of political authority as a "terrible political heresy" and a reflection of the political miseducation propagated by Radical Republicanism. He urged blacks, while it was still in their capacity, to adopt a policy that would give the current white minority a voice and representation in government proportional to their population. With increased white immigration into the state, the writing on the wall seemed clear that the days of black majority rule were numbered and that blacks would soon become the minority in South Carolina. Furthermore, while it was reasonable for blacks to expect some political concessions from whites, Delany deemed it unrealistic for blacks to expect that whites, nationwide, would consent to being governed by blacks. He blamed Radical Republicanism for infusing such political conviction in blacks. Documents 29 and 30 are comments on Delany letter to Jonathan Wright, both published in the *New York Times*. Both agreed with and praised Delany's ideas. Both echoed his gloomy and pessimistic analysis of black politics, amplified his call for minority representation, and reiterated his prediction that blacks would soon become a minority.

DOCUMENT 1

DELANY'S ADVICE TO BLACK LEADERS

Bureau R.F.A.L
Port Royal, Hilton Head Island, S.C.
February 22, 1866

To Messrs. G. T. DOWNING, WILLIAM WHIPPER, FREDERICK DOUGLASS, JOHN JONES, L. H. DOUGLASS, and others, Colored Delegation representing the political interests of the Colored People of the United States, now near the Capital and Government, Washington, D.C.

My dear Brothers: I have been watching with deep interest your movements at Washington, near the government of your country. I need not repeat to you that which you all know, and that which we have oft repeated to each other privately, in council, and through the public journals,—we are one in interest and destiny in America. I am with you; yea, if your intentions, designs, purposes, matter, and manner continue the same as those presented to the chief magistrate of the nation, then I am with you always, even to the end. Be mild, as is the nature of your race, be respectful and deferential, as you will be; and dignified as you have been; but be determined and persevering. Your position before the saged president, and reply after you left him, challenges the admiration of the world. At least it challenges mine and as a brother you have it

Do not misjudge the president, but believe, as I do that he means to do right; that his intentions are good; that he is interested, among those of others of his fellow citizens, in the welfare of the black man. That he love Caesar none the less, but Rome more. Do not expect too much from him as black men, I mean. Do not forget that you are black and he is white. Make large allowances for this, and take this as the standpoint. Whatever we may think of ourselves, do not forget that we are far in advance of our white American fellow-citizens in that direction. Remember that men are very differently constituted, and that one will dread and shun, another will boldly dare and venture; where one would succeed another might fail. Not far from where I am at present posted on the coast of South Carolina, there are several inlets, of which I will name two—Edisto and St. Helena. Of course, one pilot will shun one, another the other, each taking his vessel easily through that which he enters; while another will not venture into either, but prefers—especially during a storm—to go outside to sea for the safety of the vessel; all reaching, timely, their destination, Hilton Head, in safety.

Here, what one shuns as a danger, another regards as a point of safety; and that which one dreads another dares. What General Sherman succeeded in, General Meade might have failed in; while General Grant may have prosecuted either with success. Men must be measured and adjudged according to their temperaments and peculiar constitutional faculties.

Do not grow weary nor discouraged, neither disheartened nor impatient. Do not forget God. Think, O think how wonderfully he made himself manifest during the war. Only think how he confounded, not only the wisdom of the might of this land, but of the world, making them confess that he is the Lord, high over all, and most mighty. He still lives. Put your trust in him. As my soul liveth, you will reap if you faint not. Wait! "The race is not to the swift nor the battle to the strong, but he that endureth to the end." Bide your time.

Since we last met in council, great changes have taken place, and much has been gained. The battle cry has been heard in our midst, a terrible contest of civil war has raged, and a death struggle for national life summoned every lover of the Union to the combat. We among our fellow-citizens received the message, and eagerly obeyed the call. Our black right arms were stripped, our bosoms bared, and we stood in the front rank of battle. Slavery yielded, the yoke was broken, the manacles shattered, the shackles fell, and we stood forth a race redeemed! Instead of despair, "Glory to God!" rather let us cry. In the cause of our country you and I have done, and still are doing our part, and a great and just nation will not be unmindful of it. God is just. Stand still and see his salvation.

> Be patient in your misery
> Be meek in your despair
> Be patient, O be patient!
> Suffer on, suffer on!

Your brother in the cause of our common country,
M. R. Delany

SOURCE: Frank (Frances) Rollin, *Life and Public Services of Martin R. Delany* (Boston: Lee and Shepard, 1868), 281–83.

DOCUMENT 2
Delany to President Andrew Johnson

Port Royal Island, S.C.
July 25, 1866.

TO HIS EXCELLENCY, PRESIDENT JOHNSON:
Sir:

I propose, simply as a black man,—one of the race most directly interested in the question of enfranchisement and the exercise of suffrage,—a cursory view of the basis of security for perpetuating the Union.

When the compact was formed, the British—a foreign nation—threatened the integrity and destruction of the American colonies. This outside pressure drove them together as independent states, and so long as they desired a Union,—appreciating the power of the enemy, and comprehending their own national strength,—it was sufficient security against any attempt at a dissolution or foreign subjugation.

So soon, however, as mistaking their own strength, or designing an alliance with some other power, a portion of those states became dissatisfied with the Union, and recklessly sought its dissolution by a resort to the sword, so nearly equally divided were the two sections, that foreign intervention or an exhausting continuance of the struggle would most certainly have effected a dissolution of the Union.

But an element heretofore latent and unthought of,—a power passive and unrecognized,—suddenly presented itself to the American mind, and its arm to the nation. This power was developed in the blacks, heretofore discarded as a national nonentity—a dreg or excrescence to the body politic. Free, without rights, or slaves, mainly,—therefore things constructively,—when called to the country's aid they developed a force which proved the balance precisely called for, and essentially necessary as an elementary part of the national strength. Without this force, or its equivalent, the rebellion could not have been subdued, and without it as an inseparable national element, the Union is insecure.

What becomes necessary, then to secure and perpetuate the integrity of the Union, is simply the enfranchisement and recognition of the political equality of the power that saved the nation from destruction in a time of imminent peril—a recognition of the political equality of the blacks with the whites in all of their relation as American citizens. Therefore, with the elective franchise, and the exercise of suffrage in all the Southern States recently holding slaves, there is no earthly power able to cope with the United States as a military power; consequently, nothing to endanger the national integrity. Nor can there ever arise from this element the same contingency to threaten and disturb the quietude of the country as that which has just been so happily disposed of. Because, believing themselves sufficiently able, either with or without foreign aid, the rebels drew the sword against their country, which developed a power in national means—military, financial, and statesmanship—that astonished the world, and brought them to submission. Hence, whatever their disposition or dissatisfaction, the blacks, nor any other fractional part of the country, with the historic knowledge before them of its prowess, will ever be foolhardy enough to attempt or secession. And their own political interest will ever keep them true and faithful to the Union, thereby securing their own liberty, and proving a lasting safeguard as a balance in the political scale of the country.

As the fear of the British, as an outside pressure, drove, and for a time kept and held the Union together, so will the fear of the loss of liberty and their political status, as an element in this great nation, serves as the outside pressure necessary to secure the fidelity of the blacks to the Union. And this fidelity, unlike that of the rebels, need ever be mistrusted, because, unlike them, the blacks have before them the proofs of the power and ability of the Union to maintain unsullied the prestige of the national integrity, even were they, like them, traitorously disposed to destroy their country, or see it usurped by foreign nations.

This, Sir, seems to me conclusive, and is the main point upon which I base my argument against the contingency of a future dissolution of the American Union, and in favor of its security.

I have the honor to be, your most obedient servant.

M. R. Delany

MAJOR 104th U.S.C.T.

SOURCE: Frank (Frances) Rollin, *Life and Public Services of Martin R. Delany* (Boston: Lee and Shepard, 1868), 278–80.

DOCUMENT 3
DELANY TO REV. HENRY H. GARNET

Bureau Sub-District, Charleston
Headquarters, Hilton Head
Hilton Head, S.C.
July 27, 1867.

Rev. H. H. Garnet,
Pastor, Shiloh Presbyterian Church,
New York.

MY DEAR SIR,

In such times as these, it requires men of the greatest practical experience, acquired ability, mature intelligence, and discretional wisdom, to speak and act for the race now an integral part and essential element in the body politic of the nation. Therefore, I do most sincerely hope that you and other leading minds among our people may take your stand, speak out, and define your true sentiments in relation to the great points now agitating the public mind, especially the black man's claim to office.

The great principle always advocated by our leading men has been to claim for us, as a race all the rights and privileges belonging to an American citizen of the most favored race. But I do not think that those who have so long, so steadily, and determinedly stood up as you and others of us have done, even to a national concession of these claims, ever contemplated taking any position among our fellow-citizens, till we, at least, should be READY and QUALIFIED. It follows as a matter of course that MORE than we should be ready, before it is POSSIBLE to attain to such positions. I am sure that upon this point, there will be but one sentiment among the old-line leading men of our race, contemporaneous with us, when the subject is placed before them.

I have been induced to pen this letter to you by seeing in the telegraph proceedings of the Columbia, S.C. Convention a claim put forth by Mr. Phillips in behalf of our race, for the Vice-Presidency of the United States. I hope no such nonsense for a moment will be entertained. Our enemies would desire no heavier nor stronger club to break the heads of our friends and knock out our brains than this. We are not children, but men comprehending the entire situation, and should at once discountenance anything that would seemingly make us cat's paw and ridiculous in the eyes and estimation of the political intelligence of the world. Let colored men be satisfied to take things like other men, in their natural course and time, prepare themselves in every particular for municipal positions, and they may expect to attain to some other in time.

Mr. Phillips is a young man of 27 or 28 years of age, and consequently without any political experience, except such as acquired since the war commenced and therefore may be excused for so palpable a political blunder. I am a personal friend of his; therefore, take the liberty of speaking frankly about him.

I am Sir, for our race and country at large,
Your Friend
M. R. DELANY
Hilton, Head, S.C., July 27, 1867.

SOURCE: Martin R. Delany, *Trial and Conviction of Martin R. Delany*, unpublished pamphlet (Charleston, SC, 1876).

DOCUMENT 4
COLORED OFFICIALS

If the moral nature of office-holders could be painted on their outside, no doubt many of the high seats of dignity in the land should grow black with the color of their occupants. Most politicians, could they be brought to confess their life's maneuvering as frankly as Rousseau did his littleness; would lament much sacrifice of principle and loss of self-respect in the struggles of the career which has lifted them to place. There are few parents who after such a revelation would not prefer for their sons some quiet and obscure pursuit, rather than the cares and humiliations of an office-seeker's dependent existence. Why then should the race that has just been raised to manhood be stimulated to risk all manhood is worth in the scramble for the rewards of party, instead of being taught that their happiness and respectability depend on acquiring of self-control, and on the practice of patient industry? Why, except to appease the morbid vanity of their great misleader, and to give PHILIPS occasion for boasting that he did his worst to unfit them for their real duties by firing their ignorance with the hope of impossible distinctions?

This arch-agitator, respecting nothing but his own craving for notoriety, is doing the people he pretends to befriend a very serious mischief. The blacks have been made citizens before they are fit for the responsibilities of electors. It is the very deviltry of demagoguism to flatter them with the chimera that they are fit to take part in governing others. All among them of the least intelligence can see that the mass of the well-to-do white population owe their prosperity to industrious labor, and win any advancement by the aid of education. These are the lessons which anyone who is really their friend would seek to impress on them. He who invites them to plunge into the excitement of political strife, and cheats their credulous helplessness with the hope of its empty prizes, deserves, as this PHILIPS has often before deserved, the curses of the Republic. That Warwick of the blacks would make a Negro Vice-President, because we should thus show to the world that his people stand in social equality with our own. If, as it is said, this pitiless egotist would die contended after seeing one of them in that office, the nation might afford to pay that price to be rid of him, were it not that it better understands the duties it owe that race, and means to shun his example by consulting both conscience in dealing with them.

It is a mistake to suppose there is any logical connection between the right to vote and the right, if it be not an abuse of terms to call it so, to hold office. As the federal law now stands, any sane, unconvicted man of 21 may vote. We have chosen to ignore intelligence as a test of the elector's fitness, and have thereby taken upon ourselves a great risk and a grievous burden. But it is absurd to conclude from this that we have done away with intelligence as a ground of fitness to be elected. Yet, this is the logical basis of the demand made. Put this or that man on the ticket for the second office in the country, we are told, no because he is a fit man as well as a black man, but first because he is black, or blackish, and next because he may be fit. Turn the color argument the other way. What would be said of nomination made because the favored man is white, leaving his qualities a secondary reason? These restless reformers would have us go back to the original meaning of the word "candidate" only substituting their own barbarous coinage of "nigrate." The colored race has been put on equality with the white. As to holding office, what right has the white man ever had? Just this, and no more: the right to the free exercise of toil and his talents, if he have them, by which he may build up a character of honesty and ability, and induce the community to confide in him enough to reward him with the temporary authority of office, in the trust that the duties it imposes will be well discharged. That is all that the black man has gained in this respect by emancipation. Let him set about the work with a will. Nothing else than the accomplishment of it can entitle him to present himself for the suffrages of his fellow-citizens—far less will they tolerate his preposterous claim, founded on color, to a right which they have never had—that of governing them before he has proved his ability to govern himself. There are local offices, requiring a low grade of capacity, which the Negro may very possibly soon fit himself for. We see no objection to his aspiring to them, though we believe he would be far better and happier out of politics. But to thrust forward at once, one of a lower race, who cannot possibly have had opportunities for the requisite training in public affairs, and the knowledge of men, to fill a high post which very few indeed, after a life-long exhibitions of capacity and patriotic devotion are deemed to deserve, is the very sublimity of impudence.

The leading men of the colored race themselves make no such unreasonable claim. They understand their situation, and have no purpose to be made the cats paws of politicians. As one of their member, Major DELANY, who, in his experience as a volunteer, learned something of self-discipline and of men, very sensibly says in a letter upon the subject, "Let colored men be satisfied to take things like other men in their natural course and time, preparing themselves in every particular for local municipal positions, and they may expect to attain to some others in time."

Neither would the election of a Negro as Vice-President make him or prove him to be the social equal of the white man. Social equality is an unnatural and impossible state. No right can be pleaded for, nor can any force conquer it, nor any law impose it. It has no relations to political equality, nor does it rest upon that unprivileged right to make his way in the world, which every citizen may claim in common with every other. No man, of any color, can assert his right to be with another at the polls, or in the theater or the cars, has authority for claiming to be helped to his soup or to marry his daughter. Social distinctions spring from natural diversities, and are maintained by sympathies of feelings, of tastes, and pursuits. Put a dozen men and women of different characters together on a desert island, and in a week social distinction would have marked them apart. Can any reform reduce these inborn individualities to a flat level of common place? Radicalism here brings up against an impossible barrier, for it cannot new create human nature. But it will make the attempt, since there is no more rest for it than for the miserable spirits who in DANTE's Hell are whirled about forever among contending winds. It will attack individual preferences and the natural right to choose one's own associates, as it has attacked individual taste by sumptuary laws, and individual conscience by prohibitory ones. And the attack will be treated, as it will deserve to be, as the presumption of brutal insolence.

SOURCE: *New York Times*, August 21, 1867.

DOCUMENT 5
Delany to L. S. Langley

BUREAU SUB-DISTRICT, CHARLESTON
HEADQUARTERS, HILTON HEAD
HILTON HEAD, S.C. FEBRUARY 5th, 1868.

L. S. Langley, Esq., Member, Constitutional
Convention, South Carolina, Charleston, S.C.

DEAR SIR:

Your favor of the 3rd inst., in reply to my letter to you of the 26th ult., was received by last night's mail.

In reply to your request to permit my name to be put in nomination as a candidate for Congress from the Second Congressional District, composed of Charleston, Beaufort, Colleton and Barnwell, permit me to offer you my unfeigned and heartfelt thanks for the compliment thereby paid, confidence reposed and deference shown, because prompted by motives in strict accordance (as I know your delegation is aware) with my sense of propriety and fitness of things; acquired ability, qualified by adaptation, age and experience.

It is scarcely necessary for me to repeat what you have frequently known me to express the greatest possible discretion and prudence in these first steps in the inclipency of the enfranchisement of our race in this country. Every step taken by us should be fraught with prudence and caution, lest thereby an error prejudicial to the efforts of our friends in and out of the councils of the nations, and fatal to our cause, might be committed.

It is not necessary to our claims as American citizens, nor important to the accomplishment of that end, that a black man at this period be a representative in the national halls of legislation. This, let me insist with emphasis, the nation (the American people generally), are not ready for. And this sentiment, however undesirable, must be yielded to by us. And when they are ready for it, of course, there will be no objection, and consequently no harm done, and should they never become ready, then that will be the end of the whole matter.

Let our great and good hearted friend, Wendell Phillips, outside of the councils, claim what he pleases—it is right. His sentiments are as essential to the political life of the nation, as oxygen to animal life. And same also with the great and good statesmen inside of the council.

But too much of one at the wrong time, would assuredly produce the extinction of animal life; and too much of the other at an improper time, in like manner, prove the destruction of our hopes and cherished political issues of our friends.

Whatever they may claim at present as our rights, they do so as white men, a part and parcel of the dominant race, who desire to express for the nation, sentiments of generosity toward the black race, for their fidelity, patriotism, and deeds of military valor in the recent life struggle of the country. This they can afford to do. But we should not presume by reason of this or our numbers, to assume these positions to ourselves.

I regret the expressions of approbation in my letter of the 28th of January, of your and Mr. Whipper's course in Convention, of liberality and leniency toward the late oppressors of our race; but am as I was in regard to the Vice-Presidency, entirely opposed at this period of political experience of the country, to any person identified with the black race entering any council of the nation as a member.

I therefore most respectfully decline the proffered honor of your nomination—an honor as complimentary to me as it is liberal and generous in you to offer it.

Be pleased to make known my views in full to your delegation, with my heartiest thanks for their high consideration, and accept the warmest regards, with much.

I have the honor to be, Sir,
Your most obedient servant,
M. R. DELANY.

SOURCE: Martin R. Delany, *Trial and Conviction of Martin R. Delany*, unpublished pamphlet (Charleston, SC, 1876).

DOCUMENT 6

THOUGHTS FOR THE COLORED PEOPLE

The most important question for your earnest consideration is the destined policy of the American people, in regard to universal suffrage. Is this country ready to yield to you the same political status with the white man? This is the question which seems to us of more importance that you should fairly consider and look at it in all its bearing than any other. Your own Delany sees with sagacious eyes, the handwriting on the wall, and you have heard his eloquent voice raised in your behalf, warning you to be careful how your first steps are taken in the enfranchisement of our people. Read these few words of wisdom from his pen! "It is not necessary to our claims as Americans, nor important to the accomplishment of that end, that a black man at this period be a representative IN THE NATIONAL HALLS OF LEGISLATION. This, let me insist with emphasis, the nation (the American people generally) are not ready for. And this sentiment, however, undesirable, must be yielded to by us."

In all the political movement of the two great and powerful parties, North and West, numbering in the whole nearly 4,000,000 of voters, without adding those in the South, this one idea, as a cardinal principle, is not steadily in view! "That this country is not ready for the enfranchisement of your people." The recorded verdict of the American people is against it. The genius of American liberty is against it, and today you see it clearly marked out, in the action of the Pennsylvania Legislature, in refusing, by a large radical majority, to strike the word 'white' from their constitution. This is Steven's own state, you radical friend. Illinois, the home of your Lincoln, is against it. Ohio, Connecticut, New York, Delaware, Michigan, Wisconsin, Minnesota, and Iowa, saying nothing about the Territories, are against it. The radical leaders and your pretended friends, if the secrets of their hearts could be read, are opposed to it, and no stronger proof is needed than the result of your commission to Washington, in regard to making nominations to Congress. Why have you not a right to sit in the legislative hall at Washington, if you have a right to be voted for in state affairs? Why, the answer is very plain: IT IS NOT TO BE; if it was, this is as good a time to begin as any other. Upon the plea of policy, you are advised not to send members to Congress, because it would excite the prejudice of color, to the injury of the party. Why, do you not see, that your party is as strong today as it ever will be, and now, if ever, would be the time (if they are honest and true in their profession of friendship towards you) to give you all they promise. Beware of the wile of those cunning politicians, who preach Negro suffrage for the South but none for the North. Is citizenship less dear to you in Pennsylvania than in South Carolina? Are the boasted privileges of freedom only to be enjoyed in the South? How do you reconcile this strange inconsistency? We see but one solution: The power of your radical friends is passing away, and they imploringly appeal to the colored people of the South to bolster up their rotten and corrupt administration, upon the promise that you shall have lands, mules and office, and at the same time intend to deceive you. They have not the lands to give you, and just so sure as the sun raises and sets, just so sure will all the promises of your radical friends and allies, with the recent monstrous declaration of Beverly Nash—That you will get thirty acres of land—will prove a snare and a cheat. We beseech you to ponder well, reflect before you take that step which must separate you

from your own Southern friends. We advise you. In all sincerity, to leave the party who will betray you into ruin, when no friends are left to support you. Cultivate kind and friendly relations with the white people. Keep away from these political leagues which bend your hand and foot and rob you of your real freedom of thought and action. Want will be a hard task-master. If you listen to the cunning devices of your leaders, they will utterly destroy you in their attempt to obtain place and power. In conclusion, we have presented for your consideration a ticket for members of the legislature. You can have no objection to any of the gentlemen selected for the position. Your interest has mainly been consulted in this choice. They are your friends who, in time of need, you may confidently approach and be received with cordial feelings. They are the friends of the laborer, the tradesman, the farmer and planter. Their interest is your interest, and your destiny is with the white man of the South. "Why halt ye between two opinions; choose ye this day whom thou wilt serve."
FIDES.

SOURCE: *Daily Phoenix* (Columbia, SC), April 12, 1868.

DOCUMENT 7
UNIVERSITY PAMPHLETS: A SERIES OF
FOUR TRACTS ON NATIONAL POLITY

TO THE STUDENTS OF WILBERFORCE UNIVERSITY
BEING ADAPTED TO THE CAPACITY OF THE NEWLY
ENFRANCHISED CITIZENS,
THE FREEDMEN
BY MARTIN R. DELANY

Member of the corporation of Wilberforce University; Chief of an Exploring Party to Central Africa; Physician, Surgeon, and Practitioner in the Diseases of Women and Children; Member of the International Statistician Congress, 1860, London, His Royal Highness Albert, Prince Consort of England, President; Member of the Congress and National Association for the Promotion of Social Science, 1860, Glasgow, Scotland, Right Honorable Henry Lord Brougham and Vaux, President; Late Major of the 104th U.S. Colored Troops, U.S. Army, and Sub-Assistant Commissioner to Brevet Major-General Rufus Saxton, and Brevet Major-General R. K. Scott, Assistant Commissioners of Bureau Refugees, Freedmen, and Abandoned

Lands, U.S.A.; now Lieutenant-Colonel and Aid-de-Camp on the Staff of His Excellency R. K. Scott, Governor of the State of South Carolina

FIRST SERIES
CHARLESTON, S.C.
REPUBLICAN BOOKS AND JOB OFFICE
CORNER MEETING AND MARKET STREETS
1870

ADVERTISEMENT BY AUTHOR

THE "University Pamphlets" are but the commencement of a series of tracts intended to be written by the author as popular elementary instruction in the principles of National Polity, complimentary to the Faculty, Students, and Trustees of WILBERFORCE UNIVERSITY, the latter body of which he is a member.

These pamphlets will be adapted with special care and reference to the comprehension and benefit of the new political element in the United States—the freedmen and colored youth.

This series was originally published in four alternate numbers of the NEW ERA, Washington City, from January to March 1870.

The next series will be on the "History of Constitutional Governments," which will give a much clearer view and understanding of the importance of Constitutions, as guarantees of liberty, so essential at this time, immediately succeeding the establishment of an impartial and truly National Government.

A SERIES OF FOUR TRACTS
ON
NATIONAL POLITY

NUMBER I
CITIZENSHIP

The term *citizen*, politically considered, is derived from the Roman definition, which was never applied in any other sense—*civis ingenuus*—which meant one exempt from restraint of any kind. *Civis*, a citizen; one who might enjoy the highest honors in his own free town—the town in which he lived—and in the country or commonwealth; and *ingenuus*, free born—of good extraction.

All who were deprived of citizenship—that is, the right of enjoying positions of honor and trust—were termed *hostes* and *peregrini*, which means public and private enemies, or foreigners and aliens to the country. *Hostis*, a public, and sometimes private, enemy; and *peregrinus*, an alien, or stranger, or foreigner. As a policy, the common people or Plebeians, were sometimes classed with these, by the ruling people or Patricians; but all natives or people born in the country were citizens, and might be elevated to any position in State or the body politic, as was Cicero, to that of Consul or Chief Magistrate of Rome, who had been simply Mark Tully, (*Marcus Tullius*) a Plebeian, or poor boy from among the lower classes.

The Romans, from national pride, to distinguish their inhabitants from those of other countries, termed them all "citizens"—as in the case of the aliens and foreigners (*hostes peregrini*)—but consequently, were under the necessity of defining four classes of citizens—the better to distinguish them and prevent confusion—all but the *cives ingenui* being restricted in their privileges. This privileged class was the Patrician.

Its members enjoyed the *jus Quiritium*, which embodied, in the fullest extent, the rights, privileges and liberties pertaining to a Roman citizen.

There was one class whose members enjoyed, politically, only the *jus suffragiorum*. They had the privilege of voting, but no other political privilege. They could vote for one of their superiors—the *cives ingenui*—but not for themselves.

Such precisely was the relative condition of the black inhabitants of the United States; in some of the States they answering to the latter class—as in New York and Ohio—having the privilege of *voting*, to elevate another class to positions to which they themselves were denied.

The right of suffrage, as shown in British and American civil rights, does not necessarily imply the elective franchise. Suffrage means "a vote, voice, approbation," simply a privilege, something allowed. A privilege may sanction the rights of others, by those who do not themselves possess the rights they sanction.[3]

---

3. Noted by Delany on the document: "The truth was illustrated in France by Napoleon III's elevation of the Presidency of the French Republic in 1851. On taking the vote every man must vote 'yes' or 'no'—that is, for or against him; but the voter could not cast his ballot for himself, or any other person than Napoleon; since by his established polity no person was eligible to the position, though all had a right to give their vote for or against him. This was the exercise of the RIGHT OF SUFFRAGE, as it is called, and all that it is worth politically."

Rights are indisputable, inviolable; and in this country, political rights constitute the inherent sovereignty of the people. Where there is no acknowledged sovereignty, there can be no binding power; hence, formerly in the United States, the suffrage of the black man, independently of the white, was unavailing—worth nothing.

It must be understood that no people can be free who do not themselves constitute an essential part of the *ruling element* of the country in which they live. Whether this element be founded on a true or false, a just or unjust basis, this status in community is necessary to personal safety.

The liberty of no man is secure who controls not his own political destiny. What is true of the individual applies to a community of individuals, or society at large. To suppose otherwise, is that delusion which induces its victim, through a period of long suffering, patiently to submit to all kinds of wrong, and holds in subjection the oppressed of every country.

A people to be free must be their own ruler; each individual must in himself be an essential element of the sovereign power which composes the true basis of his liberty. This right, when not exercised by himself, may, at his pleasure, be delegated to another—his true representative.

These great truths are established in the British and American people. The people of Great Britain elect their representatives in the person of a Parliament, and the Parliament creates or elects a ruler, called Monarch or Sovereign; and in the United States they elect their representatives in the person of electors, who meet in assemblies and elect their ruler, called President. In both of these cases there is only the sovereign will of each individual and united will of the people, carried out in the persons of these rulers, to whom they delegate their authority. Otherwise, the people of neither of these countries could be politically free. The same may be said of France—the civil rights of whose people take higher ground than those of either Great Britain or the United States.

"A free agent in a free Government should be his own governor," said a great French writer. That is, as elsewhere stated, he must possess the acknowledged right to govern. This constitutes him a governor, though he delegates to another the power to govern or rule over himself.

It is plain that no one can delegate to another a power he never possessed; that is, he cannot give an agency in that which he never had a right.

It must be apparent that the political condition of the black race, previous to the rebellion, was deplorable; and a change in their status was essential before it was possible to alter their condition.

First in order, emancipation was demanded, which placed them in a normal condition in relation to their country.

In Rome—from which the political rights or claim of the individual was borrowed by the United States—citizenship, as stated, was based alone on nativity. All native-born inhabitants being citizens, the term was simply applied to the strangers and foreigners who resided among them, to gratify their pride, and thereby secure their loyalty to the country.

To place the black race in possession of equal rights, and enfranchise it with all the claims of citizenship, it was only necessary to remove all legal disabilities, and repeal all unjust provisions against it, and the black man stood in the United States a *citizen by nature*, with claims and rights as inviolable as the proudest—rights which to him became a contingency shall to his children be *inherent* and everlasting.

Will the opposers of the political elevation of the black race still continue to commit such palpable blunders in national polity as to deny that the black is a legitimate—in social polity—or legal citizen of the United States? It is time this political absurdity had ceased.

And it is now important that men of the black race make themselves masters of political science that they may grapple favorably with the great question of civilization, now the basis of national and international polity.

NUMBER II
CIVIL RIGHTS

Every member of a body politic has duties and obligations to perform, which are binding according to his relative position in society.

His general obligations are to the nation, particularly obligations to the province, district, or state, (as one of the United States) and special obligations to those with whom he is identified or classified, as German, French, Jew, Scotch, Italian, Irish, Spanish, or English. Here, in America, the special obligations of the black man are to his own people.

Civil rights imply all the privileges and enjoyments known to the body politic. These rights are not natural, but conditional, regulated by the requirements of society.

The general requirements of society are regulated by national obligations, or the obligations of state. A nation being bound to protect itself and preserve its own existence, regulates the individual, and governs society accordingly.

In France civil and political rights are one and the same—inseparable—and based upon natural rights. The right to freedom carries with it every other right and suffrage is claimed as a birthright.

To deny to the Frenchman any privilege in the body politic, is to degrade him in his own estimation, and deprive him of "one-half of his manhood." "Freedom" is his watch-word, and "Liberty" his rallying cry.

In France, Government is always regarded as despotic, where suffrage is curtailed; and, indeed, the Chamber of Deputies—representatives of the people, and the right to choose them—is as old as the advanced civilization of that people.

It was seen that Louis Napoleon, as the first step in his accession to power, in 1851, took the vote of the people. It is true that their civil rights were abrogated, when they were prevented from competing for the Presidency; because, in France, as the civil and political are inseparable, the right to vote carries with it the right to hold office.

The action above alluded to, simply shows a concession, even by Napoleon III, to those great and inherent rights as claimed by the Frenchman.

In England and the United States civil and political rights differ, and political rights carry with them different degrees of privileges. A man might have the privilege of voting and not the right to hold office; or, in other words, have the right of suffrage and not be eligible to office.

In Great Britain, Magna Charta made every person equal before the law; but in the political regulations a property qualification was required to vote and hold office. But, in America exceptions were made to one class or race of the inhabitants, who were denied both the right of suffrage and the right to hold office.

This caused much confusion and frequent embarrassment in the administration of laws, in consequence of the ambiguity of their constructions, which were as erroneous as they were unjust.

In England and the United States, as in France, the civil should have included the political rights of the people.

But an established peerage, orders of nobility and primogeniture, or land privileges, as the basis of the United Kingdom of England, Scotland and Ireland, positively prohibited these enjoyments to the lower classes, in the first case; and the National Compact, the basis of the American Union, recognizing and permitting the existence of slavery and a privileged class in the whites, in the second case prevented an acknowledgment of these great fundamental rights, as belonging to the whole people, as in France.

As a nation is bound to protect itself, to have conceded equal privilege to the common people in Great Britain would have destroyed the foundation of their government, as then constructed; and to have conceded civil rights to blacks in the United States must have, in like manner, endangered the National Compact, as slavery was the basis of the Union.

But the people of Great Britain are free, and their system of government but a matter of choice and time, which may be modified in its continual progress with satisfaction to the entire nation.

And, in the United States, by the late civil war, slavery has become extinct, the blacks enfranchised, and the civil and political rights of the whole people acknowledged.

The duties and obligations of every individual being according to his relative position in society, previous to emancipation and our enfranchisement, we had few or no obligations, because few or no responsible positions in society.

But now, having all the rights and privileges, we also have all the responsibilities belonging to society. Hence, the necessity of possessing such information and having such qualifications as to fit us for the high, responsible, and arduous duties of the new life into which we have entered.

We must possess attainments equal to the requirements of the positions we expect to occupy. Otherwise, we have no right to expect anything.

Our new political element, we are in hopes, will not fail to profit by these elementary lessons in national polity.

NUMBER III
CONSTITUTION

"The Constitution has been violated!" is an exclamation daily uttered in both Houses of Congress by the Opposition.

What is a Constitution, and for what is it intended? Let us inquire.

A Constitution is a legal guaranty of security to all the rights and privileges of the people in a country, the basis of which must be written or understood.

In all countries without these constitutional arrangements, written or traditional, the will of the ruler is law, and the liberties of the people are insecure.

The British Constitution is based on Magna Charta, a written document, which prohibits any act of government abridging or curtailing the rights and privileges of the people. Hence, no act of Parliament can be repealed, nor judicial decision reversed, that ever has been established in their favor.

The greatest political and civil rights enjoyed by the royal family and nobility must be conceded to and enjoyed by the common people of the empire; and every privilege may be extended in common to all, but none can be abrogated.

By this wise provision the only alteration to the Constitution allowable must be favorable and progressive, in strict conformity with all the provisions of Magna Charta, or the great charter of British rights.

Every act of Parliament or judicial decision, as the *habeas corpus*, the acknowledgment of Scotch and Irish peerage, ruling slavery from British soil—as in the Somerset case, West Indian emancipation, the Corn Laws, "Irish emancipation," as it is called, the rights of suffrage to the common people—each and all are additions to the Constitution, which cannot be repealed, because enhancing the liberty of the people.

The British Constitution, then, consists of a succession of liberal acts, forced by the common people from the Crown by the authority of the Magna Charta, the fundamental source of their rights.

Every act of justice, then, is constitutional, and in strict conformity with the only object and design of that instrument.

The Constitution of the United States, unlike that of Great Britain, is a document of numerical provisions, designed more for the regulation of departments of State and official duties, than for defining and guarding the rights of the people.

This instrument is conservative in character, its alteration carefully guarded against, and scarcely to be hoped for; while that of the British is progressive, continual alterations being provided for and expected.

Had the American Declaration of Independence been adopted at the time as the basis of the Constitution, it would have been to the United States, what Magna Charta is to Great Britain.

The act of 1787, limiting slavery in the Northwest territory; the act of 1808, limiting the slave trade; the instructions of 1851, to Captain Ingraham, in relation to Martin Kotzia, defining the rights of American citizens on board American vessels; the emancipation proclamation of 1863; the civil rights bill of 1866, and all the reconstruction acts of Congress promoting the rights of the people, would have only been so many clauses added to the Constitution, in conformity with the great principles of that document.

And there is little doubt that when Jefferson and his compeers framed the Declaration, they expected it, like Magna Charta, to be the basis, indeed, the Constitution itself; a guaranty of security to the rights of the people, definitely laid down as therein declared. But the whole was perverted, as sad experience has proven; and, instead of that great charter, an ambiguous document, susceptible to almost any construction concerning human rights, was shamefully imposed upon the American people and the world, as the

Constitution of a new nation claiming to have taken the most advanced position in modern civilization.

The Constitution of the United States, then, it is clearly seen, according to its structure, failed entirely as an instrument for which it was intended, previous to the late civil war. And the old line leaders in both political parties (Whig and Democrat), as statesmen, did little else, in their interpretation and legal construction of it, than mislead the American people in the knowledge of constitutional rights.

It must be understood and laid down as a proposition logically correct, that any instrument which recognizes in its provisions the violation of the natural rights of any part of the people, is a mockery in its pretensions; as the design of a Constitution legitimately must be, the enlargement and protection of the rights of the whole people.

The object of this article is to instruct a class of rulers in the elementary principles of constitutional government; and to do ample justice to a subject so important would require a series of articles on the history of Constitutions.

The new era upon us, requires new duties among a new political element; and consequently, there must be disseminated information commensurate with their requirements.

NUMBER IV
SECESSION

"These States, I affirm, were never out of the Union," declared the Hon. J. P. Stockton, United States Senator from New Jersey, while discussing the bill offered by Senator Morton, from Indiana, which again placed proud, arrogant Georgia under the stricture of the National Government.

Were the rebel "States never out of the Union?" Let me see.

Every State, in any country, has two conditions, a territorial or land, and a political or government.

When the rebellion ensued, the first effective act was to meet in general congress at Montgomery, Alabama, and declare themselves out of the Union, by absolving all relations, and ignoring all authority, withy and from the different States and Government of the United States. Immediately, all relations between these two great divisions of States, North and South, ceased, and for four long years of anxious warfare and desperate struggling, so continued.

From Montgomery, Alabama, to Richmond, Virginia, the Government of these States changed, which was as foreign to the United States as it was to France. And these facts were never denied by the Government at Washington.

But not satisfied with taking themselves out of the Union, the South endeavored to carry with them the territory, a portion of the national domain, belonging to the Union. It was this attempt of theirs, and this alone, which brought down on their offending heads, the just retribution of the nation.

Would it be pretended that these people had no right to withdraw from the United States, either as individuals or in a body, if they so desired, set up and organize themselves into a body politic for their own government and mutual protection, provided they did not encroach on the rights of any other people in so doing?

Had they immediately after the Montgomery congress, or at any subsequent period, quietly withdrawn—organized as they were—to any part of Mexico, Central, South America, or Nassau, and there set up themselves with all the "paraphernalia" of a confederacy, would the United States Government have dared interfere with them? Certainly not; nor would the law of nations have tolerated it.

What, then, was the position of the Government in relation to them? Why, it admitted their right to go, but denied their right to carry with them the territory, a portion of the public domain, belonging to the nation. The right of their political state was conceded, but that of the land or country only was denied; and it was this position alone assumed by President Lincoln, in his continual declaration that the "rebel States were never out of the Union."

What, then, is the course of Congress toward these people? Why, having withdrawn their political relations and absolved all and every interest, it is not only the indisputable right, but the imperative duty of the national council to prescribe terms and conditions upon which they may return to their allegiance.

This is both logically correct and morally right.

And Congress legislates, not on the territorial, but political relations of the late Confederate States to the Union.

Might it not be well for the opposition, who so flippantly deny the withdrawal of the rebel States from the Union, to remember these facts before claiming for them such unrestricted equal political rights as originally existed between the States? It were well that they do.

SOURCE: Martin R. Delany, *University Pamphlets: A Series of Four Tracts on National Polity.* Charleston, SC: Republican Book and Job Office, 1870.

DOCUMENT 8
ON A BLACK MAN'S PARTY

The Democratic newspapers are quite delighted and excited over what they deem to be a movement for a "Black Man's Party", and they very jubilantly predict all manner of strife and dissolution of the Republican Party. We assure them that their predictions have been so often proved fallacious that nobody, not even they themselves, put confidence in them.

We assure them that we feel no particular anxiety. The account of Messrs, Delany, Cain, and others, in Charleston, has two objective points— the States Convention and the Congressional Convention of the Republican Party. The scheme for the State Convention is one which can be easily defeated by exposure and if necessary we shall expose it fully. The second object is to defeat C. C. Bowen, and nominate in his place a colored man for Congress. This effort they, or any other Republicans, have a perfect right to make, and in making it, to use all legitimate means within the lines of the party. Having done this, they are simply bound in honor and party fealty to abide by the result whether it suits them or not.

We expect this to go on until the conventions are over, and then stop. Whoever is regularly nominated at the convention, we shall support, so we believe, will Delany, Delarge and others. But whether they do or not, we know that the solid body of Republicans will.

These men, while in the party, are strong. If they go out of it, they are weak as broken reeds. We do not believe these men intend either to leave or break up the party. But we say plainly, the Republican Party can spare them all and go right on to victory.

We repeat that while we depreciate the appeal to race, we feel no serious anxiety about it. We shall fight over our candidates, but we shall unite on them and elect them.

SOURCE: *Daily Republican* (Charleston), June 20, 1870.

DOCUMENT 9
WARD MEETING AT MILITARY HALL

A meeting of the Republican voters of Ward 4 was held last evening— call issued by order of the President of the Union Republican Club of that Ward, in order to form an effective organization for work in the approaching election. Some two or three hundred persons were present, including several from other wards. The President: Peter L. Miller.

The President stated that Colonel Delany was present, and they would be glad to hear from him. Loud calls were made for the Colonel, and he arose, thanking the audience for the compliment. He spoke at considerable length, and with great force, explaining the issues of the approaching contest, and reviewing the action of the "Palpitators" Convention recently held at Columbia. He described how the platform of the Convention was manipulated to make it acceptable to the colored man without offending the Democrats. He meant no unkindness when he stated that the platform of the convention did not mean what it said. It was almost identical with the Republican platform, and if they were sincere in their views as there expressed, why did they not come into the Republican Party at once! It was evident that it was merely a scheme to obtain power. They had promised half the offices to colored men, but as far as they have gone, have they kept their promises? No. General Butler, their candidate for Lieutenant—Governor, went so far as to say that he would give freedom and equal political privileges to the colored men. His magnanimity will be understood when I say that the colored man enjoy all those rights now, while General Butler himself labors under political disabilities (laughter). Offering privileges to the colored people that he doesn't possess himself! This act would be sublime if it wasn't so ridiculous.

And Judge Carpenter, who is he? A man who represents himself as a Kentuckian, but who instead is a wooden-nutmeg Yankee, (I am one myself) a carpet bagger, (I am one myself, but not like him) who went to Kentucky from Vermont with "saw-dust hams" and "wooden nut-megs" and now calls himself a Kentuckian. Beware of such men! When that colored woman came before him at Orangeburg, who had been robbed of her chastity by a white man, and claimed support for her children, what did this miserable Yankee recollect I say MISERABLE Yankee—who calls himself a Kentuckian, tell her? That she had no right that a white man was bound to respect—the old Taney doctrine. He is one of those people who at the North, before the war, were like serpents crawling upon their bellies eating Southern Slime. This is the character of the man who attempts to mislead colored men and to steal from them their rights and liberties. Carpenter will not dare to face us here. He promises to go into rural districts, and it is said that a Senator form Washington will come here to help him; but let me tell them that I shall follow them, and when they get through I will be heard, and if I don't make the Judge look so small that it will take a telescope as powerful as Hershel's to see him, it is because I don't know how. What we require most is unity among ourselves. We must be more united, black and white. In saying united, I don't mean that our white Republicans shall steal our dead bodies from us, as the Democrats did in Columbia, where eight aristocratic white Democrats carried an old dead "nigger" to the grave, after having "shoo flyed" off the real mourners. This was done for effect, to make capital, but we don't expect our white Republicans to do that. The speaker closed his remarks with sound advice to his hearers as to their conduct in the coming campaign. His speech was checkered with droll humor and wit, and was received by the audience with the greatest enthusiasm.

SOURCE: *Daily Republican* (Charleston), June 21, 1870.

DOCUMENT 10
Mass Meeting of Republicans

Held at Liberty Hall, Morris Street, last evening; A. J. Ransier, R. C. Delarge, J. H. Rainey

Speech of Lieut. Col. Delany

Mr. Delany being then called on said: I respond to your call. I use no deception. I know you would call on me and came prepared to speak. We are now entering upon a new campaign, and we lay down our platform so we can't be misunderstood. THE REPUBLICAN holds a lash over our backs, just the least threatening that if we don't mind ourselves they will come down upon us, and I trust therefore that I will not be misrepresented, and that my words will not be misinterpreted. We lay the basis for the new campaign, and this basis must be clearly defined. We are not equal to our white friends in many qualities, and we required therefore a principle to depend upon. We must be valued for something. We are not equal to the white race in general intelligence, and, we must therefore have an offset to be equal, and let that offset be "honesty" and "justice." I don't believe in social equality, there is no such thing. IF we want to associated with a man, we will do it, and without laws. Be let us demand as a black race (when I say "black" I take in the lightest as well as the blackest hue), let us demand justice. I take the ground that no people have become a great people who had not their own leaders. Take the world over and all nations are represented by their own people, and black men must have black leaders. We must be directors of our own people, and let it be known that neither Major Willoughby, Mr. Fox, Governor Scott, or anyone else, can lead black men. (A voice, Colonel! How would it do to follow Mr. Bird as a leader?) Well, to show that colored men want colored leaders, even Bird came to see me, at the head of a delegation, to offer me office and for counsel. He told me as long as the Reformers did what they professed he would stand by them, but let them use the word Democrat once and he is gone. He also told me that he would watch Carpenter and the others closely, and if he found anything like treachery on their part he would leave them, and I am satisfied he would soon find his mistake and join our ranks. We have no idea of forming a black man's party. It would be folly even to think of such a thing when we are only one-eighth of the population of this country—five millions of blacks and thirty five millions of whites—and the latter clearly increasing by immigration as well as by natural increase, while we have no immigrants to swell our numbers. I want it understood that we are in the majority in this state, and we would hold the political power. We are the strongest, and propose to elect to the Senate or House of Representatives. Will he not do as much for a colored man as a white man would? This is all that is claimed, and this program must be carried out. We don't want more than one-half of the offices; we don't want the minority to have all. This is justice. If a colored man is elected to the Senate or House of Representatives, will he not do as much for a colored man as a white man would? This is all that is claimed, and this program must be carried out. We don't want more than one-half of the offices, we don't want a colored governor, for our good sense tells us differently, and the will of the people indicates a different course, but we want a colored Lieutenant Governor, and two colored men in the House of Representatives and one in the Senate, and our quota of state and county offices. We must get rid of corruption. The Governor says so and everybody says so, and this issue will be met as it should be met. We must select men of integrity and veracity.

I shall help to select them, and then we shall have an honest legislature. He (the speaker) reiterated his remarks relative to Judge Carpenter, made at the Fourth Ward meeting (already reported in THE REPUBLICAN). He asked the assemblage if they firmly pledged themselves to oppose this renegade (Carpenter), and was answered with shouts of "Yes". He then attempted to close, but shouts of "Go on" urged him to continue, which he did in the same strain as above, pointing out the Congressional Districts which he wanted black men to represent—the 2d and 3d. He concluded with these words. "Now, you understand what we want, let us go on with the work. And to you colored men who are opposed to this movement, I say you dare not do anything against your race".

SOURCE: *Daily Republican* (Charleston), June 24, 1870.

DOCUMENT 11
SIDE ISSUES

Several Republican meetings have recently been held in Charleston. These were largely attended, and evinced a spirit of the firmest faith in the continued triumph of Republicanism.

But, while the masses at these meetings were right, we are sorry to say that some of the speakers were emphatically wrong, in as much as they made appeals to their hearers which were calculated to foster the most pernicious ideas concerning color or race. Land commissioner Delarge on Tuesday evening made a speech which could only be interpreted as advising the colored people to practically form a political party of their own, and to place no trust in the whites. And on Wednesday evening he made a speech which, in a more guarded way, set forth the same wretched ideas. He then even assumed to denounce a "ring" of white men, among whom he included all the state officers except the Governor and the Secretary of State.

As to the latter statement, Mr. Delarge has been misinformed. There is no such "ring". And there must never be any such clique as that. It would be a betrayal of Republicanism and the adoption of the old wicked practice of the Democratic Party.

Last evening, he repeated his advocacy of this policy of race.

As to the position intentionally or unintentionally taken by Mr. Delarge, it is suggestive only of evil; and evil continually. It is a return to the old curse of South Carolina—the political action of one race against another simply because of race.

Have Republicans indeed fought so long in South Carolina for the disenthralment of the colored people form the whites, and the destruction, as far as possible, of all political lines founded on race, only to see the colored people return evil for evil, and seek to pit their race, as a race against the whites?

South Carolina was sent to political perdition because of this action of one race against another; and she will go there again, and that immediately, if the advice of Mr. Delarge be taken.

The state having made the progress it has in Republicanism, it is easy to see the inherent weakness of any such policy, even for those who advocate it.

We will first take the case of Mr. Delarge himself, for he is the one who first publicly advocated this pernicious policy. Mr. Delarge is a Brown man. The brown men of the state are a handful as compared to blacks. Now it is very frequently asserted that there is more prejudice, more jealous watchfulness between the browns and the blacks than between the whites and the blacks. If this be so, and the lines should be sharply drawn on color, Mr.

Delarge would speedily see the unwisdom of the crusade on which he had entered. He would go up in the political balloon so high that he would never come down again.

And now Col. Delany makes speeches advocating this policy set forth by Mr. Delarge. He has made several speeches in Charleston of late, and in all these the matter of race had more prominence that the grand truths of Republicanism. But, if Mr. Delarge and all the brown men will study it carefully, this is a blow as surely aimed at them as at the whites of all classes, for Col. Delany is a black, and he plainly says black men should have black leaders. Col. Delany's extreme and impracticable views on race are too well known to need extended comment. If carried out, the result would be the arrangement of the pure blacks against the whites and browns, and he himself sent to the wall.

Mr. Ransier in his speech last night said the sensible thing. He deprecates the positions taken by Col. Delany. He thinks both races should be justly and equally considered in legislation and the distribution of power. But he advocates the election of no colored man on the ground of color, but simple because he is a man, and entitled to all the dear rights of manhood. Senator Rainey also in this gave wise and temperate counsel.

In time past white men raised the cry of "a white man's government." It is even now heard. It was and is the voice of selfishness. And so now, when on the other hand, colored men raise the question of color, it is not for the good of the party or the colored race, but for their own selfish advancement. We protest against it, and we sincerely hope that every sound Republican will promptly condemn it. We are glad to say that the speeches in question have been most heartily condemned by the thoughtful and far seeing of the colored people.

For ourselves, we expect to vote in the next election for more colored candidates than whites, but we shall vote for them not as colored men, but simple as citizens, regularly nominated by the proper Republican conventions.

Those who would lead the colored people to again force the old rigid establishment of the lines of race are their worst enemies, no matter to what race such men belong. They would lead the colored people to untold evils, and peril some of the rights they have gained through the shedding of so much precious blood, both colored and white. They are anti-Republican. Even now this talk of race, coming from colored men, sends joy to the camp of the common enemy, the old Democracy, that for generations treated the colored people as hellishly because of race. They think to gain added power from this, and it is as sure as death that, that power would be put forth against the colored people.

We write this as for the interests of no man or set of men. We write as Republicans, as life-long Republicans, brought up to love the liberty of all races of men with an intensity of love, and brought to behold, in various parts of the world, the tears and anguish and blood which have flowed from the adoption of such narrow and unstatesmanlike theories as those we have herein condemned.

SOURCE: *Daily Republican* (Charleston), June 24, 1870.

DOCUMENT 12
THE APPEAL TO RACE

Lt.-Col. Delany says he wanted a colored Lieutenant Governor, two colored members of Congress, and sundry other office in this state, and others with him are making a great pow-wow over the matter, as if somebody was objecting to this. Yet we do not know a Republican who would object to three colored members of Congress from this state. We do not know a Republican who is opposing any man because he is a colored man, and we do to believe there is one. So then, all this is merely to advance the personal interest of certain prominent colored men. It is intended, not simply to put forward colored men, but to put forward these individual colored men.

We object, then, not to these colored men, we object not to the fair use of all means to secure nominations, but we do object to the wrongful appeal to the baneful prejudices of race. Whoever is nominated in the Republican Party, we desire to see nominated not because he is black, brown, or white, but because he is, on the whole, the best man. We not only expect but desire to vote in the next election for at least as many colored men as white men. In Charleston, we expect to see more colored than whites elected. But we know full well that if the question of race is to be pointedly made by sundry leaders for selfish purposes, there will not be so many colored men elected as there otherwise would be in the states.

We say this the more boldly, because we are not candidates for any office, and we do not know even a single employee, white or colored of THE REPUBLICAN who is a candidate for any office. We say it, therefore, unselfishly, earnestly, with profound desire for the welfare of both races and of our own party.

Nor have we any fear of the result of the appeal, for the voters of our great party have good sense and honesty.

SOURCE: *Daily Republican* (Charleston), June 27, 1870.

DOCUMENT 13
REPUBLICAN MEETINGS—WARD 6

Mr. L. J. Taylor was called on next. He said that he was not prepared to make a speech, but as he had been called for he would do his best. He was opposed to certain men, and he was going to attack them whenever called on to speak, because they were, in his opinion wrong. He then alluded to a speech made by Col. DELANY, in which the latter spoke disparagingly of him, and in which he alluded to the ignorance of their race, and continued: If we had had, the same chances to obtain education as he had, we might know as much as he does. (Cries of that's so!). The speaker wanted to know, as the colonel has spoken of color, where his race would be if it had not been for white men who gave them all they had? He then reviewed the official record of Mr. Bowen and Mr. Delarge in relation to their claims upon the people for office. He said the later had dodged the issue on the Phosphate Bill, by staying away from the legislative hall when the matter came up for final disposition, and that he voted against every measure that was submitted before that body for the benefit of the people, and cited several cases. He stated that Mr. Delarge was engaged in blockade running during the war, thereby assisting in keeping his race in slavery. (Mr. C. C. Bowen at this stage arrived in the hall and was loudly cheered). After the tumult had subsided, the speaker asked the meeting whether they would again place their trust in Mr. Delarge's hands. (Cries of No, No.) He said that people who talked to them of race and color merely seek self-aggrandizement. After they place them in office, they had no further use for them. He then spoke of Col. Delany, who, he said, was an aspirant for the United States Senate. He wanted his hearers to inquire at Beaufort what the colonel did when he was stationed there in the Freedmen's Bureau, and they would find that in nine cases out of ten he had crushed the colored people. "The colonel can't fool anybody in that locality with his black leaders for black men". If you want colored men in office get good men and not those I have spoken of. The speaker then explained the disastrous result such an issue as color would have if allowed to go on, and advised all who heard him to frown down such imprudent doctrines.

SOURCE: *Daily Republican* (Charleston), July 7, 1870.

DOCUMENT 14
Grand Mass Meeting

Edgefield Alive; 10,000 People Present

The largest assemblage of people ever gathered in this town, and one of the largest ever assembled in the State, outside Charleston. Arranged by the Republicans of the County with the double objects of celebrating the Fifteenth Amendment, and Declaration of Independence.

Present also were the "Palpitators" candidate for Governor, Judge Carpenter, and General M. C. Butler, for Lieutenant Governor and Major Bacon ("The Reformers").

—delegates from Graniteville, Hamburg, Augusta and Aiken.

COLONEL M. R. Delany made a capital speech of twenty or thirty minutes. He reviewed briefly the great antislavery movement in which he participated, and said he was often misunderstood. His platform was universal suffrage, universal amnesty, and an equal division of the honors of office between the races. When he went hunting with a white man, he did not want him to divide the game by saying "I'll take the turkey, you take the buzzard." He wanted some of the turkey too. Messrs Bacon and Butler said, "We'll give you the turkey". "Will you" said the Colonel, "then you stand on my platform, and I have a church to take you right in." He said he had a good church and a good pastor, and he did not propose to change for a long time yet. The colonel said he was not prejudiced against the Southern people. Nor were other Republicans. They had welcomed General Moses, Chief Justice Moses, and a host of others. They were coming in all the time, and they were welcomed. The church door was wide open. These remarks created great enthusiasm, and were repeatedly cheered.

Source: *Daily Republican* (Charleston), July 5, 1870.

DOCUMENT 15
The Fourth in Charleston

Delarge reaffirmed his commitment to the Republican Party.
—Cain next spoke.

Colonel Delany was the next speaker. He said that he had a speech prepared which he had intended to give in day time, but he did not wish to take up their time, on account of the lateness of the hour, and he would deliver it at some future time. Being requested to go on, he continued: We must be careful now-a-days what we do say. If we dare to impart ideas, we have misconstructions placed on them. I am called an impractical theorist. There is not a bold man who is not called that. I intended today to deliver a speech which should open the eyes of my race as to their social standings in life. But I suppose the organ of our party would call that making a distinction on account of color. They want to neutralize race, wipe out the word entirely. In saying this I want my friends to understand that although I argue with the gentlemen of the REPUBLICAN, I am not at war with them. The whites have enjoyed the privilege of education, they are consequently enlightened, and it is my object to enlighten the colored people. If you depend on other people to enlighten and help you, you will find yourself again in slavery. If black men have not their own leaders, white men will lead them and when they change and become Democrats, they will carry the black people with them. If it had not been for a Douglass to battle for them many of our black men would be in the Democratic ranks now. The speaker here gave an account of his career in Virginia, how bristling with daggers and pistols, he went to the Virginia lines, and helped his brethren from bondage into the Free states. He continued: I don't want you to think that I want you to turn against your friends. Nothing of that kind. I want you to stick to them until you find the odds to heavy against them; then get away as fast as you can. They speaker was several times interrupted by questions asked by persons in the audience, to which he replied good humoredly.

SOURCE: *Daily Republican* (Charleston), July 5, 1870.

DOCUMENT 16

A Card to the Editor of the *Republican*

To the Editor of *the Republican*:
SIR: In yesterday's *Daily News* I find the following:
"Arrived at Summerville the meeting was formed and Lieutenant Colonel Delany, (colored) attempted a speech, but he was met with such a storm of yells, shouts and jeers, accompanied by blasts on the tin horns, drumming on pans, etc., that he was compelled to desist. An effort on the part of a member of the other side met with a like reception, after which the meeting was broken up and the two parties retired in opposite directions. One party reassembled in the woods and the other managed to find a vacant hall. Order being in a measure restored, each party, after some

deliberation succeeded in triumphantly electing its own set of delegates to the forthcoming Convention."

In simple justice to Mr. Milshaw and his colleagues, I would say that the above is not true, as I was listened to with respectful attention by the assembly till I was finished my remarks, when they left, having held their meeting at noon, or a little after, without one word of interruption. The other meeting had been appointed for 8 o'clock in the evening at a hall, where it was held, adjourning at a late hour.

Permit me to add that I never have nor never shall countenance disorderly proceedings at these political meetings, never yet having attended one such, and wherever I may be, I shall ever aid and assist in preventing or putting a stop to such, should it occur.

Very respectfully, sir, your most Ob't serv't,
M. R. Delany
Charleston, August 16, 1870

SOURCE: *Daily Republican* (Charleston), August 16, 1870.

DOCUMENT 17

MEETING AT MILITARY HALL

A meeting of Republicans was held at Military Hall last night—present at which was Hon. R. H. Cain as County Chairman.

Between three or four hundred people in attendance (Hon. F. L. Cardozo, Mr. Whipper). To discuss the principles of Republicanism.

Speech of Col. Delany

Mr. Clark next introduced Col. M. R. Delany. The Colonel said that he was desirous of hearing Mr. Morris of THE REPUBLICAN, but that gentleman was not present and the Colonel was urged to go on. He spoke of his entrance to Charleston with General Schimmelfennig. He deplored the present state of Congressional affairs, and thought there was no necessity for it. He thought the leaders of both races were to blame, for when leaders harmonize, the people do the same. He thought the principle and cardinal points of Republicanism were not enough talked about, and then gave a history of the party movement since 1848, enunciating as a sound doctrine of Republicanism, "Let us know no color, either white, or black, but treat a man as a man, and let Radical Republicanism be our guiding point." He said that it was he who advised the Governor to keep away from the hustlings. He advised his hearers not to trifle with Republican principles; we must remember, he said, the disparity of members of the two races, and not forget that it was the white man who gave us what we now possess and who first brought us here. He then touched upon what the consequences might be if the doctrines of Republicanism were not fairly carried out.

Source: *Daily Republican* (Charleston), August 20, 1870.

DOCUMENT 18
A Political Review: Letter from Delany to Frederick Douglass

Hon. Fred. Douglass

My Dear Sir:

It has been ten years since last we met (in your library at Rochester) to discuss and reconcile ourselves to President Lincoln's war policy. Since then slavery had been overthrown, and no "reunion" of what were, for twenty years or more, the leading colored men of the country who shaped the policy and course of our race which led to disenthralment, having taken place, and consequently no interchange of ideas by counsel, I therefore deem it of importance at the time, to take a political review of South Carolina which I think will apply justly to nearly, if not the whole, of the "reconstructed states" of the South as well as the national government.

When the war ended, the colored people of the South had little knowledge of social and political affairs, and had of necessity, to accept such leaders as presented themselves. The first of these were in the persons of various agencies, as school teachers (mostly women), the Christian Commission, Colporteurs and agent to the freedmen's affair (not the Bureau) who aided in directing their social and domestic relations.

When reconstruction commenced, political leaders were greatly required, but few to be had. Southerners (the old masters) studiously opposed and refused to countenance reconstruction, and the freedmen were fearful and would not have trusted them if they could have obtained their aid.

Those who came with or followed the army, with a very few native whites, were the only available political element to be had to carry out the measures of reconstruction.

These were readily accepted by the blacks (by this I include the entire colored people) and the fullest confidence reposed in them. Some were or had been officers in the army. Some private, some sutlers, others peddlers and various tradesmen, others gamblers and even pickpockets and "hangers-on" and "bummers". I am particularly speaking of the whites. Among them were men of refinement, educated gentlemen, and some very good men, but a large part of those active were of the lowest grade of northern society, negro haters at home, who could not have been elected to any position of honor or trust. Just such men as burnt down Negro orphan asylum and hung Negro men at lamp posts in the New York riot of 1853. In this review, I intend to speak plainly, call things by their right names, and look those of whom I speak directly in the face.

The best and most competent men were chosen to fill the most important positions in state and local government, while the others readily obtained such places as required incumbents. Indeed there was scarcely one so incompetent as not to have been assigned some position of trust.

Positioned in places of power, profit and trust, they soon sought by that guile and deception, known only to demagogues, under the acceptable appellations of Yankee, Republican and Radical, to intrude themselves into the confidence of the blacks, and place themselves at their head as leaders. So insidiously did they do this that it was not discovered by the few colored men of intelligence who held places among them till too late to remedy the fatal evil.

These demagogues laid the foundation of their power upon a basis of the most dangerous political heresy. Deception, lying, cheating, chanting "whatever can be done in politics is fair," and to "beat is the duty in a political contest no matter what means were used to effect it," are among the pernicious precepts of this moral infidelity.

Jealous of the few intelligent colored men among them, they studiously sought to divide the blacks by sowing the seeds of discord among them. This was facilitated by prejudicing the ignorant against the intelligent. These men strove and vied each with the other, regardless of consequence, to place himself in the lead of a community of blacks in both town and country, which in time was reduced to little else than a rabble mob of disorder and confusion. Trained in the Leagues as serfs to their masters, it became dangerous to oppose the teachings of these men of mischief. Because, having been recommended to their confidence at the commencement of reconstruction, their experience and knowledge in public men and matters were too limited to believe anything against them.

A knowledge of this emboldened these men to a persistence in their course of crime and corruption. Hence many otherwise, good men, both white and black, from age, inexperience or weakness were induced to accept the monstrous teachings and join with or follow the lead of these wretched imposters. Their sole object being personal gain, they cared little or nothing for public weal, the interest of the state or people, black or white, nor the Republican cause, upon which they had indecently imposed themselves. This is that which controlled Charleston politics and brought deserved defeat to the Republicans in the recent Municipal election. It was just retribution to a set of unprincipled miscreants, rioting on the people rights under the name of "Republicanism." Honest upright men of all parties, white and black, no longer able to bear it, determined to put down the abominable thing, leading Republicans, who had been standing aloof, taking an active part. Among other things, they taught the simple-minded people that suffrage was inviolably secure, the blacks being in the majority, would always control the affairs of the state in the South; that the 15th Amendment had abolished color and complexion in the United States, and the people were now all of one race. This bare faced deception was so instilled into them that it became dangerous in many instances to go into the country and speak of color in any manner whatever, without the angry rejoinder; "WE don't want to hear that, we are all one color now!"

These ridiculous absurdities were fostered by the demagogues, the better to conceal their own perfidy and keep themselves in the best positions as "Republicanism know no race" they taught.

Another imposition was that colored people did not require intelligent colored leaders; that the Constitution had been purged of color by a Radical Congress, and to be a Republican was all that was required to make a true representative. That mental culture and qualifications were only required by the proud and arrogant, that all who requested those accomplishments were enemies to both black and white, that race representation was making distinctions on account of race and color. By this means, they opposed the qualified men among the blacks, encouraged the ignorant and less qualified. They might of necessity take the lead and occupy the best places in the party. These are plain indisputable truths which will not be denied by any upright intelligent Republican, black or white.

Before the introduction of these men among them, there never was a better population, rural or town, out of which to shape a useful political element. Good-hearted, simple-minded, mostly uneducated, they were ready and willing to receive any instruction supposed for their own good, which they anxiously awaited and as eagerly sought. And could they have had the advice of the maturely intelligent, good and virtuous friend of humanity, such as was received and given by us during more than thirty years toilsome battle for liberty and right, there never could have been the cause for the complaint against us as a race now in a measure justifiable.

One most fruitful cause of mischief in the party arose from the age and want of experience on the part of the good white men who assumed the lead in politics—as well as ignorance in the most of them—and the same may be said of their colored colleagues. For the most part young men, where they possessed the required qualifications, they were deficient in experience and knowledge in politics.

To such an extent are they misled that they regularly trained themselves with firearms and marched in companies to political meetings, frequently led by miserable white men. Menacing, threatening, abusing, quarrelling, confusion and frequently rioting are common results of this most disgraceful state of affairs under which we live, all in the name of Republicanism.

The effect upon the people is wonderful. From a polite, pleasant, agreeable, kindly common people, ever ready and obliging, there is now to be met with an ill-mannerly, sullen, disagreeable, unkind, disobliging populace, seemingly filled with hatred and ready for resentment. These changes in the character of the people must have been noticed by every intelligent observer, in contradistinction to their former excellent reputation. Formerly, they were proverbial for their politeness; latterly they are noticed for the absence of it. These people are despoiled of their natural characteristics, and shamefully demoralized by renegade intruders.

These strictures had no reference whatever to the intelligent, light-minded, upright gentlemen among the white Republicans, whose examples and precepts have aided in building up society and contributing to the public good, but especially to that class who almost live in the quarters of the country people and hamlets of the towns, among the black populations, keeping them distracted with excitement, who are a curse to the community at large, and a blight in the body politic.

The social relations of the colored people is another shameful evil, which does more to weaken their strength, neutralize their efforts and divided them in politics than even the graceless intrusion and imposition of white demagogues, because being of their own household, still adhering to an absurdity, a relic of the degraded past, they cling to the assumption of white blood and brown complexion, and to such an extent is this carried, I am told, that old societies have been revived and revised, and absolute provision made against the admission among them of a pure-blooded black. Fire, military companies and even churches and graveyards, it is said, are permanently established on this basis. In one church, at least no blacks are to be seen, and in another, there is a division between the blacks and browns by different caste.

These distinctions naturally sour the blacks and widen the breach which should never have existed. What a commentary is this on the conditions of the race! Cultivated intelligence and enlightened civilization will alone remedy a humiliating condition of a people now receiving the commiseration of the education world. This canker, this leprosy must be at once healed and by a permanent purification purged from the social system of our people whose vitals it has entered, threatening death to its emaciating victims, now the scoff and derision of the Caucasoid race.

Of a piece with this, is the ridiculous aping objection raised on account of nativity. Do they not know that (unlike the white race which had various established nationalities of the highest civilization throughout the world) we cannot, as a race afford to be divided? That instead of objections, we should welcome with pride the coming among us of people of our own race, of intelligence, culture and responsibility, from whithersover they might come!

This anomalous imitation, not original, but borrowed from the other race, is not confined to class among us, but equally indulged in by many blacks and browns of every social position. Let the people learn this simple, though important lesson: that the rejection of people because of their birth place is social and political death to their race. That without intercourse and accession from abroad, intelligence, like wealth, must be limited and impotent. That the power and glory of the white race consist in their universal intercourse and unlimited recognitions.

But among these are excellent ladies and gentlemen, who, though by affinity and predilection, may belong to such associations, yet they have no sympathy with the motives that induced their formations, and therefore discard them as humiliating and will not be bound by their provisions. And to the credit of the greater of those known as "common people" among the mixed race, they entirely ignore these ridiculous distinctions, studiously refusing to recognize them—the distinction of color being propagated alone by that part known as the "highest class" among them.

To another important point, I would invite your attention—that of the course of the national government. While distinction in the rights of citizens on account of "race of color" is most pointedly prohibited, distinction on account of color is most definitely made by the government at Washington. It is a fact most noticeable in executive appointment of colored men, there are none of pure black men, the pure Negro race, but all have been most carefully selected from those having an admixture of white blood. In neither of the departments in Washington is there a single black holding a position above that of porter or lacquey, while in many, if not all of them, except the army and navy—there are those of mixed blood holding positions of clerkship—as is just and right—and other equally respectable places. Nor in no appointment requiring qualification by culture in and out of Washington, is there a pure black man or woman to be found, while many such applications have been made, but always rejected. This is no fault of our Brown brother, but that of the government, and the misfortune of the blacks. There may be these two exceptions: An ordinary black man, the keeper of a grogshop; received the appointment of postmaster, across the James River, opposite to Richmond, VA., obtained it is said at the request of a Democratic community. Also it is said that a black man, has received the appointment of Consul-General and Minister Residence to the Republic of Liberia, Africa, which required a recommendation from nearly the whole of the Republican members of Senate to obtain the notice of Mr. Secretary of State, Hamilton Fish! This minister, I am told, persistently refuses to recognize the application of a black for any position. And indeed, I am further informed that his prejudice of color caused the removal of the residence of the accomplished Haitian Minister, Colonel Romain, from Washington to New York City. Other members of the cabinet it is said largely share these feelings against the pure Negro race.

Nor, out of the six hundred colored people of North have there been any federal appointments in the Northern states to any position above that of messenger or the merest subordinate, except a post office clerkship in Boston and Chicago, one each I believe.

And what is said of Executive appointment at Washington in relation to blacks, the same I think may be safely said of the different state governments, the blacks being studiously neglected, except indeed, to persistently make appointment of incompetent black men, to position which only bring discredit to them and their race. And in not a single instance does it occur to my mind in which a competent black man has received an appointment from a state executive, with a single exception, that of the governor of a far Southern state, who appointed a black man (a special favorite of his) as one of four harbor master—the other being white—he having to employ a white man at hundred dollars a month to do his duties for him, when in the same city there were a number of well qualified black men, not one of whom ever received an office of equal significance. The fact is not ignored of the governor of South Carolina honoring a black man with an appointment of aid-de-camp on his staff, an office purely of honor, yet an honor which any gentleman might accept and is duly appreciated by the recipient.

The entire population of the African race is about five million, one-eighth of the whole American people. According to the ratio of population, they are entitled to thirty two (32) representatives in Congress, and a corresponding ratio of official appointment. Allowing one and a half million of pure blooded blacks. These, by the foregoing estimate, are entitled to about twenty six (26) representatives, with their ratio of federal offices. And yet these 3-1/2 million of people with their political claims, have been persistently neglected and almost ignored, by both federal and state governments, (except in cases of incompetent blacks for mere political purposes, to conciliate the ignorant blacks) while their more favored brethren of mixed bloods, have received all the places of honor profit and trust, intended to represent the race.

In the name of a common race, for whose liberty and equal right you and I for years have struggled, I now for the first time expose this disparaging injustice and call upon you to aid in righting the wrong. A wrong which longer to endure in silence would be an evidence of conscious inferiority and unworthiness.

Republicanism is simply the "claims to equal rights" established by our fathers in Philadelphia, 1816, by them renewed in 1829 in Cincinnati, Ohio, continued 1831 in Philadelphia; endorsed by their white brethren in 1833 in Boston as the "anti-slavery" and "abolition" of the country, the Free Soil of the Buffalo Convention, 1848, and Pittsburgh Convention 1852, when it was engrafted into politics of Republicanism, at the nomination of Fremont at Rochester, N.Y. 1856, and Lincoln at Chicago 1860.

Anti-slavery, as established by our fathers, and propagated by us and our white friends, had for its basis "justice and equal rights to all men" and for its motto; "Whatsoever ye would that others do unto you, do ye even so to them." This is "anti-slavery" as originally propagated by our brethren, aided by their white friends, continued by us, aided by our white friends and engrafted into politics. This should be Republicanism. Have these principles been adhered to under the dispensation of Republican rule? Have they not been shamefully perverted?

Both of the old parties—Democrats and Whigs—favored slavery, having as their basis the inferiority of the Negro and the right to oppress him and hold him perpetually in bondage, denied of every right but that at the option of the master. Republicanism was intended to supersede these and accord to him the enjoyment of all the rights and privileges of American citizenship.

Under the rallying cry of acting for and representing the "negro" men of every shade of complexion have attained to places of honor, profit, trust and power in the party, except the real negro himself—save such places as he had the power which to elect himself who remain today as before emancipation, a political nonentity before the government of the country.

You have now seen the elements of which the party is composed in South Carolina, and its material through the nation. Are these harmonious elements? Does the structure consist of solid materials? Can it stand the storm of political attacks from without, and strife and struggles from within? Is there no repair to be made to the structure, or is it to be left to tumble to pieces by decay and damage, from ill-usage? These are questions worthy the attention of the publicist and statesman.

There must be to make it effective a renovating reorganization in this state based upon intelligence, respectability and honesty. The discordant element must become harmonized. One class or race must not be permitted to enjoy privileges of which another is debarred. If this be continued as heretofore, devastation and ruin will come upon the party, when it will cease to exist as it would deserve to be, as no party by whatever name shall exist a single day, which does not accord and practically extend equal rights and their enjoyment to all the citizens, without distinction of race or color.

You and I have spent the best of our lives in the cause of humanity, living to see the overthrow and death of slavery, and universal liberty proclaimed in the land, and it now becomes equally our duty to crush in infancy, the offspring of the monster wherever found.

Preparatory to any action on their part with the other race as a party, the colored people must first become reconciled to themselves as a race, and respect each other as do the whites, regardless of complexion or nativity, making merit only the mark of distinction, as they cannot afford to be divided.

Having settled the above "preparatory" I would lay down the following principles as a basis of all future party actions, by whatever name it may be called, whether Republican or otherwise:

(1) Equality before the law to every person of whatever race or color, and strict adherence to the Reconstruction acts bearing upon the same.

(2) Colored people must have intelligent leaders of their own race, and white people intelligent leaders of theirs, the two combined to compose the leaders of the party. This must be accepted and acknowledged as the basis of all future political action and necessary to the harmony and safety of both race.

(3) All measure in the party must emanate from consultation of the leaders; otherwise such measures may not be respected.

(4) Demagogues and disreputable men must be discarded as leaders, and never more be given opportunity to betray their trust and abuse the interests of the people whom they assumed to represent.

I am no candidate, nor aspirant for office. I would accept of nothing that made me depend upon the position for my support or cause me to relinquish my personal business. I have spoken simply as a humble citizen, interested in the welfare of the community at large.

With the above platform to guide any future action, I close my review of the political situation.

Thanking the editor of the *Charleston Republican* for the liberal use of this column in granting this publication, I beg to remain, distinguished sir, as ever,

Your friend and co-laborer in the cause of humanity.
Charleston, August 14, 1871.
M. R. Delany.
Charleston
August 14, 1871

SOURCE: *Daily Republican* (Charleston), August 15, 1871.

DOCUMENT 19
FREDERICK DOUGLASS TO DELANY

My Dear Sir:

Your well known zeal and ability, and your long devotion to the cause of freedom and equality to all men, will, I am quite sure, obtain for the elaborate letter with which you have honored me, through the columns of the *Charleston Daily Republican*, and which is now printed in the columns of the *New National Era*, a thoughtful perusal by intelligent colored men in all parts of this country. While I heartily concur in much that you say in that letter, there are some things in it from which I as heartily dissent. It is, however, due to say that, even where I dissent from your views, I am compelled to respect you boldness, candor, and manly independence in the utterance of your convictions. Especially and sincerely do I thank you for your masterly exposure of the malign influences which surrounded the whole business of reconstruction in South Carolina and the other seceding States. I have, however, no denunciations for the carpetbaggers who assumed the leadership in the matter of reconstruction. Upon the whole, they have done pretty well—at any rate, their prominence was inevitable, and I am disposed to make the best of it. Your narrative is strong and striking, but not strange. The destitution of political knowledge among the newly enfranchised and emancipated people of South Carolina, the sullen contempt and indifference with which the old slave-holding class looked upon all efforts to bring the

State into harmonious relations to the National Government, the absence of any middle class among the native white population, possessed of sufficient intelligence and patriotism to take the lead in the needed work of reorganization, the pressing necessity for the early consummation of that work, not only reconcile me to the employment of such hands as were found ready to engaged in that work, but make me thankful that any were found to lead in its performance.

Better men might have done better work, but the same is true all around the world. The men who lay the foundations of States are not always the most scrupulous. Mingling with the adventurous, ambitious, and daring qualities needed to carry loyal white people into the South at the close of the war, there was doubtless, a tumult of motives—some the highest and best, and others base and selfish. Yet, taken as a whole, the men in whose breasts they dwelt had union, nationality, and liberty in their hearts, and were capable in some measure of serving these high interest. <u>At any rate, they were the best that could be had, and we are disposed to give them credit</u>. The wise, the thoughtful, the men of scrupulous integrity, who stayed quietly at home, avoiding all the hardships and perils of residence in those unfriendly States, should be careful in dealing out censures upon the school masters and school mistresses who hazarded everything.

As to destitution of political knowledge among the newly emancipated class—what else could have happened? You and I know that one of the worse effects of slavery is to unfit men for freedom. The abject slave to-day may be the haughty and conceited tyrant of to-morrow. The beggar suddenly raised to opulence is more offensively and insufferably insolent than the man reared and educated in wealth. Such is poor human nature. Doomed to ignorance for ages, the Negro could not be expected to cope with the white men about him at the start. If he has been the dupe of designing men it is because of his antecedents. He is subject to the same laws that govern in the case of other men. The bees and butterflies are irresistibly attracted to a garden of sweet flowers, and the cunning and designing are attracted by a crowd of simple men.

The emancipated men of South Carolina have been misled and cheated—they have been made the backs and legs upon which white men ride into power and place. No doubt of it. But the same is true of the laboring classes everywhere—wherever there are backs and legs without brains somebody is bound to ride them. When the crafty and selfish outrage the animal beyond endurance he will rise and plunge, and gyrate and, perhaps, throw the rider; but while he remains only a back and legs somebody will be found with sufficient skill and address to ride the animal.

The colored people of the South are just now going to school. It is hardly worthwhile to lament that the school is not better than it is. It is the best at hand, and the wisest course is to make the best of it. They cannot expect to get something for nothing. The best things come to any people only through suffering and toil. I rather think that the colored people of the South, notwithstanding the bad precepts they have sometimes heard, and the bad political examples set before them by their designing and unscrupulous political and social knowledge, and that they will soon be able to distinguish between a decent man and a demagogue, no matter what disguises he may assume. The outlook in North Carolina is better, and the same, I hope, will be found true of South Carolina not far hence.

I cannot agree with you in denouncing colored men for going armed to political meetings in South Carolina, nor can I agree with you that the practice is an imported one. The habit of carrying deadly weapons in the South belongs to an age considerably earlier than that of the carpet baggers. I may be wrong, but I had supposed that this practice on the part of the newly enfranchised class at the South had been impelled by a dire necessity. It is a bad practice, and one which cannot be commended in a truly civilized community, but everything in this world is relative. <u>Assault compels defense</u>. I shall never ask the colored people to be lambs where the whites insist on being wolves, and yet no man shall out do me in efforts to promote kindness and good will between the races. But I know there can be no peace without justice, and hence the sword.

One other thing: I hardly think you are quite just in what you say of the changed manners of the colored people of South Carolina. It does not seem to me that their degeneracy is so complete as you describe it to be. Were you not M. R. Delany, I should say that the man who wrote thus of the manners of the colored people of South Carolina had taken his place with the old planters. You certainly cannot be among those of the South who prefer the lash-inspired manners of the past. I know too well your own proud and independent spirit, to believe that the manners of an enslaved and oppressed people are more to your taste than those which are born of freedom and independence.

Still, even in what you say on this point, you have the advantage of me. You are on the ground, and may know whereof you affirm. I am, however, disposed to put the best face upon this complaint of yours as upon others. If there be this offensive insolence in the manners of the colored people of South Carolina of which you complain—the result of sudden elevation—time and enlightenment will surely correct the evil. Liberty has its manners as well as slavery, and with those manners true self-respect goes hand in hand with a just respect for the rights and feelings of others. Have patience, my old friend. The white people of the South have more to bear from the change in the Negro's manners than you and I have. It must be very galling to their feelings to see their former slaves, once so humble and cowering in their presence, now passing and repassing without making any one of the old signs of *obedience* and servitude. But if they can bear this new departure on the part of the blacks, you and I ought to bear our sufferings in silence. All that old-fashioned *How-do-Aunty?* And *Servant-Massa* manners are out of joint with our times. It was very pleasant in its day. It be-spoke condescension on the one side and servile submission on the other, and though pleasanter than the sound of the lash, it was part of slavery. It had a real significance then. It has none now. When the body disappears, I would not detain its shadow. But enough on this point.

There is an element of real bitterness in your letter to which I hope you have imparted a coloring deeper than the facts warrant. Is it possible that the old enemy of the darker hued people of the West Indies, which has poisoned the life blood of colored society in Haiti, imperiled its independence, and blocked the wheel of its progress has come here also? Can it be that the colored people of South Carolina are going to make such fools of themselves, as to raise such a distinction among themselves based upon a color at a moment when color has just ceased to be a crime in our country, and when human brotherhood is becoming the recognized gospel throughout the world? Are we to have, nay, have we got a caste called the *Browns* in South Carolina? You say we have, and I cannot positively contradict you. If you are right in your facts and specifications, I certainly unite with you in your hottest denunciations of that contemptible and senseless imitation of one of the meanest feelings that ever crept into the human heart.

The white people of this country have in one thing been remarkably consistent. They have hated and persecuted Negro blood wherever they have found it. Except in the State of Ohio, (where a Negro can prove that he is more white man than Negro) the man with the last drop of Negro blood in him is hated and persecuted with all the bitterness visited upon the blackest among us all. They hate the blood wherever they see it, whether in large or small quantity, whether pure or mixed, whether black as midnight or almost white. The whole thing is abominable; but we have more respect for the white man's prejudice and hate than for that of your snuff-colored Negro. Think of a man putting enmity between the blood that courses in his own veins affecting to despise the one while he respects the other! The thing is almost too absurd for contempt.

While I entirely agree with you that no discrimination should be made against black applicants for office at Washington, because such applicants are black, I am far from agreeing with you that the present Republican administration has made any such discrimination. In fact, we know of two clerks in the Departments here who are without doubt as darks as even Mr. Delany would require, and who are as capable and efficient as any others. I am not much of a logician, but I require a little closer connection between premise and conclusion than you have here shown, to consider your conclusion legitimate. There are other reasons than color and race for the limited number of colored clerks employed in the Departments at Washington—reasons which I hope will disappear in time, and which, in fact, are already disappearing. The same causes which gave the leadership in public affairs to white men in South Carolina have given the lion's share of the offices to white men in Washington. As a matter of arithmetic your figures are faultless. The mulattoes, on a solid census basis, ought to have so many offices, the blacks so many, the whites so many, the Germans so many, the Irish so many, and other classes and nationalities should have offices according to their respective numbers. The idea is equal and admirable in theory; but does it not already seem to you a little absurd as a matter of practice? The fact is, friend Delany, these things are not fixed by figures, and why men are what they are cannot be so fixed. According to the census, the colored people of the country constitute one-eighth of the whole American people. Upon your statistical principle, the colored people of the United States ought, therefore, not only to hold one-eighth of all the offices in the country but they should own one-eighth the property, and pay one-eighth of all the taxes of the country. Equal in numbers, they should, of course, be equal in everything else. They should constitute one-eighth of the poets, statesmen, scholars, authors, and philosophers of the country. The test should be impartially and stringently applied, if applied at all, and should bear equally in all directions. The Negro in black should mark every octave on the National piano. In every company of eight American authors that can be named we ought to be able to name one black author, and so through all the varied departments of American activity. The Negro should edit just one-eighth of all the newspapers; he should be the author of just one-eighth of all the books written and printed in the United States; and, in a word, be one-eighth in everything. Now, my old friend, there is no man in the United States who knows better than you do that equality of numbers has nothing to do with equality of attainments. You know, too, that natural equality is a very different thing from practical equality; and that though men be potentially equal, circumstances may for a time cause the most striking inequalities. Look at our newly emancipated people, read their history of ignorance and destitution, and see their present progress and elevation, and rejoice in the prospect before them. You are too broad not to comprehend, and too brave to shut your eyes to facts; and in the light of these your octagonal principle certainly will not work.

I note what you say of Hon. Hamilton Fish, the Secretary of State of the United States, and the removal of Col. Romain, the ex-Haitian Minister, from Washington to New York, and cannot but think you have done the Secretary of State great wrong in what you say on that subject. Hamilton Fish may not be an old-fashioned abolitionist, but he certainly is a gentleman, and incapable of mean and underhand dealing towards anybody. At any rate, some better witness than "they say" or "it is rumored" will have to appear before I shall be convinced that your reproaches of this gentleman and statesman are just.

In conclusion, my dear old friend, let me assure you that I rejoice in every honor of which you are the recipient, and hold you worthy of all that have been bestowed upon you, and of still higher promotion. Let me also assure you of my cordial co-operation with you in all well-directed efforts to elevate and improve our race, to break down all unjust and mischievous distinctions among them, and secure for them a just measure of the political privileges now so largely monopolized by our white fellow-countrymen.
Very truly yours,
Frederick Douglass.

SOURCE: *New National Era* (Washington, DC), August 31, 1871.

DOCUMENT 20

S. N. GAILLIARD ON DELANY

GENTLEMEN: In conformity with my promise, I now proceed to give you my opinion concerning Major Delany's letter. Your first question was, "why he addressed that letter to Mr. Douglass at this time?" I can only impute his motive to the fact of Mr. Douglass' recent appointment, and my opinion is that he wrote to him in a public way with the hope that his letter would reach the ear and eye of the Administration, and it might give him an appointment as a representative of the "pure black man."

Secondly, Major Delany says that "when reconstruction commenced political leaders were greatly required, but few to be had." Now the question, where was the major? I will tell you. He was in Hilton Head in the capacity of a Bureau agent and, I learn, busily engaged in selling the cotton, corn and other produce belonging to the poor freemen, which makes him very unpopular with them now. Well, in the year 1867 or 68, I can't remember which, a delegation was appointed by the Republicans of Charleston, after a consultation with the leading men in other counties to communicate with him (Delany), asking his consent to be placed in a position by which he could become a "leader." He gallantly refused, "saying the time had not come," and did not take any part in the reconstruction of the State. My opinion is he ought to be the last man to growl about "leaders."

Thirdly, you ask my opinion relative to what he says about the "Social relations of the colored people." I believe that social relationship must and will regulate itself. It is a fact that no one will deny, that there are persons who believe that they are superior to others because of a light or brown hue, and are not disposed to associate with "black people." As to "superiority," if they are silly enough to believe that color is the test, then I would leave them to revel in the glories of their mistaken idea. Nobody has a right to find fault with them. I believe that the paragraph in the Major's letter is quite out of place and very impolitic, and has a tendency towards causing an estrangement between the "blacks and browns." Social relationship affects individuals only. Every man has the right to select his own company, and form associations with the same if he chooses.

Politics affects the whole people; therefore, there is such dissimilarity that while we can afford an estrangement socially, we cannot afford it politically. For the political downfall of one is the downfall of the other. In "Politics" we must work in union. The Major, in probing that old sore, that time alone can cure, is doing the state and country more harm than his philosophical endowments enable him to perceive, for the blacks are just as proud and happy as the browns, or any other color dare to be.

To be rational and politic, if I was the writer, I would advise the voters never to select a man to office who would be likely to discriminate in official patronage or otherwise on account of color. By doing so, every individual will take it in a political aspect, and it is my opinion that this would do more towards harmonizing the conflicting elements, than anything else that could be said or done.

The major says "Black leaders for black men." This reminds me of the diabolical dogma enunciated by Cain, Delany and Co., in the campaign of 1870. That dogma that almost caused the defeat of the Republican Party in this (Charleston) county. The man that would set forth such an unwholesome doctrine must be guilty of one or two evils: If he does it with a view to his own aggrandizement, knowing as he ought the direful consequences that must inevitably accrue from it especially when carried out as preached by the Major and Co., in the last general campaign. Then he must be a.... And if he does it, not having political sagacity enough to know that it must result detrimentally to the political interests of the black man, then he is insensible to the plainest facts, and unfit to be a "leader." For whilst we are in the majority in this State; we must not forget that we are vastly in the minority in the United States. The moment we inscribe that motto on our banner (figuratively speaking), namely! "Black leaders for Black men," we will cause such a line (not of sects, as the major says about some imaginary church) to be drawn, that nothing short of the millennium can erase or destroy it. Our white friends, both north and south, will leave us to "paddle our own canoe" and we, not having sufficient of the necessaries to stem the tide, will drift with the "ebb" into the abyss of political destruction.

Prudence would dictate as a motto "The best Man" be he as black as it is possible to be, or as white as a lily, if he will carry out the principles of Republicanism without fear or favor. Then let him lead or anything else, regardless of his color; there will be no need for division lines. As a party, keep in view that maxim, "United we stand, divided we fall."

I was asked what I thought of the Major as an aspirant for office. I don't know if it is your purpose to act or propose him for an office, but in case it be so, I should say, judging from the anxiety manifested last fall whilst a candidate for the United States Senate, that he would accept an office, though he would have to "depend upon it for a support."

Yours respectfully,
S. N. GAILLIARD.

SOURCE: *Daily Republican* (Charleston), August 22, 1871.

DOCUMENT 21

THE *NEWS AND COURIER* ON DELANY TO
FREDERICK DOUGLASS, AUGUST 17, 1871

The letter of M. R. Delany, addressed to FREDERICK DOUGLASS, and published in the REPUBLICAN of this city, on the 15th inst., is a remarkable document, deserving attention and should be printed in papers North and South for the information of all parties. It throws light on very much that is little understood, and it is like a straight sword with two cutting edges. Delany evidently has written from conviction and quiet observation. He is a Northern colored man possessing some education, and takes upon himself the character of an active advocate of "humanity" along with Douglass, in efforts to "overthrow slavery." After seeing this "overthrow" and watching from his standpoint the operations of his brethren as freemen and citizens for six years, he deems it of importance at this time to take a political review of South Carolina, and thinks that his review "will apply justly to nearly if not the whole of the reconstructed States of the South as well as the National Government."

We think Mr. Delany's views are worthy of examination and that some deductions may be drawn from what he presents as facts, which may be unexpected to him, though perfectly logical. We quote:

> When reconstruction commenced, political leaders were greatly required, but few to be had. Southerners (the old masters) studiously opposed and refused to countenance reconstruction, and the freedmen were fearful and would not have trusted them if they could have obtained their aid.

While we admit the truth of this statement, we urge upon those who have charged us with opposition to reconstruction, a consideration of the admission, that if the former master had pursued a different course, "the Freedmen were fearful, and would not have trusted them," were the dregs of the Federal army—the harpies who FOLLOW the tracks of war—who had every selfish interest in stirring up ill feeling and destroying the confidence of these "simple-minded people," who otherwise would naturally have trusted their old master. But Mr. Delany describes these first leaders with a masterly pen.

> Those who came with or followed the army, with a very few native whites, were the only available political element to be had to carry out measures of reconstruction. These were readily accepted by the blacks (by this I included the entire colored people) and the fullest confidence reposed in them. Some were, or had been officers in the army; some privates, some sutlers, others peddlers and virtuous tradesmen, others gamblers, and even pick-pockets, "hangers-on" and "bummers". I am particularly speaking of the whites. Among these were men of refinement, educated gentlemen, and some very good men; but a large part of those most active were of the lowest grade of Northern society, negro-haters at home, who could not have been elected to any position of honor or trust. Just such men as burnt down Negro orphan asylums, and hung Negro men to lamp posts in the New York riot of 1863. In this review I intended to speak plainly, call things by their right names, and look those of whom I speak directly in the face.
>
> The best and most competent men were chosen to fill the most important positions in State and local governments, while the others readily obtained such places as required incumbents. Indeed, there were scarcely one so incompetent as not to have been assigned some position of trust.

Position in places of power, profit and trust, they soon sought by that guile and deception known only to demagogues, under the acceptable appellations of Yankee, Republican and Radical, to intrude themselves into the confidence of the blacks, and place themselves at their head as leaders. So insidiously did they do this that it was not discovered by the few colored men of intelligence who held places among them till too late to remedy the fatal evil.

These demagogues laid the foundation of their career upon a basis of the most dangerous political heresy. Deception, lying, cheating, stealing, "whatever can be done in politics is fair," and to "beat is the duty in a political contest, no matter what means are used to effect it," are among the pernicious precepts of this moral infidelity.

Jealous of the few intelligent colored men among them, they studiously sought to divide the blacks, by sowing the seeds of discord among them. This was facilitated by prejudicing the ignorant against the intelligent. These men strove and vied each with the other, regardless of consequences, to place himself in the lead of a community of blacks in both town and country, which in time was reduced to little else than a rabble mob of disorder and confusion. Trained in the leagues as serfs to their masters, it became dangerous to oppose the teachings of these men of mischief. Because, having been recommended to their confidence at the commencement of reconstruction, their experience and knowledge in public men and matters were too limited to believe anything against them.

A knowledge of this emboldened these men to a persistence in their course of crime and corruption. Hence, many otherwise good men, both white and black, from age, inexperience or weakness, were induced to accept the monstrous teachings and join with or follow the lead of these wretched imposters. Their sole object being personal gain, they cared little or nothing for public weal, the interest of the state or people, black or white, nor the republican cause, upon which they had indecently imposed themselves. This is that which controlled Charleston politics and brought deserved defeat to the republicans in the recent municipal election. It was just retribution to a set of unprincipled miscreants, rioting on the people's rights under the name of "Republicans." Honest, upright men of all parties, white and black, no longer able to bear it, determined to put down the abominable thing; leading Republicans, who had been standing aloof, taking an active part.

Will northern and western statesmen, and all good citizens, weigh well this description of men, who by means so vile foisted themselves upon our state and city Governments—seize the sword of power, and the treasury of the people—imposed taxes for the express purpose of enriching themselves, winked at iniquity, pardoned convicted criminals, and sitting in high places with women of ill fame and men worse than themselves! Can insult to a brave people take a viler form than this? A prisoner, INNOCENT, robbed, manacled, and then SPIT upon, to be taunted because he did not help himself! Will the world believe Major Delany's statement? If so believe also that the people of South Carolina have been FORCED to remain under a government composed in a 'large part' of the 'lowest grades of northern society,' 'peddlers,' 'sutlers,' 'gamblers,' 'pick-pockets' 'hangers-on,' 'bummers,' Negro murderers and burners of orphan houses! This is the admission, nay, the positive declaration of one behind the scenes, an intelligent colored man, concerning his own party and its leaders in South Carolina.

When it has suited the politicians North and West, they have bitterly complained of the state of which slavery reduced the colored people of the South—their semi-barbarism—and troublesome character, etc., etc. That this was and is both a slander and falsehood, Mr. Delany thus proves:

> Before the introduction of these men among them, there never was a better population, rural or town, out of which to shape a useful political element. Good-hearted, simple-minded, mostly uneducated, they were ready and willing to receive any instruction supposed for their own good, which they anxiously awaited and as eagerly sought. And could they have had the advice of the maturely intelligent, good and virtuous friend of humanity, such as was received and given by us during more than thirty years toilsome battle for liberty and right, there never could have been the cause for the complaint against us as a race now in a measure justifiable.

And we add, if they had been left to the care and instruction of those who had been their best friends all their lives, they would never have changed their conduct—though they never might have voted for pick-pockets and gamblers to rule over them. We are told further, by Mr. Delany, and we insist that the HONEST men of the North and West notice this, and that, "to such an extent are they misled that they regularly trained themselves with firearms and marched in companies to political meetings, frequently led by miserable white men. Menacing, threatening, abusing, quarrelling, confusion, and frequently rioting, are common results of this most disgusting state of affair under which we live, all in the name of Republicanism."

Mr. Delany further remarks that:

The effect upon the people is wonderful. From a polite, pleasant, agreeable, kindly common people, ever ready and obliging, there is now to be met with an ill-mannerly, sullen, disagreeable, unkind, disobliging populace, seemingly filled with hatred and ready for resentment. These changes in the character of the people must have been noticed by every intelligent observer, in contradistinction to their former excellent reputation. Formerly, they were proverbial for their politeness; latterly they are noticed for the absence of it. These people are despoiled of their natural characteristics, and shamefully demoralized by renegade intruders.

Would a word of this be believed if stated by any member of the Democratic Party? But we now have some deductions to make which, though evident to those who have endured the lawlessness of the Negro under his new teachings and through him the political position of the gamblers and pick-pockets in power. The cause of all the cry in this state about Ku-Klux, and of all the violence which unhappily has disgraced some parts of our country, is to be traced directly to the teachings Major Delany mentions. These led to erroneous views of the duty of the laborer, and false ideas of right and wrong and then followed constant stealing of hogs, chickens, stocks of all kind, then of corn and cotton from the field, so that in some sections of our state many a planter gave up his plantation in despair. Appeals were made to those in authority for protection, but in vain, and when a rascal was caught in the very act of stealing cotton, if convicted, he generally escaped punishment, until patience ceased to be a virtue and the law of self-defense came into play.

Then punishment began—this led from one step to another—both sides or parties growing more reckless and determined, until the miserable moral disorder culminated in the tragedy at Union. We will continue our review of the very important paper of M. R. Delany.

SOURCE: *News and Courier* (Charleston), August 17, 1871.

DOCUMENT 22

THE *NEWS AND COURIER* ON DELANY TO
FREDERICK DOUGLASS, AUGUST 18, 1871

We are willing to admit that there are "intelligent, high-minded, upright gentlemen among the white Republicans" and, for that matter, we think there are some, perhaps many, among the blacks. We have never heard

Major Delany's name mixed up with 'gamblers', 'pick-pockets', or villains of any kind, and believe him to be a conscientious man, who writes from conviction and well established premises. For this reason we attach importance to his utterances, and we are justified in demanding that his evidence shall be admitted and believed, our own to the same tenor having been systematically ignored. This letter is divided—we presume unintentionally—into three great and important divisions, political, social and ethnological. We have presented those points which specifically bear upon the political aspect, and we touch now his social deliverances. We desire to do this with great delicacy and with a sincere sympathy with the cultivated minds of those among the blacks, who desirous of seeing their race elevated, are bearing and incubus which cannot be fully realized by any besides themselves. Mr. Delany in his letter continues:

> The Social relations of the colored people is another shameful evil, which does more to weaken their strength, neutralize their efforts and divided them in politics than even the graceless intrusion and imposition of white demagogues, because being of their own household, still adhering to an absurdity, a relic of the degraded past, they cling to the assumption of white blood and brown complexion, and to such an extent is this carried, I am told, that old societies have been revived and revised, and absolute provision made against the admission among them of a pure blooded black. Fire, military companies and even churches and graveyards, it is said, are permanently established on this basis. In one church, at least no blacks are to be seen, and in another there is a division between the blacks and browns by different caste.

Without concurring in the above extract in full, especially where the assumption of superiority in the brown man is imputed to an absurdity, a relic of the degraded past, we feel assured that the cause of complaint DOES exist to a very great degree, and we think was in existence in a still higher degree during the time of slavery. In fact, we know that this feeling prevails to a great extent among the lighter colored citizens, because we have been so informed by some of them. As unpleasant as it is, it is however a natural sentiment, and has its counterpart in the minds of colored peoples against the whites, when positions are changed. A white man in Africa meets with no sympathy; his color is in many districts obnoxious to the blacks. Nevertheless we sincerely regret that in this our country this feeling exists, and do hope that the sensible and intelligent men of both shades will use their best endeavors to promote harmony and good feelings among themselves. But in their own class, there is after all much that is corrective, and their 'SOCIETY', is an imitation of that which exists among whites. We again quote from Mr. Delany:

> But among these are excellent ladies and gentlemen, who, though by affinity and predilection, may belong to such associations, yet they have no sympathy with the motives that induced their formations, and therefore discard them as humiliating and will not be bound by their provisions. And to the credit of the greater of those known as "common people" among the mixed race, they entirely ignore these ridiculous distinctions, studiously refusing to recognize them—the distinction of color being propagated alone by that part known as the "highest class" among them.

Society is arbitrary. Ladies and gentlemen will associate in 'sects' and 'circles', and as with whites, so with blacks. 'The common people among the mixed race entirely ignore these ridiculous distinctions." Did it not occur to Major Delany when he wrote the sentence that he proclaimed a fact which is of more consequence to his race than all theorizing reasoning or even education can be? If mulattoes and blacks do readily and truly meet on the platform of labor, we may hope the time will come when on one place at least—all will be equal. If that fails, we have no expectation that he or his descendants will live to see much improvement in the social status of the blacks in this country. The letter passes now to a consideration of the action of the national Government in the selection and appointment of officers:

> To another important point, I would invite your attention—that of the course of the national government. While distinctions in the rights of citizens on account of "race of color" is most pointedly prohibited, distinction on account of color is most definitely made by the government at Washington. It is a fact most noticeable in executive appointment of colored men, there are none of pure black men, the pure Negro race, but all have been most carefully selected from those having an admixture of white blood. In neither of the departments in Washington is there a single black holding a position above that of porter or lacquey, while in many, if not all of them, except the army and navy—there are those of mixed blood holding positions of clerkship—as is just and right—and other equally respectable places. Nor in no appointment requiring qualification by culture in and out of Washington, is there a pure black man or woman to be found, while many such applications have been made,

but always rejected. This is no fault of our Brown brother, but that of the government, and the misfortune of the blacks. There may be these two exceptions: An ordinary black man, the keeper of a grogshop; received the appointment of postmaster, across the James River, opposite to Richmond, VA., obtained it is said at the request of a Democratic community. Also it is said that a black man, has received the appointment of Consul-General and Minister Residence to the Republic of Liberia, Africa, which required a recommendation from nearly the whole of the Republican members of Senate to obtain the notice of Mr. Secretary of State, Hamilton Fish! This minister, I am told, persistently refuses to recognize the application of a black for any position. And indeed, I am further informed that his prejudice of color caused the removal of the residence of the accomplished Haitian Minister, Colonel Romain, from Washington to New York City. Other members of the cabinet it is said largely share these feelings against the pure Negro race.

Nor, out of the six hundred colored people of North have there been any federal appointments in the Northern states to any position above that of messenger or the merest subordinate, except a post office clerkship in Boston and Chicago, one each I believe.

We presume the statements in the above extracts are in the main correct. It may be that the Government has not been able to find black men of suitable education to fill offices. The mulatto has had in this respect many advantages. He has often had facilities for improvement, denied to his black brother, and thus being ready to fill offices requiring intelligence, he had been preferred. But with all proper allowance for this, we are fully persuaded the main reason lies deeper, and it may be doubted whether the Government will ever be able to overcome or destroy this underlying reason. We must deal with principles and with prejudices as we find them, always being governed by the supreme law of rectitude in our convictions, though often failing to reach the high standard of perfect right, and we must not expect, in this sin-stricken world, to account for all anomalies and evils that exist. Major Delany says: "I INTEND TO SPEAK PLAINLY, CALL THINGS BY THEIR RIGHT NAMES, AND LOOK THOSE OF WHOM I SPEAK DIRECTLY IN THE FACE." This is most manly and honorable. It is rights to do so and we honor him for his independence. We claim the same privilege. We have reached that part of this letter which leads us to present some opinions with which its writer will not agree. We intend no discourtesy, but we want to look things directly in the face ourselves, as must any thinking man in this country. We are face to face, with the STUPENDOUS

FACT—the existence among us of, as is said five millions of people of a different race and color, whom claim perfect equality with the dominant race, as their right. The subject will be continued in our next issue.

Source: *News and Courier* (Charleston), August 18, 1871.

---

document 23

The *News and Courier* on Delany to Frederick Douglass, August 19, 1871

If we understand the remaining portion of this extraordinary letter, part of which we present below, the 'animus' of it is to claim the instant eradication from the minds of the white citizens of this great country, any opinion and every prejudice which now prevents an entire acknowledgement of the equality of races—the admission of the intelligent leaders of their own race—as colored men, into the counsels of party, and this for all future time. In short, the proposition is that there are to be in this country two races, one black, one white, which are to have equal power and rule, and to exist in harmony, working together peacefully for the common good, holding offices in proportion to numbers, and theoretically every eighth term to elect a black man as President of the United States; and an urgent call is made upon Frederick Douglass to aid in this Herculean task. The cry is:

> You and I have spent the best of our lives in the cause of humanity, living to see the overthrow and death of slavery, and universal liberty proclaimed in the land, and it now becomes equally our duty to crush in infancy, the offspring of the monster wherever found.

This is obscure. We cannot surely say what percentage this 'offspring' has, or who is the 'monster,' but we suppose it must refer to race 'caste'.

We think Major Delany and Frederick Douglass will have an unusually severe experience in this behalf. We have fairly before us, in this review, two great facts:

1st: The existence in this country of two distinct races.

2nd: The existence of a fixed universal prejudice against one of them, the weaker, in the minds of the more powerful.

And, yet, as resulting from the LEGISLATIVE ACTS of the STRONGER, the stigmatized race are placed as EQUALS in civil rights and before the law! Let us look a moment at the 'status' of the Negro in the division of the human family into races. It is a favorite statement of these times, that the Negro, by slavery, was 'oppressed', 'degraded', 'robbed of rights', and for all this he has and ought to have, the sympathy and 'commiseration of the educated worlds.' The Negro type is not of yesterday, and its natural home is not America. The "race has been known for about 4,000 years as inhabitants of a part of Africa. In the long field and broad duration of Negro life, not a single civilization, spontaneous or borrowed, has existed, to adorn its gloomy past." The whole of Africa, South of ten degrees North latitude, shows a succession of human beings, with intellects as dark as their skin. SLAVERY has ever existed among them, in its worst forms; even Cannibalism is not infrequent, and to this day, the little we know of this miserable people is as a glimmering light, upon a mass of moral and social degradation beyond description. Slavery was the means by which five millions of the descendants of these hopeless beings were elevated to a position second to no other laboring people in the earth according to Major Delany's description of them. Had it not been for slavery, would not this letter writer himself, instead of being the educated, intelligent man he is, be now engaged in his fetish worship, and beyond the pale of hope. Great ends have been accomplished by Negro slavery in this land—and those now living here are in a far higher position than the 'race' upon their native soil. But looking at the Negro as he is there, and has been for thousands of years, was it not natural for progressive nations to regard him as an 'inferior' long before American slavery existed? That only deepened a pre-existing sentiment which is all but universal in this country.

The Government of this country succumbs to its power—not theoretically, but practically. Facts stated by Mr. Delany show this clearly, and also that state Governments are equally under its influence. He says:

> And what is said of Executive appointment at Washington in relation to blacks, the same I think may be safely said of the different state governments, the blacks being studiously neglected, except indeed, to persistently make appointment of incompetent black men, to position which only bring discredit to them and their race. And in not a single instance does it occur to my mind in which a competent black man has received an appointment from a state executive, with a single exception, that of the governor of a far Southern state, who appointed a black man (a special favorite of his) as one of four harbor master–the other being white—he having to employ a white man at hundred dollars a month

to do his duties for him, when in the same city there were a number of well qualified black men, not one of whom ever received an office of equal significance. The fact is not ignored of the governor of South Carolina honoring a black man with an appointment of aid-de-camp on his staff, an office purely of honor, yet an honor which any gentleman might accept and is duly appreciated by the recipient.

Can this sentiment—prejudice—feeling or whatever else you may please to call it, be removed? We cannot anticipate future events, but so long as the old Free states use the name of the 'black man' as a bugaboo to frighten their children, so long at least the prejudice will exist. We believe there is now more real sympathy in the South for the Negro than at the North, or we think our people are disposed to treat him in his capacity with all due consideration, to give him a fair share of the offices suited to his abilities, and to aid him in his efforts to improve his physical condition, but we doubt the expediency on his part of attempting to obtain concessions which are not judicious, or to strive for utopian theories. As for some good advice to the colored people Major Delany concludes his letter by laying down some principles as a basis for future party action:

> Preparatory to any action on their part with the other race as a party, the colored people must first become reconciled to themselves as a race, and respect each other as do the whites, regardless of complexion or nativity, making merit only the mark of distinction, as they cannot afford to be divided.
>
> Having settled the above "preparatory" I would lay down the following principles as a basis of all future party actions, by whatever name it may be called, whether Republican or otherwise:
>
> (5) Equality before the law to every person of whatever race or color, and strict adherence to the Reconstruction acts bearing upon the same.
>
> (6) Colored people must have intelligent leaders of their own race, and white people intelligent leaders of theirs, the two combined to compose the leaders of the party. This must be accepted and acknowledged as the basis of all future political action and necessary to the harmony and safety of both race.
>
> (7) All measure in the party must emanate from consultation of the leaders, otherwise such measures may not be respected.

Demagogues and disreputable men must be discarded as leaders, and never more be given opportunity to betray their trust and abuse the interests of the people whom they assumed to represent.

With this basis what security is there for our colored citizens to abandon their old associations, turn their backs on those to whom they always go with perfect confidence in times of trouble, and who will stand by them when their political friends, who are now only using them, will have left them forever. In many respects we coincide with the views expressed in this important letter, and call upon its author to aid in the clearance of this worse than 'Augean Stable' which he has so graphically described.

SOURCE: *News and Courier* (Charleston), August 19, 1871.

DOCUMENT 24
Major Delany's Letter Refuting Delany's Allegation of Republican Party Bias

We publish a few weeks since a communication from our correspondent, 'R. J. H.,' in which he referred to the following extract from a letter by Major DELANY:

> There may be these two exceptions: An ordinary black man, the keeper of a grogshop; received the appointment of postmaster, across the James River, opposite to Richmond, VA., obtained it is said at the request of a Democratic community. Also it is said that a black man, has received the appointment of Consul-General and Minister Residence to the Republic of Liberia, Africa, which required a recommendation from nearly the whole of the Republican members of Senate to obtain the notice of Mr. Secretary of State, Hamilton Fish! This minister, I am told, persistently refuses to recognize the application of a black for any position. And indeed, I am further informed that his prejudice of color caused the removal of the residence of the accomplished Haitian Minister, Colonel Romain, from Washington to New York City. Other members of the cabinet it is said largely share these feelings against the pure Negro race.

The statement in regard to the appointment of the 'postmaster across the river' is incorrect in every particular; and wishing to do justice to all parties concerned, we propose to lay before our readers the true state of the case, and at the same time furnish proof that will peremptorily forbid any future controversy in the matter. The facts are these: The postmaster referred to (James H. Cunningham, of Manchester, Virginia) is a very worthy and intelligent colored Republican. He was not appointed at the request of the Democratic community in Manchester or elsewhere, but he obtained his position at the solicitation of Hon. CHARLES H. PORTER, M.C. of the Richmond (Va.) district who has ever been, and is always ready to promote the interests of every known Republican in the district as far as lies in his power: . . .

The former incumbent of said office (Mr. JAMES M. MOODY, an appointee of ANDREW JOHNSON, and an active opponent of the Republican Party) was also the happy possessor of a 'groggery'—the latter business being conducted in the same room in which the postal affairs were carried on. It will be readily surmised by our readers that this state of things must have been particularly unpleasant to a majority of the citizens, and especially was this the case in Republican quarters. When, however, Mr. CUNNINGHAM took possession of the office he at once removed the bar-room to another part of the building, in that persons coming to the post office should not be compelled to receive their mail in a liquor dispensary; and we are truly pleased to chronicle the fact that Mr. C. has since abandoned the liquor traffic altogether. We append copies of two letters, made from originals on files in the post office Department, which will abundantly show that Mr. CUNNINGHAM'S appointment was procured by Mr. PORTER, and will also establish how rightfully the latter sought to dispose of anti-Republican office-holders:

14 WEST CLAY STREET
RICHMOND, VIRGINIA
September 2nd, 1869.

Hon. George Earle, First Assistant and Acting Postmaster General, Washington, D.C.
Sir,

I have the honor to request that James M. Moody, Postmaster at Manchester, Chesterfield County, in this state, be removed, and James H. Cunningham, of the same place appointed in his stead.

Mr. Moody is an active supporter of the rebel party whereas Mr. Cunningham is a thorough Republican, and competent, honest, and of good moral character.

I will add that his appointment will meet with the cordial approval of the Republican Party of Manchester.
I am, very respectfully,
Yours obedient servant,
(SIGNED) CHARLES H. PORTER.

Source: *New National Era* (Washington, DC), October 12, 1871.

DOCUMENT 25

South Carolina Obligations 1

To the Editor of *the New York Times*:

The undersigned is now in the city on business in the interest of South Carolina, and desires to assure the community that the nomination of Gen. F. J. Moses for Governor of South Carolina was intended to raise the credit of the state.

Gen. Moses is in favor of immediately providing for the payment of the interest on the public debt, meeting every obligation due at maturity, opposed to Blue Ridge, Greenville script, and will strictly adhere to the decisions of the Court on the subject.

He could not have received the nomination from those who alone had the power to give it, had he not been in favor of every legal and legitimate measure tending to promote the credit, interests and integrity of the state.

All bondholders and those interested in South Carolina securities may call at the Freedmen's Bank, No. 185 Bleecker Street, where we will be found every day until Saturday, from 10 a.m. till 4 p.m. and will be pleased to satisfy all gentlemen interested that the credit of the state will not be permitted to perish.

I am, sir, very respectfully, your most obedient Servant.
M. R. Delany
Member State Executive Committee.

Source: *New York Times*, September 25, 1872.

DOCUMENT 26
South Carolina Obligations 2

To the Editor of *the New York Times*:

"A Bond-holder in Trust," in a note dated on the 26th inst. makes the following pertinent inquiry, and request that a reply be made through the TIMES! Did Gen. Moses in a speech in Charleston, say "that if he were elected Governor he would repudiate the debt of the state, and did not care to have the state credit good in New York?"

The Judge Melton made a like speech, but only worse, that others say in their speeches that "the debt shall be scaled to nine millions."

Will "the interest on the January and July, as well as the October and April bonds, be paid soon?"

To these questions I would respectfully reply that neither Gen. Moses nor Judge Melton made such declarations in a speech at Charleston, the writer of this being present at the time alluded to and heard every word which dropped from their lips. And if such expressions were attributed to them in the public prints, they must have been reported by newspaper correspondents, as there were no such reports of their speeches in either of the Charleston journals.

No person who has the capacity and intelligence to comprehend the integrity of the state and import of our obligations, with the influence to affect public sentiment, would have ever talked about "scaling the debt down to nine millions." The thing is simply nonsensical, because intolerable, and therefore, impracticable.

In regard to the interest on the bonded debt, I can only reply that I know the intention of the new government, as the first step toward restoring the credit of the state is to pay off the interest due on the debt.

Be assured that there will be no "repudiation, nor the semblance of it," by the people of South Carolina. The State is full of resources, her population industrious and producing, her staples abundant and valuable and her revenue equal to the demands of her liabilities. A change in the administration of her government will prove this.

M. R. Delany
No. 185 BLEECKER STREET, NEW YORK
Monday, Sept. 30, 1872.

Source: *New York Times*, September 30, 1872.

DOCUMENT 27
REV. R. H. CAIN TO GOV. FRANKLIN J. MOSES

Columbia, S.C., May 18th 1873.

To His Excellency Gov. F. J. Moses, Jr

Dear Sir—Your precious time, and arduous duties, are so pressing that I cannot intrude upon you in person, to express my impressions and desires. I therefore drop you these lines hoping that the same respectful consideration, which you have always accorded me, in person, may be accorded to my written communication. Dear Sir—we have ever been the best of friends, since we first met in your office in Sumter in 1866. I have reposed confidence in you—and whatever promises made to me. You will remember the mutual pledge made between us, prior to your nomination for governor, relative to Charleston appointments. I do not ask you to do anything that would embarrass your administration, nor make the appointment of a man, who would do harm by his appointment. I have felt much concern about my friend Delany, and my pledges to him made, before he consented to abandon his opposition to your nomination for Governor. It was principally on my personal representation to him, and my declaration, that you have been grossly maligned, and misrepresented by those men who sought your defeat, that I brought him over from the opposition—believing what I stated relative to your honorably, maintaining our rights, and keeping your pledges made to the colored men who would stand by you, he became your advocate, and our mutual friend. I had assured him on the honor of a gentleman that you would not break faith with him, he has constantly held on, while all others have declared to him, that you would not give him an appointment, nor keep faith with me, in his behalf. I do hope sir, that you may disappoint those who thus traduce you. Permit me to say, that it is certainly impolitic to break faith with friends, it is dangerous however insignificant they may be, it would be better to have one unwise officer, than to have a thousand of his friends against you in the future. Gov. Scott broke faith with those who served him most faithfully, and when the time came none would trust him. I hope sir, that you will not make his mistake. Keep this promise and he proves inefficient, remove him and you throw on him the blame, and deprives those who are now, and may be, in the future too ready to find a flaw against your re-election—on further advancement, for Col. Delany's condition is a needy one, he has staked all, on your word; for heaven's sake do not cast him away. He has many strong friends, who sympathize with him, and desire to see him placed where he may render the state some service, while he makes a living for his wife and children. You know doubtless what it is to be without money, without friends, without a position; with pressing necessities. I appeal to your generous nature, to your honorable pledges made to him, to me and to others. Do not permit other considerations, less potent, prevent your doing a simple justice, to those who have done much to serve you in the past, and are ready to do in the future. Dear Sir, you will pardon this seeming importunity on my part. Nothing but the unbounded regard and confidence in your noble, and consideration would have prompted me to venture this freedom, with the highest consideration for your Excellency, and the complete and triumphant success of your administration.

I remain your obedient servant
R. H. Cain.

SOURCE: Franklin J. Moses Papers, Box 4, Folder 3, South Carolina Department of Archives and History, Columbia.

DOCUMENT 28
DELANY TO JUSTICE JONATHAN WRIGHT

Charleston, February 10, 1874

Hon. J. J. Wright, Assistant Justice,
Superior Court, South Carolina
Columbia, S.C.

MY DEAR SIR,
I see by the recent convention held by the young men of Richland County, at which you spoke and gave some excellent counsel, that much interest and alarm were manifested by them at the influx of white immigration.

THIS IS BUT THE EARLY CURRENT of that immigration of which I frequently cautioned the people concerning in 1866, at Hilton Head, and among the Sea Islands; and spoke of it at the great ratification meeting at Epping Hall (now United States Courthouse) Charleston, 1868, and more particularly at the club meeting of Republicans at Beaufort the same year, (I, being then in the United States army, stationed at Hilton Head) and subsequently at other times when you were present. I remember the club meeting particularly, as the suggestion made by me met with determined opposition, and one of the most prominent leaders of the party there at the time arose in the meeting and advised the people that there need be no fears of any such thing ever taking place, as it was simply impossible ever to outnumber the colored people in South Carolina and Mississippi, where the blacks now had the preponderance. You must remember this at the Beaufort club meeting. I spoke of general amnesty, and this too, was 'pooh-poohed!' I simply desire to say that this tide of emigration having now set in will go on to completion—that is, it will not cease till the white population in the state sufficiently outnumbers the blacks to secure to the whites the basis of

A RULING ELEMENT

The object of the 'Granges' or immigration movement in this state, as you very well know, is to neutralize the black ruling element, by reducing or exceeding its majority. And my candid opinion is, that the whites in the South generally, and South Carolina in particular, prefer as agricultural, mechanical, and laboring elements the blacks to the whites, and that this immigration scheme never would have been organized had they, from the past and present aspect of things, not been led to believe that we, the blacks, were influenced, controlled and led in our political actions without principle or a will of our own, and that so long as we outnumbered them, they will never get a chance to participate in the political affairs of the state. This is my sincere conviction, after much observation and intelligent inquiry.

BUT THE THING IS NOW DONE,

And it is a fixed fact that in five years, if not less time than this, the black population (I include all people of color) will be in the minority in this state. What our race requires is proper information to rightly direct it. This has been too long neglected, and should have been given by those who led them in politics. What I desire to say is that it is your duty, as it is that of every intelligent man among us, who aspire to a leadership, loves his race, has the capacity, and is versed in the great principles of political science, and consequently, the philosophy of popular succession, to warn his people of a great approaching reality, which, sooner or later, will verify itself in history. That, having prospectively lost the popular preponderance and consequent certainty of representation in all departments of government, local, state and national, our only hope and chance of its future security is in the principle of

CUMULATIVE VOTING

Which secures MINORITY representation as well as majority. Let our Legislature be wise enough now, while it is in the power of our race to do so, to take such measures as to secure, by constitutional enactment, the right of minority representation, which, while it immediately secures to the whites of the state, irrespective of party, a pro rata representation, or representation in proportion to numbers, it secures to the black race the same ratio of representation in counties where whites have the majority, and when they shall preponderate in population in the state, which they most assuredly will, at no distant day.

THE WHITE RACE IS TRUE TO ITSELF, and it is useless and doing injustice to both races to conceal the fact, that in giving liberty and equality of rights to the blacks, they had no desire to see them rule over their own race. And the blacks may as well know this at once; that there is no scheme that can be laid, no measure that may be entered into, nor expenses so great, which they will not incur to change such a relation between blacks and whites in the country. Rest assured of this, that there are no white people North or South who will submit to see the blacks rule over the whites in America. We may as well be plain and candid on this point, look each other in the face, and let the truth be known. Radicalism, as taught by political leaders for selfish motives and personal gain, has led the masses of our untutored race to believe otherwise, and act accordingly. But this is dreadful,

TERRIBLE POLITICAL HERESY

Which should receive the stamp of condemnation by every true friend of mankind and a just government, black and white. They are, as they should be, willing to have us participate; to concede to us our legitimate and reasonable share as citizens, but not an absolute and supreme control in political affairs.

I have the honor to be, Sir,
Your friend and fellow-citizen
M. R. Delany.

SOURCE: *New York Times*, February 21, 1874.

DOCUMENT 29

ON DELANY'S LETTER TO JUSTICE WRIGHT

One of the colored leaders in South Carolina has written a letter warning his race on the dangers which await them in the near future, unless they now take measures to secure a voice in affairs wherever the whites are in the majority by the adoption of minority representation. This advice is timely, and it is to be hoped, in the interest of both races, that it will be followed. Negro supremacy in South Carolina has not been an unmixed blessing, and when whites obtain the numerical superiority, as they shortly will from immigration, they are not likely to be any more liberal in their policy than the blacks have been. Unless the blacks now permit the whites their proportionate participation in affairs, they are certainly in their turn to be entirely excluded, and the relations of the two races will thus be always disturbed. Major DELANY has proved himself a sincere and intelligent friend of his race by the advice he has given them on this matter, and we hope he will have the assistance of such enlightened colored men in his state as Mr. Elliott on the task he has undertaken. If the Negroes now having the power will base the government of South Carolina on the whole people, their capacity for public affairs will never be denied in the future.

SOURCE: *New York Times*, February 16, 1874.

DOCUMENT 30

MINORITY REPRESENTATION: A COLORED ADVOCATE
IN FAVOR OF IT IN SOUTH CAROLINA

Major M. R. Delany, a colored man, who held a commission in the Union Army during the latter years of the rebellion, and who has lived in South Carolina since the war closed, has written a letter on the relations of the races in the state, to Hon. J. J. Wright. Mr. Wright is also a colored man and for some years has been one of the Justices of the Supreme Court of the state. Major Delany, after speaking of the increased white immigration, and expressing the belief that within five years, Negroes will be in a minority in South Carolina goes on to say:

> What our race requires is proper information to rightly direct it. This has been too long neglected, and should have been given by those who led them in politics. What I desire to say is that it is your duty, as it is that of every intelligent man among us, who aspire to a leadership, loves his race, has the capacity, and is versed in the great principles of political science, and consequently, the philosophy of popular succession, to warn his people of a great approaching reality, which, sooner or later, will verify itself in history. That, having prospectively lost the popular preponderance and consequent certainty of representation in all departments of government, local, state and national, our only hope and chance of its future security is in the principle of cumulative voting which secures MINORITY representation as well as majority. Let our Legislature be wise enough now, while it is in the power of our race to do so, to take such measures as to secure, by constitutional enactment, the right of minority representation, which, while it immediately secures to the whites of the state, irrespective of party, a pro rata representation, or

representation in proportion to numbers, it secures to the black race the same ratio of representation in counties where whites have the majority, and when they shall preponderate in population in the state, which they most assuredly will, at no distant day. The white race is true to itself, and it is useless and doing injustice to both races to conceal the fact, that in giving liberty and equality of rights to the blacks, they had no desire to see them rule over their own race. And the blacks may as well know this at once; that there is no scheme that can be laid, no measure that may be entered into, nor expenses so great, which they will not incur to change such a relation between blacks and whites in the country. Rest assured of this, that there are no white people North or South who will submit to see the blacks rule over the whites in America. We may as well be plain and candid on this point, look each other in the face, and let the truth be known. Radicalism, as taught by political leaders for selfish motives and personal gain, has led the masses of our untutored race to believe otherwise, and act accordingly. But this is dreadful, terrible political heresy which should receive the stamp of condemnation by every true friend of mankind and a just government, black and white. They are, as they should be, willing to have us participate; to concede to us our legitimate and reasonable share as citizens, but not an absolute and supreme control in political affairs.

SOURCE: *New York Times*, February 21, 1874.

CHAPTER 4
The Independent Republican

Introduction

Neither Delany's letters to Frederick Douglass and Justice Jonathan Wright nor his repeated public outrage against Radical Republicanism stemmed the tide of radicalism and what he characterized as its excesses in South Carolina. His anticorruption ideas and his advocacy of caution, gradualism, moderation, and reconciliation with former slave owners fell on deaf ears. Convinced that Radical Republicanism was leading blacks to the abyss of self-destruction, Delany joined a coalition of "liberal" Republicans and conservatives to launch the Independent Republican Movement in 1874. The IRM was a splinter group comprising disgruntled elements of the Republican Party who ostensibly wanted to reform the rampant corruption in state politics, which they blamed on Radical Republicanism. This group had earlier attempted to stage a coup within the Republican Party. At the State Nominating Convention of 1874, this group, composed mostly of conservatives and ex-Confederates sympathizers of the old system, nominated two candidates, Judge John T. Green, an ex-Confederate officer, and Martin Delany, for governor and lieutenant governor, respectively, to challenge the Radical Republican candidates Daniel H. Chamberlain and Richard Gleaves (a black man), for governor and lieutenant governor.

This conservative attempt to hijack the radical Republican Party failed abysmally. The Radical Republican candidates won the nomination. The margin of loss, especially for Delany, is revealing. He lost to Richard Gleaves by a margin of eleven votes to ninety-seven. Thus, the attempt by conservative elements within the Republican Party to hijack the party and steer it along a more moderate and conciliatory course failed. The Green-Delany ticket was defeated. But not dead! About three weeks later, these conservatives launched the IRM in Charleston to challenge the Radical Republicans in the ensuing election. The Green-Delany ticket was back. The objective of the movement was to topple Radical Republicanism and redirect South Carolina politics along reconciliatory paths. The IRM generated quite a momentum, awakening state conservatives from their political apathy. They mobilized and came out to vote in record numbers. As one conservative put it, the IRM was their opportunity "to kill the snake of radicalism." The election saw increased white participation. Nonetheless, the IRM lost. Blacks remained solidly behind the Republican Party, and their vote was crucial to the party's victory.

The opening selection (doc. 1) in this chapter is a meeting of the coalition at which Delany delivered a speech emphasizing the need for racial harmony. He urged blacks to turn away from Radical Republicanism and embrace local whites. He opined that they shared common interests despite political differences. He warned blacks to no longer remain blindly loyal to Radical Republicans but to reconcile with and embrace local whites with whom they supposedly shared common interests and challenges. He believed that their coming together (blacks representing labor, local whites representing capital) would redeem the state to the benefit of all. Delany declared this racial unity as the key to the redemption of the state. Document 2 highlights Delany's address at the IRM Nominating Convention. He reiterated his contention that blacks had been manipulated, misled, and exploited by Radical Republicanism, which he blamed for the rampant corruption in the state. He called for a "New Departure," urging blacks to embrace local whites and abandon the Republican Party. He advocated nomination and election of honest people and mostly local whites who he believed would win the people's confidence. He maintained that changing the political landscape and culture in South Carolina required the cooperation of blacks and local whites. He attributed black economic poverty to the influence of "bad leaders" who have misadvised and misguided the people. He called on blacks to pursue this "New Departure" and quit following so-called leaders and friends. They should reconcile instead with "the intelligent and honest white men of the state." He also called for a government that would reform the rampant political abuses and corruption. Delany insisted that in order to advance, whites and blacks in South Carolina had to unite. He considered this union vital to the future prosperity of the entire state. He rejected calls by some Radical Republicans for social equality, which he characterized as "the great bugbear." Amid thunderous applause, he reassured the mostly white and conservative audience that the racial unity he envisioned for the state did not imply social equality. He did not believe that social equality should or could be enforced by any legislation. It would "regulate itself." Delany strongly affirmed his opposition to social equality, much to the delight of his audience.

At the IRM State Convention (doc. 3), Delany was formally elected as the candidate for lieutenant governor to run alongside gubernatorial candidate John Green, an ex-Confederate soldier and judge. In his acceptance speech, Delany pledged to work for racial harmony and equal justice for all regardless of race. He also promised to adhere only to principles and policies that advanced the interests of blacks and whites. He reiterated his adherence to Republican principles. Delany reminded the audience that the IRM grew out of disaffection with and the desire to correct the ills of the Radical Republican Party. He was committed to challenging and ending the politics of racial division that had alienated blacks from local whites. He would pursue justice for everyone regardless of race. At the next ratification meeting (doc. 4), Delany castigated the Radical Republicans for not advancing the interest of blacks but instead sowing seeds of racial discord in the state. This divisive policy was the Radical Republicans' strategy of controlling blacks. Delany believed that change was imminent, evident by the growing unity and cooperation of blacks and local whites. He called for reconciliation between "men who held high offices of trust under the old state government, and me, Martin R. Delany, a John Brown Abolitionist." His speech elicited wild cheers. He also contended that blacks have been led astray by their own kind. The IRM, he reassured, would change everything. It would introduce a new policy and improved relationship between blacks and local whites. The existing system of Radical Republican rule was, he opined, riddled with corruption, and he urged blacks to acknowledge that the Democratic Party was not the enemy. Blacks should no longer be scared of and alienated from Democrats. He insisted that Radical Republicans had misrepresented and maligned Democrats in order to retain the loyalty of blacks. Delany vowed to no longer remain a prisoner of such false consciousness. He suggested that Democrats had done much more for the state and for blacks than they had been given credit for. He insisted that the label "Democrat" should no longer be cast as a negative one.

Delany wanted blacks to realize that Radical Republicans had not fulfilled for blacks one fundamental principle of politics, "that politics are intended for the benefit of the people," and thus far Radical Republican policy had been divisive and selfish, resulting in economic misery to blacks. Delany described the IRM as a movement designed to turn blacks in a new direction (a new departure). He argued that Democrats had been unfairly misrepresented and declared his determination to fight radicalism and reverse its course. He promised to fight for just cause and the truth and was willing and ready to face the political retaliations that he felt were sure to come from the Radical Republicans. He informed the audience of an impending conspiracy and false indictment by the Radicals, whom he accused of driving a wedge between blacks and former slave owners and, in the process, damaged the economic fortunes of the entire state. Delany called for a new political relationship between blacks and local whites. He reassured his black listeners that the Democrats had been misrepresented by Radical Republicans. Delany declared that Democrats had in fact contributed more to the Underground Railroad than had Republicans. This revisionist history was all music to the ears of his largely conservative audience, composed mostly of members of the old state system—the system that had once enslaved blacks and had fought a bloody Civil War against their freedom. They responded with thunderous applause and sang the "Bonnie Blue Flag," the anthem of the former Confederate states.

At the next IRM meeting in Greenville (doc. 5), Delany told blacks it was in their and their state's best interests to cooperate with local whites. Their interests were intertwined. He urged blacks to vote only for men who would advance those interests. Documents 6 and 7 are commentaries in the *News and Courier* on Delany's campaign activities. The paper editorialized about the IRM Nominating Convention, Delany's nomination, and his call for racial reconciliation and anticorruption efforts. The paper reported that Delany's speeches made quite an impression on the "first gentlemen of South Carolina," who reciprocated kindly by proclaiming him the pride of his race. They described Delany as an educated black man who espoused "true patriotism and statesmanship" and who was working to strengthen "the cause of Honesty and Reform." The paper characterized Delany as someone "exceedingly Black," yet able to deliver "the utterances of an educated man and the sentiments of true patriotism and statesmanship." Delany, the paper observed, acquitted himself "so completely" with "the first gentlemen of South Carolina" (representatives of the old order).

DOCUMENT 1
INDEPENDENT REPUBLICANS: CONSERVATIVES AND REPUBLICANS IN A COMMON CAUSE

Call for a meeting of the citizens of Charleston, irrespective of party to cooperate in measures to secure a fair election, about four thousand persons assembled in front of City Hall last night. The crowd was composed of whites and colored citizens—every profession, trade and occupation in the community was represented.

President—the Hon. H. D. Lesesne

Vice-Presidents: Mayor G. I. Cunningham, Ex-Gov. William Aiken, Coroner Aaron Logan, E. D. Seabrook, Senator S. E. Gailliard, etc.

Remarks of Maj. DELANY

The chairman then introduced as the first regular speaker, Maj. M. R. Delany, who said: Mr. Chairman, this is one of the most extraordinary occasions that we have longed hoped for in Charleston. Most of you know my political sentiments; therefore, I will not detain you with any lengthy expression of them. The speaker then alluded to the perfect which prevailed in the vast multitude before him, and accredited it to the general principle that as are the leaders so are the followers. Most of the past disturbances at most meetings in the city he thought due to the prompting of those who ought to and did know better. The people of South Carolina have but one common interest, and they should act with a view to serve that common interest. It was great political heresy to suppose that because a man is opposed to his neighbor in political opinion, he must also be in antagonism with him in his private relations. What was most to be desired is that the whites and the blacks in this state should know and understand their duties towards each other, so act as to stand together and work for their mutual weal and prosperity. The speaker said that for a long time he had stood alone in his party, and had been denounced for entertaining such opinions, but the day is gone, he said, when we can be made to believe that everything the Republican Party did was right. The black men of this state have at least learned that they were dependent upon the whites just as the whites dependent upon them, and that it is in their interest to work with, rather than against whites. In speaking of the present commissioners of election, he said it has been authentically stated that the Governor of the state has openly declared that he would not put men in office as commissioners of election who would count in whom they choose. (A voice, 'they won't come in by a jug fall.') If there is one prominent characteristic in my nature, it is justice. I must say that I do not consider Peter Gregorie an unjust man. Of the other two, I can't say anything, but I believe Gregorie to be honest. The speaker then dwelt upon the importance of their adoption of the resolution that would be offered, and concluded by impressing upon his audience the fact that each man, black and white, represented a portion of the two fold basis of the land—labor and capital. The black man and the white man must work in cooperation together, and by this mutual cooperation would be worked out the redemption of the state, and prosperity and happiness for the whole people (cheers).

Source: *News and Courier* (Charleston), October 2, 1874.

DOCUMENT 2

The Independent Republican State Nominating Convention: Hibernian Hall

Col. M. R. Delany was invited to address the convention. He reviewed, very briefly but forcefully, the history of reconstruction in the state, and the causes which led to the establishment of the present condition of affairs. He said that, in the early days of reconstruction, the colored people had asked the native whites to come forward and aid them in establishing the government. This they refused to do, and the colored people, being themselves unable to comprehend the situation, were driven to the necessity of going to those who had come here from the North. A consequence of this was the mistaken ethics of politics into which the colored people were led. Among other things, and by far the most erroneous, was the belief taught by the Sixth Ward New York politicians, that whatever was done in politics was right. In this way, the colored people were taught to believe that it was right to vote minors, women and girls, even to go to the graveyard and rake up names of the dead and vote them. But the colored people had now resolved upon a new departure. These teachers had never done a single thing for the benefit of the colored race. The only instance was in the establishment of the Land Commission, which, under cover of giving lands to the Negroes, was used to put money in their pockets (that's so). He then went on to say that in his opinion, if this convention should nominate suitable candidates, the Honest Government League would coalesce with the Independent Republican, and the tax-payers would sanction and support them (applause). He then touched upon the question of taxation, showing that if rents were high and the poor people suffered, it was because the landowners were ground to death by taxation, that if the poor had to pay exorbitant prices for the necessaries of life, it was because burdensome taxes were tacked on to the cost of the material. All this has been brought by the bad leaders and bad advisers of the colored people. They are tired of this now and wanted a new departure, (cheers). The colored leaders of the people who were following the white leaders were only following them for the money that they paid them, and the black men must look for other followers. The time has come when the black man must stand up side by side with the intelligent and honest white men of the state, like a tower of strength and stop all this, (applause). This departure from the old double-dyed corrupt wing of the Republican Party was but the natural consequence of their corruption (applause). He said further that he had the assurance that the tax payers of the state would endorse any movement on the part of the Republicans which looked to a reformation in the state government. If this convention placed such candidates in the field as would be acceptable to the tax payers, he was confident that the conservative convention, which meets on the 8th of the month, would endorse such candidates, and not nominate anybody in opposition to them. He warned the convention then to look carefully to their action, and to give an earnest to the people of the state of their desire to affect a reform of past abuses. A union of the blacks and whites would bring about such a state of affairs as would enable the laborer to demand the highest price for his labor and the capitalist to pay it (applause). None but the blacks and whites could accomplish this. He had one more word to say, and that was in reference to the great bugbear, SOCIAL EQUALITY. He said he had a family of which he was just as proud as anybody. But social equality must regulate itself. He would not allow anybody to dictate to him who should eat at his table (Applause). The blacks were imitative creatures and until it became fashionable for white men to sit down at the table with black men, there was no danger of black men insisting upon sitting down to the table with white people (Applause and laughter). It was all a bugbear, and no man with common sense would give a bawbee for any law which would compel a black man to sit down at the table with a white man, or which would compel a white man to receive a black man at his table (Great applause).

SOURCE: *News and Courier* (Charleston), October 3, 1874.

DOCUMENT 3
THE INDEPENDENT REPUBLICAN STATE CONVENTION

The Independent Republican State Convention met at twelve O'clock, on Saturday—nominations of both Green and Delany.

After this earnest and graceful speech, which was applauded to the echo, the president introduced Col. Martin R. Delany, "the honest exemplar of the honest colored men of South Carolina."

SPEECH OF COL. MARTIN R. DELANY

This is one of the most extraordinary occasions of my life. I have not words to express my gratitude to you for this manifestation to your regard and confidences in nominating me for the second office in the gift of the people of South Carolina. I have but little to say to you now, for you have already heard me frequently upon the various phases of our relations to each other; but this much I will say to you, that I have entered into this great movement with no other design than, if elected, to second to the utmost extent the integrity of the chief magistrate of the State. I will go further than this, I will pledge all of the intelligence, all of the power of intellect that I possess, all of the integrity of character, to bring about between the two peoples of this state, blacks and whites, those relations that will tend to the promotion of each other's mutual welfare (cheers). I shall not act (in the sense in which it is understood) as a party man. I shall know no other party than that which shall have for its object the interest of the whole people, black and white, of the state of South Carolina (cheers). I shall strive to correct, so far as my own race is concerned, one or two errors in the Republican Party as it formerly existed. We are standing upon a new platform, so far as party acts are concerned. In our party there were three points of consideration: 1st we were formed as a Republican party in contradistinction to the Democratic party; next, we had factions in our own party, which was all wrong; and next, one part of our party was taught as a fundamental principle that they must stand in direct hostility to one portion of the people which formed the community in which they lived. I shall endeavor to correct this. It is my province to say that, because, when I look upon my race, I see that it has all and everything to lose in a contest such as might be brought about by antagonism of races. This being true, I have but one more remark to make. I do not intend to lower my standard of manhood in regard to the claims of my race one single step. I do not intend to recede from the rights that have been given us by the beneficence of a just Congress of the nation one single hairsbreadth; but I do intend, in demanding all this, to demand the same equal rights and justice for every citizen, black and white, of the state of South Carolina. And upon this line I will fight it out if it takes all winter (cheers).

Source: *News and Courier* (Charleston), October 5, 1874.

DOCUMENT 4
Green and Delany

A Rousing Ratification Meeting Last Night

A mass meeting of Independent Republicans was held at the City Hall, last night, to ratify the nomination of Judge Green and Major Delany as Governor and Lieutenant-Governor.

When the applause which followed Judge Green's speech had subsided, the chairman introduced,

COL. MARTIN R. DELANY,

The Independent Republican candidate for Lieutenant-Governor, who spoke as follows:

FELLOW-CITIZENS—I propose to say very little tonight after the speech of my distinguished leader and, in that little I intend to call attention to a few points that underlie this movement. In the first place, let me ask you what were the reconstruction acts of Congress established for? Certainly not for the white people, because they were already in the enjoyment of all their rights and liberties. It must have been then for the benefit of the colored people in the South. And just here let me ask you, what benefits, have the colored people in South Carolina derived from the propagation of Republican sentiments? ('None!', from the crowd). One thing it has done, and that is to keep up a continual strife, parading a huge scare crow by means of which they keep you in a state of continual fight, making you believe that you are in a constant danger of losing your liberties unless you have certain leaders to back you up and protect you ('that's so'). This is what Republicanism has done for us, and the result has been to keep up a constant hostility between the whites and blacks ('Yes! Yes!' from the crowd). Such a party is not worth the effort to keep it in existence. It cannot be denied that, after the introduction of Republicanism in South Carolina, the colored people became divided among themselves, and it was to the interest of their leaders to keep up these dissensions and divisions. Just let any two men come here from the North, and go to hunting office, and in less than three months they will have the colored people arrayed in open hostility between themselves, on one side shouting "hurrah for massa Jim!" (Laughter). But a change is coming over the people. Only a few nights ago was presented, on this very spot, one of the strangest spectacles that has ever been seen in South Carolina. That was a citizens' meeting, and on the platform sat gentlemen—some of the first white men in South Carolina, men who had held high offices of trust under the old state government, and me, Martin R. Delany, a John Brown Abolitionist (cheers). I have been asked by some of my brethren, if the white men are anxious to unite with the colored men in an effort for honest government, why did the cotton pressmen the other day turn off black laborers and employ white men? I answer, for the reason that the leaders of the black men had created dissensions among them and persuaded them to do what they ought not to have done. They led them astray ('that's so' from the crowd). And I tell you now that no people in this condition can advance in civilization. It is the mission of this independent movement to put a stop to this policy, and to lay down and mark out for you new lines of duty, to establish between you and your white fellow-citizens new and peaceable relations, to teach you that there is something else to do than to shout "Hurrah for Republicanism and Damn Democracy." The hour for this has passed. A remarkable feature of the old Republican movement in this state is that it never produced a single statesman since the establishment of the reconstruction acts. Why? Because there were always a few men at Columbia who filled the offices and led the party, and every man in the party had to accept their advice and follow the policy laid out by them or be silenced. These men, my fellow-citizens, have become so accustomed to rule that they do not hesitate to adopt any device or any measures to coerce the people to their ends. In this very campaign, before the meeting of the State Convention, a high state official came to Charleston with the message that if a delegation was sent there without being instructed to vote for a certain candidate they would not be admitted. The same officials have since declared that certain men must rule in this county. It was the fight against this impudent dictation that the Independent Republican party arrayed itself, and it is now high time that your eyes be opened to your duty in this matter. To prevent you from acting right they have raised the cry that this was a Democratic movement. Why this very day I saw a colored brother rush down to the wharf exclaiming, "Great God, what do you think! Maj. Delany has turned Democrat!" (Laughter). They also accused Judge Green of being a Democrat. And how do they prove it? Why by Attorney-General Melton's statement, that he had himself gone to Judge Green and for two hours begged and beseeched him to consent. Judge Green said that he was not wealthy and could not afford to spend the money necessary to carry on the campaign and because he consented afterwards to become the candidate for the Independent Republican party, he is called a Democrat. Was he any the less a Democrat when Attorney-General Melton begged him to consent? (No! No!) I tell you my brethren that the whole policy of these masters of yours is to make you believe anything they say. They want you to remain like you have always been here-to-fore—a set of young blackbirds with your mouths open and eyes shut, waiting to swallow blindly anything that the old bird chooses to drop in them, no matter whether it is grasshopper or a scorpion (Laughter). But they find out now that you are getting to be old birds, and that you are opening your eyes. ("Dat's so" from a gray headed colored man in the crowd). And we are no longer to be frightened by the old bugbear of "Democrats." Why, it was the Democrats who gave us freedom. And we are never to learn anything from the Democrats? Look at Frank Blair. He commanded the 12th Army Corps, which swept like a besom through the state under Sherman in his memorable march to the sea, and burnt Columbia, and yet, Democrats voted for him for Vice-President in 1868, while we poor devils don't dare to vote for a good man because he is a Democrat (Applause). Why, if one of us was starving and stopped in the street to pick up a piece of bread from the gutter, and a Northern man was near and shouted "Democrat", you'd drop it and run. (Laughter). So my duty is to teach my people these truths and I say right here that I don't intend to be deterred, even by the thirty indictments that I understand are to be brought up against me by some lying scoundrel (cheers). Let these swindling adventurers come with their indictments, and I promise to make the place too hot to hold them (yells and cheers). Who believes that the indictment against Mayor Cunningham is anything but a political prosecution? ("That's so" from the crowd). This thing has got to stop. If any vagabond can attack an honest citizen in this way, whose character will be safe? I'll tell you the plot they made up: they intended first to trump up an indictment against me; but they were afraid that the colored people would say that they were prosecuting a black man and it would react against them. They therefore turned their attention to Mayor Cunningham, the chief magistrate of your city. The meaning of this is that these fellows will resort to anything. They are determined to have you under their feet, and to make you sub serve their interests. It is time, however, for you to have your eyes open, and to learn that politics are intended for the benefit of the people, and that the policy, which divided a community is pernicious and is only devised to carry out the selfish ends of the men who devised it. It was in consequence of the hostility created by these men between the two races; that white men are brought here to labor when our streets are full of idle colored men (That's so). The white people here, I am sure, would rather have colored labor, but they could not be expected to employ it as long as it were arrayed in hostility against them. For myself, I am determined that it shall not be said that there is not a black man with the courage to warn my people against this. It is time to look things in the face; to recognize the fact that the whites and blacks should cultivate amicable relations between themselves, neither race abating one single right, but both working together harmoniously for the public peace and prosperity (Applause). These truths the people must learn. There must be new political relations between the races. Remember my brethren, that the white people have said that, if the blacks would lay down their own platform and nominate honest men for office, they would come upon it and unite with them in working out the salvation of the state (Applause). Just here I want to tell you something that I don't want the white people to hear. Before and during the War, I was conductor on the Underground Railroad. You all know what that was—a society to carry off slaves and give them freedom. This required money. I tell you we got ten dollars from a Democrat where we got one dollar from a Republican and, what is more, we didn't refuse the money because it came from Democrats. Don't let us now refuse assistance because it comes from Democrats. Let us, in this new issue, extend our hands to every honest citizen of the state, and go on to certain success and triumph in our effort to redeem the state (Applause).

At the conclusion of Col. Delany's speech the band played the "Bonnie Blue Flag," which produced another hearty cheer from the crowd.[1]

SOURCE: *News and Courier* (Charleston), October 7, 1874.

DOCUMENT 5

A VOICE FROM THE MOUNTAINS: ANOTHER ROUSING MEETING IN GREENVILLE—SPEECHES FROM GEN. KERSHAW AND COL. DELANY

Special Dispatch to *the News and Courier*

GREENVILLE, S.C., October 15—Col. Delany and Gen. Kershaw made rousing speeches here tonight to the largest mixed audience ever assembled in Greenville. Delany made a tremendous effort to convince his colored brethren that their interests and the interests of the whites were inseparable,

---

[1]. "Bonnie Blue Flag" was the anthem of the former Confederate states.

and that the prosperity of both races depended upon the inauguration of peace and good will between the people, black and white, of the state. The whites turned out en masse to hear him speak, and the voice of all was that he made the best speech of the campaign. He sifted the Bond Ring and advised the colored people how to secure good government by voting for men who had the interest of the entire people at heart. Delany spoke two hours, and it was a telling address. The strongest straight-out Democrats have agreed to go unanimously for the Green ticket. T. A. Davis, colored, a representative of Charleston, spoke next. He made a red-hot speech and had the undivided attention of the colored people. Gen. Kershaw then took the stand and endorsed the remarks of the previous speakers. He said they embodied his sentiments and he was willing to stand on that platform. . . . The county is aroused and nothing short of an earthquake can stop the great wave that is overflowing the sentiments of these people in favor of the Independent Movement. The Up-country sends greeting cheering words to the people of the Low country, and will guarantee 25,000 Majority for the Independent honest movement before we strike the Low country where we expect to meet a still greater majority.

SOURCE: *News and Courier* (Charleston), October 16, 1874.

DOCUMENT 6

THE CAUSE OF FAIR DEALING AND PEACE IN CHESTER

Correspondent of the *News and Courier*

CHESTER, OCTOBER 21—The Conservative and Independent Republican parties assembled at this place today for the purpose of hearing Gen. Kershaw on the part of the former and Messr Delany on the part of the latter. In consequence of the imperfect manner in which the notice of these meetings disseminated there were not too many persons from the country present as would have been the case had the appointments been fully known. As it was, the courthouse was about as full as it could hold, one-third being colored people. It is not my purpose to give any idea of the substance of the speeches made. It will be sufficient to say that they were all addressed to the one grand idea—the thorough reconciliation of the white and colored people in the interest of honesty and good government. Gen. Kershaw made a speech which characterizes the man. It was a political essay, full of truth, sincerity and fairness, and more than this, abounding in a cheerful hopefulness for the races and regeneration of South Carolina. He was listened to throughout with the most eager interest, for as he stands first, of all men, in the hearts of the people of South Carolina. It was the wish of our citizens to take advice from his lips. The efforts of Col. M. R. Delany produced a most profound impression on both white and colored, particularly on the former. From the fact of his being so exceedingly black, it has caused extreme surprise wherever he has gone to hear voicing from his mouth the utterances of an educated man and the sentiments of true patriotism and statesmanship. His complexion, too, recommended him to the jet blacks of his own race, and I could see it excited a feeling of pride in the colored people that one of their own genuine men should acquit himself so completely alongside of the first gentlemen of South Carolina.

Source: *News and Courier* (Charleston), October 24, 1874.

DOCUMENT 7

Major Delany

The candidate of the Independent Republicans and Conservatives for the office of Lieutenant-Governor is doing gallant work in the up-country. It is a surprise and gratification to the whites to hear wise, generous and statesman-like words from the lips of a black man, and the colored people are proud to see that a man of their own race can worthily stand side by side with Kershaw and McGowan, in the advocacy of fair-dealing and peace. Major Delany has, by his good work, strengthened the cause of Honesty and Reform.

Source: *News and Courier* (Charleston), October 24, 1874.

CHAPTER 5

TRIAL AND CONVICTION

INTRODUCTION

After the failure of the Independent Republican Movement, in early 1875 Delany returned to the Republican Party a disappointed and humbled man. His political apostasy had, however, created a deep resentment within the party. Yet despite the resentment, Delany initially found favor within the new administration. Newly elected governor Daniel H. Chamberlain had campaigned as a reform candidate and pledged, if elected, to put in office only honest officials regardless of past or present political affiliations. One reflection of this was his appointment of Martin Delany as Trial Justice for Ward 3 of the City of Charleston. However, while Chamberlain was willing to be magnanimous and appoint political opponents to offices, many within his party could not easily forgive and forget Delany's anti-radical ideas, especially his cozy relationship with state conservatives and ex-Confederates. It seemed it was a matter of time before they would make their resentment public. But the moment came sooner than anyone expected.

Shortly after the IRM defeat, Delany was invited to New York to address a gathering of distinguished gentlemen in Irvin Hall. This audience was composed of philanthropists and financiers, potential South Carolina state bondholders he had earlier appealed to on behalf of Governor Franklin J. Moses. Delany saw this as an opportunity to highlight the challenges posed by radical politics while also extending his anti-radical crusade northwards. He recounted his now familiar criticisms of radical excesses in South Carolina, blaming Radical Republicans for misleading blacks and establishing a reign of violence, political instability, and racial antagonism. This speech, according to Delany, so enraged the radicals back in South Carolina that they decided finally to conspire against him and destroy his political career. The indictment he alluded to earlier in the IRM campaign seemed about to materialize. In a letter to his esteem friend Frederick Douglass, Delany detailed a litany of offenses that the radicals purportedly accused him of and that became, he contended, the basis of a widespread conspiracy to punish him.

Document 1 reproduces the full text of a lengthy letter Delany wrote to Douglass and intended to publish as a pamphlet. In it, he recounted details of ten offenses the radicals charged him with, including his persistent opposition to black political assertiveness, his advocacy of political moderation and accommodation, concession to white superiority, call to deemphasized social equality, castigation of black officeholders, opposition to a proposal for a black mayoral candidate for Charleston, and campaign against and contribution to the defeats of radical candidates in the Charleston municipal election of 1875. All these culminated in Delany's being sued, tried, and found guilty of grand larceny. He gave a detailed explanation of the circumstances that led to the grand larceny conspiracy, underlining the political character of the lawsuit. As he explained, it all started when he ran a land and note brokerage business and was entrusted with the sum of two hundred dollars, proceeds from the estate of the deceased father of a client, one Mrs. E. B. Richardson. He then invested the funds, along with those of other clients in county claims, expecting profitable returns and thus profits to his clients. Despite several state appropriations from the county, Delany's claims were not honored. He was left with but one conclusion: this was clearly, in his view, an attempt to humiliate and embarrass him, a punishment for his political views and activities. This situation led to the grand larceny indictment.

Delany characterized the lawsuit, trial, empaneling of the jury, testimonies, and trial as a grand scheme of radical conspiracy to destroy him politically and humiliate him publicly. The outcome, according to Delany, was a foregone conclusion. He described the jury as composed mainly of political adversaries whose mayoral candidate he had campaigned against and helped defeat in the last municipal election in Charleston. Some of the jurors had run for offices and lost. They took less than ten minutes to render a verdict. He was found guilty and sentenced to twelve months in the penitentiary. Delany vowed never to relent or compromise on his convictions. He would continue to "advocate the rights of the whole people of the state, without regard to race, color, or politics." He urged Douglass and other leading blacks to recognize the threat posed by such radicalism before it consumed every member of the black race. Today it's Delany, he stressed, but someone else would definitely be next if these powers were not confronted and stopped.

Document 2 is a commentary on the indictment by the Charleston *News and Courier* defending Delany and characterizing the grand larceny episode as politically motivated. The paper observed that Delany had been a fervent advocate of moderation and racial reconciliation, anathema to the radicals who persecuted him. The paper also recounted the circumstances leading to the grand larceny case showing that Delany was not guilty of the charges. It characterized the entre process as abusive, vindictive, and designed to convict "an innocent man" who had fallen out of favor with his party. The paper appealed to the public for consideration. The *News and Courier*'s plea seemed to resonate in some quarters. Soon there were petitions to Governor Chamberlain urging pardon for Delany. Documents 3, 4, and 5 are letters to Governor Chamberlain from C. C. Bowen, Circuit Judge J. P. Reed, and two citizens of Charleston County, George E. Johnston and Aaron Logan recommending pardon for Delany and the remission of his sentence. Bowen suggested that Delany was willing to refund whatever was lost by his client and had in fact given him (Bowen) the money for transfer to the church. Reed raised doubt about the fraudulent charge. Johnson and Logan corroborated that the money had actually been given to Bowen, who for some unknown reason had yet to hand it over to the trustees of the church. They pleaded with the governor to pardon Delany "one of the few of our race of whom, we are proud to claim."

Document 6 is a letter of intimidation from one Reverend N. N. Hunter to Delany threatening further lawsuits if Delany did not return some money owed to certain residents of James Island. Delany wrote a letter to W. R. Jones, Governor Chamberlain's secretary (doc. 7), in which he denied the allegation in Hunter's letter. He characterized the allegation as yet another example of the statewide conspiracy and denied any direct involvement in any transaction in James Island. Document 8 is a letter to Chamberlain from R. S. Tharin expressing interest in Delany's trial justice position should it become vacant "by Death, Resignation, or other cause." Document 9 is a letter Delany wrote to Secretary Jones expressing disappointment that "friends" who had promised to raise money on his behalf seemed to have reneged. He would now take up the matter himself and seek help from "friends of another party—as I have not got the means within myself—to raise the money." Delany claimed to have once raised the money and given it to a "friend," who seemed to have misused it (possibly Bowen).

Document 10 announced Delany's pardon with the confirmation that the money had been refunded to the church. Document 11 is a letter of gratitude to Governor Chamberlain from Delany and a pledge to support and work for his renomination in the coming election. Delany stressed two significant points in this letter: first, he acknowledged political disagreement with leading black Radical Republicans, and second, he underscored and lamented his financial and economic disadvantaged status in comparison with these other black politicians. Finally, to function effectively for Chamberlain's reelection, Delany requested "a thousand mile RR [railroad] ticket" that would enable him canvass the state and meet with notable members of the executive committee to advocate for the governor.

DOCUMENT 1
Delany to Frederick Douglass: Trial and Conviction

CHARLESTON, SOUTH CAROLINA
February, 28th, 1876
Hon. Frederick Douglass
Washington, District of Columbia.

MY DEAR SIR AND FRIEND:

When we last met in 1872, the situation in the South, and my position there, was a long and earnest theme between us, and I think then, we did not materially differ, as to the duties and policy of our race as part of the fixed industrial and political elements. The constantly increasing and alarming intrusion of the worst class of white political adventurers from the North, was with us, a subject of the deepest interest.

So long as the black man can be made to serve the purpose of this class, he may consider himself secure; but the moment he ceases to do this, he becomes the object of resentment and opposition, if not attack and punishment. To these adventurers, he at once becomes offensive. Such, as an individual, I have ever been, and in a series of short articles, in this pamphlet, I propose to lay before the country, the true character of so-called radicalism, as it exists in the state of South Carolina, and the alarming extent to which it has gone, in subverting the rights and liberties of the people, especially those who oppose them whether white or black, as exhibited in my own case.

In the worst times of *ante bellum* days, during the existence of an institution that was national and recognized by the Constitution, defended by the North and South, supported by the Supreme Court and Treasury,

Army and Navy of the country, you and I could write, speak of, and oppose policies and parties which supported it, boldly and fearlessly. But since the overthrow of that institution and the power of those who supported it, we dare not oppose the infamies of radical rule under these adventurers and new masters of the whole people, without the fear of the loss of liberty, by ignominious convictions, through conspiracy and perjury. And you must remember, that our race it is, which is made the instruments of this most intolerable state of affairs in the hands of a class through the state, worse than that of the abominable gang of ruffians, who during their civil war, undertook to draw up and try as criminals, the respectable people of London. It is not republicanism that is doing this, but imposters, intruders, villains by that name

My dear Douglass, it is due to the joint position once occupied by you and I in the cause of the rights of man and our common country; to the honors which I have received in foreign lands; to the honors received in our own country, especially those of the suffrage of one half of the people of South Carolina for the second office in their sovereignty, an honor which any man might well covet; it is due to the distinguished Chief Magistrate, who has honored me with the official position which I now occupy, to vindicate an unsullied reputation against as vile and bareface a conspiracy as ever disgraced civilization. An outrage only to be reconciled with the character of those who originated it and loaned their aid in carrying it out.

The rights of the people are always insecure, when the ignorant, venal, low and vulgar, get the power in their own hands.

FIRST OFFENCE:

During the session of the Constitutional Convention at Columbia, 1867; a young member offered a resolution claiming for our race the nominee in the next national Convention for the Vice Presidency of the United States. On seeing this in the telegraphic news of the first paper which reached me, I at once wrote the following letter (taken from the New York *Daily Tribune*, Tuesday, August 6th 1867): Those who demanded that the Vice-Presidency should be offered to the Blacks will learn from the sensible and patriotic letter of Major Delany, a colored soldier, that the "one sentiment among the old line leading man" of that race is that "no such nonsense should for a moment be entertained." "Our enemies," he says "would desire no heavier, nor stronger, club with which to break the heads of our friends, and knock out our brains than this." *Tribune*.

The following letter is addressed to the Rev. H. H. Garnet, Pastor, Shiloh Presbyterian Church, New York, by Major Delany, a colored soldier:

Bureau Sub-District, Charleston
Headquarters, Hilton Head
Hilton Head, S.C.
July 27, 1867.

Rev. H. H. Garnet,
Pastor, Shiloh Presbyterian Church,
New York.

MY DEAR SIR,

In such times as these, it requires men of the greatest practical experience, acquired ability, mature intelligence, and discretional wisdom, to speak and act for the race now an integral part and essential element in the body politic of the nation. Therefore, I do most sincerely hope that you and other leading minds among our people may take your stand, speak out, and define your true sentiments in relation to the great points now agitating the public mind, especially the black man's claim to office.

The great principle always advocated by our leading men has been to claim for us, as a race all the rights and privileges belonging to an American citizen of the most favored race. But I do not think that those who have so long, so steadily, and determinedly stood up as you and others of us have done, even to a national concession of these claims, ever contemplated taking any position among our fellow-citizens, till we, at least, should be READY and QUALIFIED. It follows as a matter of course that MORE than we should be ready, before it is POSSIBLE to attain to such positions. I am sure that upon this point, there will be but one sentiment among the old-line leading men of our race, contemporaneous with us, when the subject is placed before them.

I have been induced to pen this letter to you by seeing in the telegraph proceedings of the Columbia, S.C. Convention a claim put forth by Mr. Phillips in behalf of our race, for the Vice-Presidency of the United States. I hope no such nonsense for a moment will be entertained. Our enemies would desire no heavier nor stronger club to break the heads of our friends and knock out our brains than this. We are not children, but men comprehending the entire situation, and should at once discountenance anything that would seemingly make us cat's paw and ridiculous in the eyes and estimation of the political intelligence of the world. Let colored men be satisfied to take things like other men, in their natural course and time, prepare themselves in every particular for municipal positions, and they may expect to attain to some other in time.

Mr. Phillips is a young man of 27 or 28 years of age, and consequently without any political experience, except such as acquired since the war commenced, and therefore may be excused for so palpable a political blunder. I am a personal friend of his; therefore, take the liberty of speaking frankly about him.
I am Sir, for our race and country at large,
your friend,
M. R. DELANY
Hilton, Head, S.C., July 27, 1867.

SECOND OFFENCE:
At a caucus of the colored members of the State Nominating Convention, 1868, then sitting in Charleston, it was decided upon to nominate a colored man for Congress, and Mr. L. S. Langley was assigned the duty of corresponding withy the person designated. At that time, reconstruction was incomplete, and the status of the black race was undetermined; the feelings of the common people of the North, North-west and West still seething and wrankling with emotions of the war, were in no mood to tolerate any such advanced move as this; which in reply to this, I sent the following letter to Mr. Langley (taken from the *Charleston Daily News*, of Saturday, March 21st, 1868). Of this letter, there have been many misconstructions, and some silly and mischievous ones;

The following letter from M. R. Delany, an intelligent and well educated colored man, who lately held the commission of Major in the United States army, and who is now, we believe an ATTACHE of the Freedmen's Bureau, has been sent to us for publication. As a manifesto from a Negro leader, disclosing authoritatively the purpose of the Radical party, with regard to the black race in the future, it is very interesting and significant;

BUREAU SUB-DISTRICT, CHARLESTON
HEADQUARTERS, HILTON HEAD
HILTON HEAD, S.C. FEBRUARY 5TH, 1868.
L. S. Langley, Esq., Member, Constitutional
Convention, South Carolina, Charleston, S.C.
DEAR SIR:
Your favor of the 3rd inst., in reply to my letter to you of the 26th ult., was received by last night's mail.
In reply to your request to permit my name to be put in nomination as a candidate for Congress from the Second Congressional District, composed of Charleston, Beaufort, Colleton and Barnwell, permit me to offer

you my unfeigned and heartfelt thanks for the compliment thereby paid, confidence reposed and deference shown, because prompted by motives in strict accordance (as I know your delegation is aware) with my sense of propriety and fitness of things; acquired ability, qualified by adaptation, age and experience.

It is scarcely necessary for me to repeat what you have frequently known me to express the greatest possible discretion and prudence in these first steps in the inclipency of the enfranchisement of our race in this country. Every step taken by us should be fraught with prudence and caution, lest thereby an error prejudicial to the efforts of our friends in and out of the councils of the nations, and fatal to our cause, might be committed.

It is not necessary to our claims as American citizens, nor important to the accomplishment of that end, that a black man at this period be a representative in the national halls of legislation. This, let me insist with emphasis, the nation (the American people generally), are not ready for. And this sentiment, however undesirable, must be yielded to by us. And when they are ready for it, of course, there will be no objection, and consequently no harm done, and should they never become ready, then that will be the end of the whole matter.

Let our great and good hearted friend, Wendell Phillips, outside of the councils, claim what he pleases—it is his right. His sentiments are as essential to the political life of the nation, as oxygen to animal life. And same also with the great and good statesmen inside of the council.

But too much of one at the wrong time, would assuredly produce the extinction of animal life; and too much of the other at an improper time, in like manner, prove the destruction of our hopes and cherished political issues of our friends.

Whatever they may claim at present as our rights, they do so as white men, a part and parcel of the dominant race, who desire to express for the nation, sentiments of generosity toward the black race, for their fidelity, patriotism, and deeds of military valor in the recent life struggle of the country. This they can afford to do. But we should not presume by reason of this or our numbers, to assume these positions to ourselves.

I regret the expressions of approbation in my letter of the 28th of January, of your and Mr. Whipper's course in Convention, of liberality and leniency toward the late oppressors of our race; but am as I was in regard to the Vice-Presidency, entirely opposed at this period of political experience of the country, to any person identified with the black race entering any council of the nation as a member.

I therefore most respectfully decline the proffered honor of your nomination—an honor as complimentary to me as it is liberal and generous in you to offer it.

Be pleased to make known my views in full to your delegation, with my heartiest thanks for their high consideration, and accept the warmest regards, with much.
I have the honor to be, Sir,
Your most obedient servant,
M. R. DELANY.[1]

THIRD OFFENCE:

I was sent for in March or April to attend the great Ratification Meeting, held at the Epping Hall, now U.S. Court Room, when all the candidates for state offices would be present.

As might be expected, at that meeting there were much though well meant, doubtless, ill-timed and extravagant advice. I by a designed arrangement of some friends, at my own request, being kept till near the last, that I might learn the spirit and disposition of the speakers.

I advised my own race to moderation of action and sentiments, in all that they said and did, reminding them, that we are only one-sixth of the entire population of the country, that the white people are the ruling element of the nation, and must take the first rank, and would have the first and choice places, though we would get some; that in conceding rights to us, they had no intension to surrender their own; that whatever we claim for ourselves, we should take care not to interfere with the rights of others. That we must not in finding room for ourselves undertake to elbow the white people out of their places.

At the conclusion of my speech, there was a buzz in the great throng, and on passing out, many murmurs of disapproval of what I had said, spoiling many of the misguided radical harangues made that night, one gentleman, now a prominent leader, expressed himself aloud saying: "that man should never be permitted to hold office in this state!" The crowd of colored people speaking with expression of disapprobation of what I had said to them, because their radical leaders present, made them believe, that it was against their interests and rights. The adventurers even made them believe that I was against my own race, and had been sent to the meeting by the old planters in their interests. And such was my third offense, as they designedly interpreted.

---

1. This portion of the letter also appears in chapter 3, document 5.

FOURTH OFFENCE:

My fourth offence, consisted of a "Political Review," a letter addressed to you through the columns of the Charleston *Daily Republican*, dated August, 14th, 1871, from which the following are a few extracts:

> When reconstruction commenced, political leaders were greatly required, but few to be had. Southerners (the old masters) studiously opposed and refused to countenance reconstruction, and the freedmen were fearful and would not have trusted them if they could have obtained their aid.
>
> Those who came with or followed the army, with a very few native whites, were the only available political element to be had to carry out the measures of reconstruction.
>
> These were readily accepted by the blacks (by this I include the entire colored people) and the fullest confidence reposed in them. Some were or had been officers in the army. Some private, some sutlers, others peddlers and various tradesmen; others gamblers and even pickpockets, and "hangers-on" and "bummers". I am particularly speaking of the whites. Among them were men of refinement, educated gentlemen, and some very good men, but a large part of those active were of the lowest grade of northern society, negro haters at home, who could not have been elected to any position of honor or trust. Just such men as burnt down Negro orphan asylum and hung Negro men at lamp posts in the New York riot of 1853. In this review, I intend to speak plainly, call things by their right names, and look those of whom I speak directly in the face.
>
> The best and most competent men were chosen to fill the most important positions in state and local government, while the others readily obtained such places as required incumbents. Indeed there was scarcely one so incompetent as not to have been assigned some position of trust.
>
> Positioned in places of power, profit and trust, they soon sought by that guile and deception, known only to demagogues, under the acceptable appellations of Yankee, Republican and Radical, to intrude themselves into the confidence of the blacks, and place themselves at their head as leaders. So insidiously did they do this that it was not discovered by the few colored men of intelligence who held places among them till too late to remedy the fatal evil. These demagogues laid the foundation of their power upon a basis of the most dangerous political heresy. Deception, lying, cheating, chanting "whatever can be done in politics is fair," and to "beat is the duty in a political contest no matter what means were used to effect it," are among the pernicious precepts of this moral infidelity.

Jealous of the few intelligent colored men among them, they studiously sought to divide the blacks by sowing the seeds of discord among them. This was facilitated by prejudicing the ignorant against the intelligent.

These men strove and vied each with the other, regardless of consequence, to place himself in the lead of a community of blacks in both town and country, which in time was reduced to little else than a rabble mob of disorder and confusion. Trained in the Leagues as serfs to their masters, it became dangerous to oppose the teachings of these men of mischief. Because, having been recommended to their confidence at the commencement of reconstruction, their experience and knowledge in public men and matters were too limited to believe anything against them.

A knowledge of this emboldened these men to a persistence in their course of crime and corruption. Hence many otherwise, good men, both white and black, from age, inexperience or weakness were induced to accept the monstrous teachings and join with or follow the lead of these wretched imposters. Their sole object being personal gain, they cared little or nothing for public weal, the interest of the state or people, black or white, nor the Republican cause, upon which they had indecently imposed themselves. This is that which controlled Charleston politics and brought deserved defeat to the Republicans in the recent Municipal election. It was just retribution to a set of unprincipled miscreants, rioting on the people rights under the name of "Republicanism." Honest upright men of all parties, white and black, no longer able to bear it, determined to put down the abominable thing, leading Republicans, who had been standing aloof, taking an active part.

Among other things, they taught the simple-minded people that suffrage was inviolably secure, the blacks being in the majority, would always control the affairs of the state in the South; that the Fifteenth Amendment had abolished color and complexion in the United States, and the people were now all of one race. This bare faced deception was so instilled into them that it became dangerous in many instances to go into the country and speak of color in any manner whatever, without the angry rejoinder; "we don't want to hear that, we are all one color now!"

These ridiculous absurdities were fostered by the demagogues, the better to conceal their own perfidy and keep themselves in the best positions as "Republicanism knows no race," they taught.

Another imposition was that colored people did not require intelligent colored leaders; that the Constitution had been purged of color by a Radical Congress, and to be a Republican was all that was required to make a true representative. That mental culture and qualifications were only required by the proud and arrogant, that all who requested those accomplishments were enemies to both black and white, that race representation was making distinctions on account of race and color. By this means they opposed the qualified men among the blacks, encouraged the ignorant and less qualified. They might of necessity take the lead and occupy the best places in the party. These are plain indisputable truths which will not be denied by any upright intelligent Republican, black or white.

These strictures have no reference whatever to the intelligent, high-minded, upright gentlemen among the white Republicans, whose examples and precepts have aided in building up society and contributing to the public good, but especially, to that class who almost live in the quarters of the country people, and hamlets of the towns, among the black population, keeping them distracted with excitement, who are a curse to the community at large, and a blight in the body politic.

FIFTH OFFENCE:

The fifth offence, consisted in a pamphlet said to have been written by me, called "Political Battle Axe, For the Use of the Colored Men of the State of South Carolina in the Year 1872," by Kush. Even this, was referred to in Court on the Trial.

This pamphlet, was very widely circulated, was found in all parts of the state, and seems to have been simultaneously scattered through every county. Though it had an unknown author, it was at once attributed to me and created quite a sensation, much interest, and general murmuring. It had incorporated at the conclusion, a Constitution for the political guidance of a society called, "The Young Men's Progressive Association."

And this seems really to have been the first effective wedge in the ranks of the reckless radical republicanism in the state. As quickly following the appearance of the "Battle Axe" a "Progressive Association" among the young men was organized, and immediately thereafter, a scheme was set on foot, a committee of three hundred organized, a correspondence entered into with a learned and distinguished gentleman of the state of an opposition candidate, and all the details of a bolt completed, being the first suggestion of such a move in our state. This was politically known as the "Willard Movement" and gave great dissatisfaction to the regulars. "Vengeance" was then sworn against me.[2]

---

2. Delany did not deny authorship of the "Battle Axe." It seems curious that the sequence of events following its publication mimicked what Delany did in real life.

SIXTH OFFENCE:
My sixth offence was embodied in two letters addressed to a distinguished gentleman[3] of the black race occupying a high place in the state, (whom I refrain from naming here, as he took umbrage at the liberty of addressing my letter to him at the time) dated Feb. 10th, and March 17th, 1874, in which I advocated general amnesty, cumulative voting or minority representation, and cooperation in political actions by whites and blacks of the state, as the only guarantee against a displacement of the blacks by emigration, which would most certainly be encouraged to neutralize the political misrule of republicanism.

SEVENTH OFFENCE:
The letter written by me the same year, in reply to a committee of colored citizens, requesting my views in relation to a colored mayor for Charleston, in which I told them that the credit of the city would be blasted by destroying confidence everywhere in our financial and commercial relations. The state having been ruined under the suffrage of the colored race, the city of Charleston was the only part of it left, that gave us credit abroad, advising against any such movement, as the most impolitic that could at the time be set on foot.
And these offenses became magnified.

THE CROWNING OFFENCE:
The "Crowning act of infamy," an offence never to be forgiven, and sworn to be punished, was that on the fourth day of October, 1874, I dared receive the unanimous endorsement of the Conservative Convention sitting in Columbia, as the nominee for Lieutenant-Governor on the Independent Republican ticket, cooperating with conservatives. This was an offence unbearable, a sin never to be forgiven, and only to be remitted for by the most condign punishment.

THE AGGRAVATING OFFENCE:
After the election, in which the state came well nigh being carried for the conservatives, reducing the majority from forty thousand to ten, I went to New York City, and under the auspices of the most distinguished gentlemen for positions of, wealth, and education, in the most select and Aristocratic Hall in the great Metropolis (Irving Hall). I addressed a meeting presided over by Col. William Cullen Bryant, editor, scholar, poet and

---

3. This is a reference to Justice Jonathan Wright.

statesman, supported by the equally venerable Hon. Peter Cooper, the millionaire, Philanthropist, proprietor and donor of the great Cooper Institute, and many other distinguished gentlemen without regard to politics.

From this aggravation of a sin (the Conservative nomination) there was no redemption this side of the grave, and punished I must be even unto death!

Though seven years to this time have elapsed, since mustered out of my four years service as a major commanding the United States army, they have persistently opposed and prevented my nomination or appointment to any office, either state or federal, till I received the nomination of the Independent Republicans and Conservatives to the high and honorable position of Lieutenant-Governor of the state in 1874, and four months since, the office of Trial Justice, which I now hold. Crush me to earth, they were determined upon, and all because I could not be used, was above their influence, and would as I ever shall, oppose dishonesty, corruption and imposition upon the people's rights, under the disguised mockery of politics and law. "He has gone far enough, he shall be put down!" they said as I passed by the City Hall one day, shortly after returning from the North. The "Solicitor" was heard to bet that he would have me in the Penitentiary in two weeks after the meeting of the Court!

I shall not forget in this connection to acknowledge the generous course of Gen. H. G. Worthington, the Collector of the Port of Charleston, in tendering and appointing me, as Inspector of Customs, which I held till relinquished to run for the above mentioned office. This he did, in the face of the opposition of these very pretended Republicans.

TENTH AND MOST IRRITATING OFFENCE:
In the last Municipal election for Mayor and other officers of Charleston, I took an active part, conducting a weekly paper,[4] as the representative organ of the colored population, against fraud, and in favor of good government, closely contesting every inch of ground, and determinedly disputing every claim put forth. The close of the contest gave us the city government.

Many were the cunning and plausible devices brought in to this contest, well adapted to deceive, all of which were met and dispersed, routing our opponents with surprise and dismay, dispelling every hope of carrying the state, because of their failure in carrying the city.

In this, I was charged with having dealt a heavy hand, and for so grave an offense, I must pay the severest penalty known to the criminal law excepting death. And that would have been the penalty, could it legally have been inflicted.

---

4. This was the *Charleston Independent*.

GRAND LARCENY:

January 1871, I entered into a general business of Land Agency, and Land and Note Brokerage. The buying of state and county claims and pay certificates was a general business at that time, the investment being considered safe and good.

In April of that year, I was called upon to act as the Agent of Mrs. E. B. Richardson, and aid her in getting out letters of administration on the estate of her father, Telemachus Baynard, who died on John's Island. I did so, becoming an appraiser, with two other gentlemen, legally chosen.

On visiting the place to appraise the property, when about to return, we were informed that there were to hundred dollars in money in the house, said to be funds belonging to a religious society, of which the deceased was a trustee, holding the funds. The money was given in trust to me as the agent of Mrs. Richardson, to be accounted for to the society, at the same time it was stated, there had been much wrangling and quarrelling about the money. The men claiming to be trustees wanting to take it without responsibility, while the widow of the deceased refused to give it till her daughter came and took out letters of administration.

There had been as reported to me quite a stir among the members of the society concerning the funds, many objecting to them being delivered to the persons who made the demand. Several called upon me at different times, begging me to retain the money, till their dispute was settled. Using my discretion in the matter, I determined to secure it by investing it in county claims which at the time I was daily buying, for which I never paid less, but frequently more than fifty cents on the dollar. This I did, but supposing at the time, that the money would be realized in the fall of the fiscal year, as was expected by all who dealt at the time in this class of paper which mainly consisted in the monthly salaries of county employees, such as constables, deputy coroners, many of the deputy sheriffs, witnesses at courts, and jurors, till the rule of court by Judge Graham compelled the payment of jurors on the presentation of their tickets at the counter of the county treasurer, as the Judge's was paid.

After waiting in expectation and promises which are well remembered by all of the people of this county for these back payments, till the order came that none could be paid till special appropriation for the payment would be made by the legislature, and they began to depreciate to fifteen and twenty cents on the dollar. I had an injunction sued out and judgment, on one thousand and fifty-one dollars, all held in trust by me for others (except eighty dollars) for the express purpose of securing these funds at par and with interest, so that not a dollar of the assets could be lost by depreciation in value.

Mr. Sheriff Mackey who was a lawyer, obtained the injunction for me, at the same time that he obtained one for himself on twelve thousand or more dollars, these being the first suits entered against the county for those deficiencies.

An appropriation for these back claims, as is well known to all, was made, and all remember the first installment of sixty thousand dollars reported. And though mine was the second judgment on file in the Commissioner's and Treasurer's office, Col. Mackey received his twelve thousand dollars, and the remainder of the forty-eight thousand was exhausted, and not a cent paid on the one thousand and more dollars due to my claim. Another sixty thousand of that appropriation was received by the treasurer, and all paid out as before. And up to the present, from year to year, appropriations have been made for back claims against the county, and every other creditor preferred, when a simple rule of court as the late Hon. Judge Graham frequently promised, would only be necessary to obtain the payment of that judgment, in which is the sum of two thousand dollars of money belonging to the Wesley Society, which was the cause of this suit for Breach of trust and Grand Larceny.

And this material fact I desire to impress upon the public mind, that I never did use the money, invested it for safe keeping as the agent of the administratrix into whose hands it fell, till the people who claimed it settled their dispute, and secured it by injunction, and judgment to prevent the contingency of a loss, and IT IS THERE NOW SECURED by judgment, in the office of the Clerk of the Court.

I never claimed that judgment only as an agent in trust for others, and not as a party in interest, except eighty dollars as stated.

I subsequently offered to transfer from the judgment to the trustee Messrs. Brown and Rivers, the amount of the money I received, but they as frequently declined to accept saying that, "they did not understand these things." At one time in the summer of 1874, I took Mr. Brown to the door of the office of the Clerk in the Court House, to make the transfer, but he turned away saying that he would "see me again."

During the same season Dr. Webster (the head of this whole matter) called on me at the Custom House where I was an Inspector of Customs, when I went directly to the Court House with him to make the transfer to the amount of the money invested, where the judgment or claims on file were shown to him by Mr. Lee, one of the clerks. Mr. Winkler being out just at the time, but Mr. Webster seeming satisfied as was thought, at seeing that there was a judgment secured, would not wait.

There are two other material points of fact to which I invite the public attention, to the last of which Mr. Lee, the clerk referred to, will testify.

The encumbrance of two hundred dollars placed upon the judgment by a law firm against me, was done without my knowledge or consent, and evidently in anticipation of this suit to embarrass me. I protest that I knew nothing about it and the parties who entered it know that I did not. Yet it was declared to the jury that I had it done in my own interest and had actually sold this to satisfy a debt against me. The transfers made to Messrs. A. G. Coleman, E. G. Schwartz and Sampson Green, it was declared from the same source to the jury, were portions of the judgment sold off by me to these parties, when they were all original claimants in the judgment to the amount received by each of them, I holding for the two, first on their own account, and on account of Sampson Green for Mrs. Richardson, the administratrix.

To the latter, A. T. Smythe, Esq., can confirm, as Green, through him, sued on his transcript from the judgment, when he satisfied himself that I was not his debtor, but simply the agent of another. And to conclude this part of my statements, I should not neglect to say, that to Messrs. Campbell and Whaley, through whom Mr. Webster sued for the Church, I several times offered and urged them to accept of a transfer from the judgment to them, their share of the money claimed by the trustees, but they declined to settle the matter in that way. But I believe that they never obtained judgment against me. That perhaps is the reason they declined to accept the transfer.

I should here state that the same person, Dr. Webster, sent me a postal card of intimidation (Political) stating that he was coming out with a newspaper, and if I did not comply with his demand in paying the money, he would attack my character. He did so, as during the canvas, a few weeks later, about ten days before the election, he published a letter in his paper, over his own initials, accusing me with robbing a Church! This letter was hastily read at all of their political gatherings.

THE LAW SUIT:

I left New York after the middle of May of last year, 1875, after spending some weeks North endeavoring to enlighten the people of both races as to the true state of our political affairs, the causes, the character of the people whom we desire to come into the state, and those whom we did not want. My course and position while absent were well known at home, because the leading papers wherever I spoke, noticed my speeches, some of which were noticed here as I am informed.

I had arrived but a short time in Charleston, till this suit was entered in a Trial Justice office against me for Breach of Trust and Grand Larceny by this Rev. Alonzo W. Webster, D.D., he making two or three black men make the affidavit, these black men being local preachers under him, he being the presiding elder.

From October 1875, it was continued to the next or February term of the Court of General Sessions, 1876.

THE TRIAL ... PANELING A JURY:

A handsome little black child, about four or five years of age was led by a black man, an employee of the Sheriff's office, into the court room, and seated on a chair at the table. The solicitor entered immediately after announcing that he was ready.

The child was stood up on the chair by the same black official who led it into the court room, and directed to take a ballot, when with child-like innocence it was bent to thrust in his hand, when it was seized by the official with an admonition, which did not require to be repeated, as at each drawing the child carefully inserted its hand leaning and peeping into the hat that it might be certain not to disturb the arrangement till the panel was complete. In this case a special panel was drawn, though I was willing to accept of either of the two fixed juries Nos. 1 and 2, as they stood on the general panel or venire. I never before understood a packed jury.

THE TESTIMONY:

It is not my purpose here to sift the testimony of those who were trained to swear against me, as the fact that I was convicted on the statements herein set forth of my transactions in the money matter, makes its own comment beyond a controversy. A more shameful misstatement, misrepresentation, and barefaced perversion of truth, never was perpetrated in a court of justice. Falsehood after falsehood was declared by one of the witnesses, and shamefully reiterated by the counsel for the prosecution. It is enough to make one shudder and the flesh to creep on its bones, to contemplate the reckless perversion of truth, exhibited on that occasion. It was a deep seated conspiracy, with a determination to crush me, and everything was resorted to, in furtherance of that end.

THE SOLICITORS:

The state, the nation, the world at large should know, the point at which the Charleston Bar, of which a Wardlaw, a Duncan, an O'Neil, a Petigru, and such lights of learning and literature, with their compeers both dead and living, once members, has arrived in the progress of such legal management as that of the present prosecuting attorney.

This functionary, without comparison, I venture to state, in Belle letters literature and forensic eloquence, a specimen of which I shall give, that people abroad may understand the character of those by whom we are now mastered; commenced his pleading by the declaration, that of fourteen years at the bar, it was the happiest moment of his life. That he never felt so strong in all his life before, because he had for the first time before him, the very character he wanted.

Then, in a tirade of an unbroken stain of full one half hour, of low, coarse and vulgar abuse, of sneers and jeers, of jibes and butts, and mockery, at my pretended respectability, integrity, morality, learning and veracity; placing himself squarely before me, with extended arm, his fingers nearly touching my nose, with all the vehemence which he could command, he three times exclaimed as I give it here, increasing the emphasis to the climax as he observed the smiles of sanction in the countenances of his jury as they glanced with nods of the head at each other: "You tell a DAMNED INFERNAL LIE! It is a DAMNED INFERNAL LIE!! You are a DAMNED INFERNAL LIAR!!!" This was the language of the solicitor of the Charleston Bar, in open court, in a plea which by his own admission, was the greatest thing that he ever made, and the happiest hour of his life! What have not the Charlestonians been reduced to? Have they a Modoc Indian at the head of their Bar?

THE JURY:

The following is the list of names of the jury which convicted me, all respectable men, one of whom stooped whispering into the ear of a lawyer who passed out from the jury box: "He's good for the penitentiary!" They returning in less than ten minutes with a verdict of guilty.

E. R. Cowperthwait, Foreman
Daniel B. Dupont
D. P. Johnstone
EDWARD WESTON
JOHN CROSS
THOMAS M. HOLMES
Alva Gage
BENJAMIN MONCRIEF
Edward N. Wilson
HENRY ARTOPE
Benjamin S. Roper
G. W. Klinck.

There was one remarkable coincidence about these gentlemen, all of them happened to be those who are opposed to the election of Mayor Cunningham, whom I supported, and did much toward the defeat of the candidate which they supported. And some of them were candidates for offices of honor or profit, on their side hence, I had aided in their defeat!

History shall have their names. Their verdict was a foregone conclusion. Those in capitals are all colored men. ALBUS ET NIGER OMNIA FRATER NOBILE.

THE SENTENCE:

Some time was spent on the day of sentence in searching out points of law on the motion made by my learned and able counsel, E. E. Seabrook, Esq. I requested the sentence if it had to come, as his honor was refused the motions.

"I should prefer to find some law if possible to avert a sentence. Indeed, it will give me a great deal of pleasure if I could!" said the Judge. "But it would only be nominal," said his honor, "as to take an appeal to the Supreme Court, has made a sentence necessary."

There was but one object on the part of those who brought on this base and shameful prosecution at the head of whom was this man Webster, and this so-called solicitor, which was to disgrace me so in the estimation of the respectable native white citizens who had supported me for the second office in the state, that they would henceforth discard me, and by the telling of the blacks that I was sent to the state's prison, I could never again have political influence enough to check them in their deception and imposition.

With the same faithful adherence to the cause of universal liberty as in ANTE BELLUM days, shall I continue to advocate the rights of the whole people of the state, without regard to race, color, or politics, if doing so, it shall necessitate the driving of such wretches into their native haunts, never more to be seen among respectable men.

PERSONAL:

I believe that his honor the Judge, was deceived from the first by this solicitor, and did not till after judgment, really understand the true state of the case.

And I here take pleasure in recording the generous course of Col. Bowen, the Sheriff, who refrained from the exercise of his authority over me during the entire trial. Also to his gentlemanly assistant, the first deputy Sheriff, Mr. Dingle, who treated me in like manner. And to Mr. John Bonnin, sub-deputy, for uniform attentions in the court room during the entire proceedings, also to Mr. Dover, a sub-deputy. Both of the latter being men of my own race.

A conspiracy to send an innocent citizen to the state prison for the purpose of disgracing and humiliating him to destroy his political influence, is one of the greatest as well as the meanest and most cowardly outrages ever perpetrated in a civilized country; and the men who could aid in so vile an act, are capable of anything dishonorable to accomplish their ends.

They are moral assassins, unequalled by any KU-KLUX however vile, cruel and revolting; the creatures and offshoots of a terrible conspiracy, a hydra-headed monster, whose heart is in Orangeburg, and its body entwined and coiled through every community in the state, with its vilest hideous head in Charleston.

This conspiracy is in waiting for the citizens, whom those vile wretches hate, and have attempted upon others and failed, I being their first victim. The outrage is fearful and too monstrous to be a reality. The serpent must be driven from its lair.

Now let them succeed and go on in this last scheme of prosecution of theirs to hold the reins of power, and keep their feet on the people of the South, by using our race as the political instrument of their oppression, let them continue to promote strife between the races, the eye of the whole North and West being already turned in this direction, and their minds made up, and the first occasion for the murmur of a conflict of races, and the whole country will rise up and rush to arm with such force and power, that Sherman's invasion compared with which, would be but children's school play.

Extermination will be their theme
Their watch-word, "Every Negro in the grave!"
Until from Withlacooche's stream
To where the Rio Grande laves;
One simultaneous war cry,
Will bust upon the midnight air;
And rouse the black man, but to die!
Midst weeping, wailing and despair!

When our race, shall only be remembered among the things of the past! And it is for us, I mean the colored men of leading intelligence, to avert this dreadful; this fearful thing in time.
M. R. Delany
To Hon. Frederick Douglass
(to be printed in pamphlet form)

SOURCE: Martin R. Delany, *Trial and Conviction of Martin R. Delany*, unpublished pamphlet (Charleston, SC, 1876).

DOCUMENT 2
The Charges against M. R. Delany

Several newspapers, noticing the recent conviction of Martin R. Delany on the charge of grand Larceny, have forthwith proceeded to brand him a thief and hypocrite, and a bright and shining example of the insincerity of Republican "reform". The bare fact that Mr. Delany received the votes of almost all the conservatives in South Carolina last year, for an important office, should have induced his critics to inform themselves fully as to the truth of the case, before accepting the mere issue of a trial, in these days, as conclusive proof of guilt on the part of the accused. We have been for a long while conversant with the facts of the transaction in question, which have been published in this paper; and the issue of the trial does not alter our conviction that the accused is honest, that he attempted no fraud, and that recent action had its origin in political differences and was prosecuted with partisan zeal.

The whole record of Col. Delany, from the beginning of the Reconstruction process, has been creditable to him and diametrically opposed to that of his political enemies. He has never failed to urge moderation on the part of his race, an alliance with whites, and an utter repudiation of worthless adventurers and low demagogues. He has been a stumbling block in the way of Ring leaders, and they wish to be rid of him.

The facts of the transaction which led to Delany's trial are about as follows: In 1871 Delany established a general land and commission agency. The purchase of State and County claims was, at that time, a general business, the investment being considered good. In April of that year a fund of two hundred dollars was placed in his hands, as agent of a Mrs. Richardson, for a religious society, of which her husband had been trustee. There had been wrangling as to the proper person to receive the money, and Delany was requested to hold it. He invested it in County claims, expecting them to be paid in the fall with the other claims. Subsequently payment of the claims was refused, without special legislation. The claims began to decline in value. Delany then sued out an injunction, and judgment was entered for $1,131; all except $80, being held in trust by him for others, in order to secure these claims at par with interest so that not a dollar should be lost by depreciation. This judgment, and one obtained by Sheriff Mackey for $12,000, were the first obtained against the county. An appropriation for $60,000 was made for these claims, and though Delany's judgment was second, he received nothing. Another appropriation of the same amount was paid out over his head. Subsequent judgments have been made in the same way, and still this judgment is unsatisfied. It is still secured by judgment in the office of the Clerk of Court of Charleston County. The $200 entrusted to Delany by Mrs. Richardson is included in this judgment. Delany subsequently offered to transfer the judgment to the trustees of the society, but they refused to accept it. Similar offers were several times made and refused. A law firm placed an encumbrance of $200 upon the judgment for a claim against Col. Delany. The persons to whom transfers of parts of the judgment were made were all original owners. The attorneys for the Church refused to accept a transfer of that part of the judgment which covered its claims.

It is for the alleged wrongful conversion of this money that the action was brought. On the trial the solicitor was so abusive and vindictive as to be rebuked by the court. The testimony adduced was remarkable, and the whole matter seems to have been a well organized scheme to betray the Court and jury into wronging an innocent man. There is hardly a man in South Carolina who has had the money of others in his possession, and invested it for safe-keeping, who could not be charged with fraud with as much reason as Delany was. No doubt he was and is liable for the money and judgment for the amount has been recovered against him. But there was no ground for criminal prosecution.

We trust that those papers which have published the fact of Delany's conviction will do him the justice to explain what were the circumstances. That he is a colored man and a Republican, and out of favor with "the Party", is additional reason why unusual consideration should be shown him in his undeserved trouble.

SOURCE: *News and Courier* (Charleston), March 23, 1876.

DOCUMENT 3

C. C. BOWEN TO GOV. D. H. CHAMBERLAIN

Charleston, S.C.
April 3rd, 1876.

Hon. D. H. Chamberlain
Governor,

I would respectfully recommend the pardon of Maj. Delany lately convicted in the Court of Sessions of Breach of Trust, he having signified his willingness to pay over the amount due to the society to which it belongs, and having deposited in my hands the sum of two hundred and five dollars ($205.00) the amount due, which upon his request for

executive clemency being granted, will be immediately turned over to the Trustees of the said society.
Very Respectfully
Your Obedient Servant
C. C. Bowen.

SOURCE: Daniel H. Chamberlain Papers, Box 11, Folder 33, South Carolina Department of Archives and History, Columbia.

DOCUMENT 4

The State vs. Martin R. Delany
JUDGE'S RECOMMENDATIONS

In view of the former good character of the defendant, and a doubt that may be reasonably entertained as to whether he acted with a fraudulent intent in the breach of Trust which he was convicted, I recommend that the imprisonment in the penitentiary to which he was sentenced, be remitted and pardoned, upon condition that he first pay to the Trustees of the John Wesley Church, the sum of money which he consented, Two hundred and ten dollars—with interest from the date of conversion, and also the cost of the prosecution, that the Church and the County may be saved harmless.
J. P. Reed
Judge 1st Circuit
April 27th, 1876.

SOURCE: Daniel H. Chamberlain Papers, Box 14, Folder 16, South Carolina Department of Archives and History, Columbia.

DOCUMENT 5

PETITION FOR DELANY'S PARDON

Charleston, S.C.
August 19, 1876.

To his,
Excellency D. H. Chamberlain,
Governor of South Carolina,
Hon. Sir,

We the undersigned colored citizens of Charleston County, most humbly petition as ask your Excellency attention and consideration to the unfortunate situation of our friend, "Brother" and "Companion" COL. M. R. Delany. We some months ago sent to your Excellency a petition based on certain conditions for his pardon (namely the paying of certain moneys $282.00). Two hundred and eighty two dollars, at that time, if your Excellency will please to look among the papers sent to you, you will find a letter from the Hon. C. C. Bowen, telling your Excellency that the money for the Wesley Chapel was paid, and was in his hands, waiting for the Trustees to forward receipt for and receive the same. The Trustees did go and have receipted for the money and their receipts if not in your possession, are in the hands of C. C. Bowen, and have kept back for reason best known to him (C.C.B.). M. R. Delany is dear to us, whatever may be his faults, and if we had the money we would willingly pay, YES a thousand times over, rather than seeing him going to the penitentiary. Some of us are public officers, doubtless you are aware, of the County affairs, for paying her creditors, but a large number of your petitioners have no money and find it hard at this time to make daily bread for ourselves and families, we can safely say that two-thirds (2/3) of the people of Charleston today are living on one meal per day, but we hope, the above clause will not be wanted to impress you with our unfortunate condition for that is not the subject which compels us to ask of you, and from the interposition of your executive clemency in his behalf, we want and only want Delany pardoned. The record of the Court will show that the money originally sued for, and claimed by the Wesley Church of John's Island, is today in the hands of the Court. M. R. Delany, Governor, happened to be one of the few of our Race of whom, we are proud to claim, we have waited long to hear of you on the letter of C. C. Bowen, we trust that you will soon relieve us of our painful anxiety by an early reply, being satisfied that its issue is sufficient to justify you in granting the pardon prayed for by your petitioners, and believing and hoping it will come.
We have the honor to subscribe ourselves,
Your Excellency, Constituency and Petitioners
George E. Johnston
Aaron Logan.

SOURCE: Daniel H. Chamberlain Papers, Box 14, Folder 4, South Carolina Department of Archives and History, Columbia.

DOCUMENT 6
Rev. N. N. Hunter to Delany

CHARLESTON, S.C.
APRIL 22, 1876.

Mr. Martin R. Delany,

Sir; this will inform you, that unless the persons money on Jas Island is returned them by you, in both cases, that in which they had books given them by you, and also have the money returned them in the matter of the flash tract of land—that at the next term of the Court of Gen. Session they will commence proceedings at law in such cases made and provided against you. A number of these persons as you are aware are members of the Presbyterian Church on the Island whose cause were brought before and heard by the late R. C. Delarge, Esq., and you. Then promised us (I as their friend) that you would soon return them their money. Now it must be returned without further delay.

Rev. N. N. Hunter.

SOURCE: Daniel H. Chamberlain Papers, Box 12, Folder 2, South Carolina Department of Archives and History, Columbia.

DOCUMENT 7
Delany to W. R. Jones, Esq.

Secretary to Gov. Chamberlain

Charleston, S.C.
May 18th 1876.

W. R. Jones, Esq.,
Private Secretary.
Sir,

I have the honor to state that the day before E. A. Seabrook, Esq., my counsel left Columbia, he showed me the letter from his Excellency through you to him, concerning which he was to call upon his Excellency, after which write me.

As I have not heard from him, I desire to comply with what was implied in your letter in reference to myself.

In regard to Mr. Hunter's statement, the James Island officer of which he speaks, I had no direct transaction with any people there about land. I leased a place from Mr. Julius T. Moses—the Hunt Plantation—subletted it through

Dr. W. G. King, their Agent in the place, to whom I receipted for the money paid in the name of said person; the people who rented and were on the place where they had been for years, and still are, measured out their own land, farmed it, continued on the place, and I never before the day I received a note from Hunter, noted the same day of that sent to his Excellency, had I ever heard or known, that there was a word of complaint or discontent. The reception of the note from Hunter completely surprised me.

The Johns Island matter which he refers to, is the same which is now secured by Judgment with that Church money, in the office of the C.C. of Charleston County, and for which I have no responsibility whatever, never having had any transactions with these people directly, never having seen them, only as the woman Mrs. Richardson, with whom they traded, brought them to me as her agent, to have their business adjusted.

Mrs. Richardson (now Mrs. Moultire) was once sued through Hunter by these people before DeLarge, when I was summoned as a witness and what came of the matter, I never heard—except that he never tendered a decision—till I received this note from Hunter. His statement that I "promised to pay them" is a gratuity, as logically false as it is morally wrong and unjust.

The whole thing has been manufactured for an occasion and purpose which is apparent; and why, I do not know, as I always heretofore, treated him with the respect and deference due his position and pretensions.

Please convey to his Excellency, the contents of this note and the assurance with which,
I have the honor to be, Sir,
Your most obedient servant,
M. R. DELANY.

SOURCE: Daniel H Chamberlain Papers, Box 12, Folder 23, South Carolina Department of Archives and History, Columbia.

DOCUMENT 8
R. S. THARIN TO GOV. D. H. CHAMBERLAIN

Charleston, S.C.
June 1, 1876.

Gov. D. Chamberlain,
Your Excellency will doubtless remember that I made formal application for the office of Trial Justice of Ward No. three in this city; but that, for executive reason, no appointment was then to be made.

Afterwards, Major Delany, your opponent in the canvass received the appointment for reasons sufficient in your Excellency's judgment, with which I imagine not.

Now in today's "News", I see local showing Delany's reliance upon his position as derived from your Excellency's appointment.

Grant was removed by executive proclamation, and subsequent events have placed Delany on no higher level than that which Grant occupied in Court.

If your Excellency, for reasons of State, should retain Delany, of course I am still an outsider. But, I think, I may very respectfully suggest that I am ready to accept the office should it become vacant by Death, Resignation, or any other cause, which would leave your Excellency in a situation to make the appointment.

The same objection as to time of appointment would hardly inhere, and the letters of Col. Simms, Major Gayer, and the petition for the office signed by Judge Bryan, Gen. Simms and Hon. G. G. Magrath have been forwarded to the executive office. Some of the documents went up during your Excellency's absence from Carolina.

I have the honor,
Your Excellency,
To be, and remain, with highest consideration,
Your Excellency's obedient servant
R. S. Tharin.

SOURCE: Daniel H. Chamberlain Papers, Box 12, Folder 34, South Carolina Department of Archives and History, Columbia.

DOCUMENT 9
DELANY TO W. R. JONES

Secretary to Gov. Chamberlain

Dear Sir,

I have the honor to acknowledge the receipt of the note dated the 3rd and post-marked the 5th, this morning.

I thank his Excellency for the opportunity of writing him directly on this subject, as I have been concerned and perplexed about the delay, as the matter was in the hands of "Friends" who volunteered to do those acts of kindness for me, which it was reasonable to suppose could be much easier accomplished, as well as more agreeable than I could, for which I thanked them most kindly.

It has been several weeks since—more than a month, I am certain—that they informed me, that they had in hand the receipt of the Trustees of the Church, and the Certificate of Clerk of Court. And I am certain that more than two months ago, I gave to my friends my note for the money to be paid to the Trustees, as I had no money, and they thus proposed to pay for me, and to be my obligation.

On frequent inquiry I would learn that the receipt has not been sent his Excellency, but could not exactly learn the cause of delay. Of course, this gave me uneasiness, but I could not intrude myself between his Excellency and the gentlemen with whom he was in communication and institute an enquiry, as though I had no confidence in them. I had and did fully confide in their integrity in offering me their friendship.

I saw after the reception of your note today, one who had communicated between me and the others in this matter, showed him the note and stated my ultimatum, which is that I shall proceed immediately among my friends of another party—as I have not got means within myself—to raise the money necessary to meet these requirements, and communicate directly through you with his Excellency on the subject. It shall be attended to at once by myself in person, and I shall wait no longer on friends.

I should say to his Excellency in justice to myself, that I once raised this money since this litigation ended to meet these demands, when it was placed in the hands of a party who volunteered to attend to it as a friend—two weeks previous to the offering of these gentlemen now acting for me—but instead of paying it in my behalf, they expended it in paying on a mortgage against real estate of theirs!

This was severe on me, but of course I had to bear it, and could not disclose it on my account so as not to expose them.

I shall hope to communicate in a few days my progress in, to me, very important and very delicate matter.

Please make known to his Excellency immediately, the contents of this communication, and the assurance of my high appreciation of the favor he designed in writing me.
I have the honor to be sir,
Your most obedient servant
M. R. Delany.

Source: Daniel H. Chamberlain Papers, Box 13, Folder 13, South Carolina Department of Archives and History, Columbia.

DOCUMENT 10
THE STATE VS. M. R. DELANY
FRAUDULENT BREACH OF TRUST AND GRAND LARCENY
PARDON GRANTED

The defendant was convicted of fraudulent Trust and Grand Larceny at February 1876 term of Court of General Sessions for Charleston County and sentenced to twelve months imprisonment in the penitentiary. The facts of the case seemed to be these: that the sum of about two hundred and ten dollars was placed in his hands in trust for Wesley Church, a religious society in John's Island which sum he invested in his own name in County warrants. Said warrants were not paid by the county and with other similar claims were sued on and judgment against the county obtained. Said judgment is still unsatisfied. The petition sets forth the previous good character of the defendant and the fact that the fraudulent intent was not proven.

His Honor Judge Reed states that in view of the former good character of the defendant and a doubt that may be reasonably entertained as to whether he acted with a fraudulent intent in the breach of trust which he was convicted, I recommend that the imprisonment in the Penitentiary to which he was sentenced be remitted and pardoned, upon condition that he first pay to the trustees of the John Wesley Church the sum of money which he consented, <u>two hundred and ten dollars</u>, with interest from the date of the conversion and also the cost of the prosecution that the Church and the County may be saved harmless.

The Sheriff of Charleston County having certified to me that the said has been placed in the hands of the Trustees of the said Church, I hereby grant the pardon.

SOURCE: Daniel H. Chamberlain Papers, Box 14, Folder 16, South Carolina Department of Archives and History, Columbia.

DOCUMENT 11
DELANY TO GOV. D. H. CHAMBERLAIN

Charleston, South Carolina
September 1st 1876.

Governor Chamberlain
Sir,
Many thanks to your Excellency for great and beneficent favors.

The first thing now to be done should be the <u>securing</u> of your <u>nomination</u> by the Convention.

This I think can be done through the chairman of the State Executive Committee. General Elliott and I are personal friends. Though we differ in political matters and I wish that I can do more with him than most any other colored man in the state, when I have occasion to approach him on any matter of public policy of interest.

He knows that I am sincere in all of my measures, do not dissemble, have no duplicity, and therefore, he always listens with respectful attention to my propositions. I must have an interview with him immediately, to show him the importance of putting you in nomination, which I think he will adhere to.

I did not see him when here, as I did not desire to do so, preferring to confer with him at home.

I regret that I am so circumstrained in consequence of my position, that I cannot command means as I should, and as the respectable men do generally. But if I could obtain a thousand mile R.R. tickets, so that I can hold frequent interviews with him, I believe that I can be instrumental in getting the General to favor the measure.

I shall not be in the convention, as I never have been in one as a delegate, but have always as an outside influence among the people, which was effective in many measures of policy before the conventions.

If the suggestion be favorable in your opinion, and it be your pleasure, please let me hear from you at your Excellency's earliest convenience.
I have the honor to be sir,
Your most obedient servant
M. R. Delany.
P.S.

As I have commenced Business, I shall of necessity have to make frequent short visits in whatever form of canvassing as many do, hence the most favorable facilities for transportation by R.R.
M. R. D.

Source: Daniel H. Chamberlain Papers, Box 14, Folder 18, South Carolina Department of Archives and History, Columbia.

CHAPTER 6

A New Departure

Introduction

Delany's pledge to remain faithful to the Republican Party and work for Chamberlain's reelection was dated September 1, 1876. Less than three weeks later, Delany was nominated president of a National Independent Organization of Colored Men, a movement formed by a group of black conservatives opposed to Radical Reconstruction and working to support Democrats in the coming election. His presidency would extend to states "south of North Carolina," including South Carolina, Georgia, Alabama, Mississippi, Louisiana, and Florida. Document 1 is Delany's letter accepting the nomination and outlining his vision for the movement. He depicted it as a movement for reconciliation with southern whites and the promotion of racial harmony. He stressed the need for blacks and whites to work together (via the triple alliance of land, labor, and capital) for mutual benefits. Delany envisioned the emergence of "one great southern party" of both races working together and unified in mutual love and respect; blacks and whites working together "conceding and supporting each other's just and legal claims." The result, he hoped, would be a union of "one people and one party" committed to the development of the nation.

With the National Independent Organization nomination, Delany's switch to the Democratic Party seemed a fait accompli. He became actively involved in the activities of a growing number of Colored Democratic Clubs. The emergence of these clubs in several counties in South Carolina shows that Delany's disaffection with Radical Republican rule was not an aberration, though it was unpopular. Documents 2 and 3 are reports of meetings of the Colored Democratic Clubs of Wards 3 and 4. Delany addressed both meetings, reiterating his call for racial harmony and appealing to blacks to switch allegiance to the Democratic Party and work for the election of its gubernatorial candidate, Wade Hampton. He also explained why he joined the Democratic Party. He insisted that Democrats had changed. He described Democrats as honest and faithful people who could be trusted to keep their campaign promises with regards to respecting and protecting the rights of blacks. The Democratic Party had launched a campaign platform that promised to uphold and respect the rights and privileges of blacks. This was Delany's primary consideration for switching political affiliation.

Delany became actively involved as a campaign speaker for the Democrats. Document 4 is an excerpt from a campaign rally at which Delany delivered speeches accusing Radical Republicans of a litany of offenses, including exploiting blacks, misrepresenting the Democratic Party, and fomenting racial discord in the South. He denounced Republicans for exploiting and perpetuating black ignorance to enhance their political power. In a curious revision of history, Delany contended that blacks had been misled and misinformed into equating Democrats with slavery. He called on blacks and whites in South Carolina to unite solidly in support of Wade Hampton and the Democratic Party. He reiterated that, if elected, Democrats would keep their campaign pledges. He believed that the Democratic Party would establish a government that would restore confidence in the state economy. Such confidence was only possible through racial harmony, and in Delany's view, only one party would promote this goal—Democratic Party. Document 5 is an article in the Columbia *Daily Register* (a conservative paper) commending Delany for his crusade for racial harmony, describing him as "the most original, correct and forcible thinker among the Negroes of this country." The writer called on blacks to heed Delany's warnings and abandon the Republican Party.

Democrats won the 1876 election and the ensuing compromise left blacks in South Carolina and in the entire South without the protective presence of the federal government. For a brief period, it seemed Delany's optimism would be vindicated. Among few blacks appointed to offices by Governor Hampton, he was reappointed to the trial justice position in Charleston. But this honeymoon was not destined to last. Ultra-conservative members of the

Democratic Party who had strategically assumed a low-key posture during the election campaign quickly seized control of the government and unleashed a reign of terror on blacks, particularly those in positions of political authority whose responsibilities and aspirations seemed to challenge the status quo of white supremacy. Delany was not spared. Documents 6 and 7 are petitions for the removal of Delany as trial justice on grounds of incompetence. The petitioners alleged that he was "unfit for the office" and that he administered the position in "a manner disreputable to the present administration of the State." Delany wrote to Governor Wade Hampton to challenge the allegations and requested the opportunity to vindicate himself (doc. 8). Delany was, however, not without his supporters. A group of thirty-one Charleston citizens sent a counter-petition to Governor Hampton in support of Delany's retention, describing Delany as "cool, deliberate" and of "broad experience" (doc. 9). The petitioners denounced the call for Delany's removal as politically motivated.

With the ultraconservatives (or Redeemers, as they referred to themselves) in full control of the government in South Carolina, nothing could stem the tide of reprisals against black officeholders and blacks in general. South Carolina had become inhospitable for blacks. They increasingly turned toward emigration, inaugurating a Liberian exodus movement. In response to the petition for and counter-petition against his removal, Delany joined and became actively involved in the exodus movement, thus returning to his old back-to-Africa scheme. Documents 10, 11, and 12 embody his contributions to the movement. The first was a letter Delany, now relieved of his position as trial justice and in his capacity as chairman of the Committee on Finance, Warehouse, and Transportation and a member of the board of directors of the Liberia Exodus Joint Stock Steamship Company, wrote to H. R. Latrobe, president of the American Colonization Society, to request assistance for the movement. Specifically, Delany asked for help with a loan of $1,680 to enable the company to pay off its bank loans and thus remain solvent.

The last two letters are addressed to William Coppinger, also of the American Colonization Society. By this time Delany had vacated his official positions within the exodus movement but remained a member. He discussed at length his ordeal with Radical Republican persecution in South Carolina and the difficult position he now found himself in. He recalled how he had been victimized for his anti-radical political views and rendered jobless and poverty-stricken. He reiterated his determination to relocate to Africa and requested some financial assistance. He recalled how in the late 1850s he had planned to relocate to Africa until his plans were interrupted by the Civil War. Delany specifically requested assistance with securing employment that would give him steady income with which to realize his dream of returning to

Africa. The first letter to Coppinger was dated August 18, 1880. By December, it was clear that Delany had not received any positive response. He then wrote a second letter dated December 18, to which he attached his war records and pleaded for help with securing the job of "Door Keeper of the US Senate." Delany received no job offers from the Senate.

DOCUMENT 1

The Black Man's Political Movement: Delany to Rev. Garland H. White

Charleston, S.C.
September 18, 1876.

Rev. Garland H. White
Halifax, N.C.

MY DEAR SIR—Your communication to me came some time since, conveying the request of the National Independent Organization of Colored Men, that I should accept of the Presidency of all the states South of North Carolina, was duly received and favorably replied to, when I promised to set forth my acceptance through the column of some public journal. Circumstances, not herein necessary to name, have prevented till recently my doing so.

In such an organization by the colored men of the country the first step should be guided by wisdom, with care and caution. One miss and unguarded step might be fatal. We are not to set up ourselves as the censors of a government and critics of a constitution organized by an assemblage of as wise men as have been known to modern civilization; nor, through ignorance, assail Democracy nor Republicanism; the two fundamental and greatest principles which can underlie any government. It is only the perversion of these principles with which we have to deal, and the abuse of them that is the subject of complaint.

By the National Independent Party, as I understand it, the object is to form an organization composed solely of colored men for the express purpose of protecting their interests as a race, regardless of either of the old party ties. What they have to look to is not the promotion of these old party interests, but the harmonization of our race as a race with the race originally comprising both of the old parties. We have more vital interests at stake than simply Democracy and Republicanism, as these have been made safe and secured to us by the constitutional provisions of the Thirteenth, Fourteenth and Fifteenth Amendments.

The nation is now composed of two great political race elements, whites and blacks; and of two great sectional divisions, North and South. These divisions, before the war, were different in their industrial, social and political relations; the Southern section being designated as "peculiar institution," the constituent representation of the South being based on a different elementary ratio to that of the North. This, then, was the constitutional compromise for the promotion of harmony in the country.

Of the two races, the greater part of one, the African or our race, belongs to the South, who, comprising the agricultural element, are the producers of the rich and important staples of this section of the country. We, then, produce the labor, and the white race the capital; we are the laborers and they are the capitalists. Capital and labor must go together; and without harmony and mutual association they cannot be available.

What should be our line of duty, then, both black and white? Why, as before the war the Southern section had its peculiar institutions, social and political, let us now, after the war, have the same nominal institutions adapted to the change and new state of things, by the clasping of hands, and a combination of the two races in one great Southern party, based on the common interest of all the people of both races, inseparably connected, regarding and respecting alike each other's rights, conceding and supporting each other's just and legal claims, promoting peace, friendship and confidence, till we shall be in our domestic relations only known as one people and one party in interest, developing the rich resources of the soil scarcely yet commenced.

If this be the object of the Independent Party to unite in one common interest, industrial and political, in each State, both races in the South, regardless of the two old political parties in either sections of the country, then am I with you always, even to the end. We must be the judges of our own interests and leaders of our own race. In national politics, each race may use their own judgment as to the candidate they may support.

I am, dear sir, with the deepest heartfelt interest in this movement, your friend, and that of both races.
M. R. Delany.

SOURCE: *News and Courier* (Charleston), September 19, 1876.

DOCUMENT 2
The Campaign in the City: The Colored Democracy of Ward 4

A successful meeting of the Colored Democratic Club of the Fourth Ward was held at the Club room in Mazyck Street last evening, and some real wholesome doctrines were advanced by leading colored men.

J. Chaplin, the President stated that its object was for the purpose of discussing the best means of bringing the colored people to a sense of their situation and their duty, if for no other reason than their own self-preservation, to vote for Hampton and reform.

Col. Martin R. Delany was then introduced and, in a quiet and conversational style, made a characteristic speech, during the course of which he said that from his advent into political life he had advised the colored people to strike hands with their native white people, whose interests were identical with theirs. The two races constituted the elements of government—they are inseparably connected—and, unless they live in harmony, it would be impossible for them to live usefully together. The present movement, headed by Gen. Hampton, was of great importance to the colored people, and the expressions of Gen. Hampton and his supporters on the ticket went to show that they meant equal rights to all. He had, he said, been struck with the opening of Col. Simpson's remarks at Marion, where he said: "I see before me today beautiful women, gray-haired, Sires and gallant men, both white and black," showing by this simple expression that he, the candidate for Lieutenant-Governor on the Democratic ticket, thought it no detraction to the brave soldiers before him to include and recognize that there were gallant colored men present also. The radicals told the colored people that their party was the party of freedom, and that under its banner alone could they expect to enjoy that equality guaranteed them under the law. On the other hand, the Democrats said that they recognized the Thirteenth, Fourteenth and Fifteenth Amendments of the United States Constitution, and proposed to give the colored people every right and privilege guaranteed them by the law. What more did the colored people want? They didn't want to be hugged and kissed? The Radicals say: "Oh, this is only to gain votes." Cannot the colored people afford to trust their own native white people for two years when they have trusted alien adventurers for eight years? At Kingstree, the blacks and whites rode in one grand procession together. The Radical leaders again said to the ignorant colored people: "Oh, that's only to bring the colored people over." That was just what the whole people wanted. They wanted both races to live amicably together. In several of the counties the colored race had representatives on the county tickets, showing that it was not the intention of the Democrats to oppose the colored men, but only to oppose that class of colored men and white men who were corrupt and unfit to hold office under a free people. Col. Delany gave some good sound advice in this strain, and touched upon the point of Hampton being the first man in the South to advocate that the colored race be allowed the right of voting. He said he remembered it well, and he remembered how Morton and Andrew and Others at the North had opposed it, and so strong was the opposition that even Nash issued a cartoon representing Gen. Hampton asking Nash to dine with him, and Nash declining, with the apology that he had promised to "sleep with Mars Pinckney."

SOURCE: *News and Courier* (Charleston), October 10, 1876.

DOCUMENT 3
THE CAMPAIGN IN THE CITY: MEETING OF THE COLORED DEMOCRATIC CLUB OF THIRD WARD, OCTOBER 21, 1876

Col. Martin R. Delany was then loudly called upon, and in response delivered a very sensible speech, making his point so clear that his colored hearers could not fail to understand. He said that the reason he had left the Republican Party and joined the Democratic Party was that Wade Hampton and his party were indeed in earnest in establishing the true Jeffersonian Democracy and had been faithful to their pledges in the past, and he was sure they would be equally faithful in the future. He did not want his colored hearers to think he was personally opposed to Mr. Chamberlain; he had found that Mr. Chamberlain was in bad company and it was his object to break that company up. He had found it an exceedingly hard task to make his colored friends believe that the Democrats were in earnest in giving the colored men a fair representation, and to illustrate that fact he would state that Democrats had voted for him for their Lieutenant-Governor in the Independent Movement. He had used his influence in getting the colored men of this city to do as the German and Irish citizens had done, come together and submit the names of parties whom they had nominated to represent them; but they would not do this, and the Democrats had actually to reach out and take them by their wool and gave them a representation. This act alone was, in his opinion, enough to show that they meant to do what they had promised.

At the conclusion of Col. Delany's remarks, which were frequently interrupted by applause, the meeting adjourned.

SOURCE: *News and Courier* (Charleston), October 13, 1876.

DOCUMENT 4
The Campaign in the City: A Meeting in Hibernian Hall Last Night. An Enthusiastic Gathering of White and Colored Democrats.

COL. M. R. DELANY.

The next speaker was received with tremendous applause. He would not promise to make a speech, but he was here to identify himself with the Democratic Party of South Carolina. The trouble in this state was that the people of his race had been in the commencement misled by the evil advice of bad and designing men. The mistake has been that his people were once raised to the highest pinnacle of man's ambition without being educated up to the point. If their leaders had had an interest in the people of South Carolina, white and black, they would have educated them and fitted them to fulfill the duties of citizenship. But they had not such intention. Their object was to keep the black people in ignorance so as they could secure their suffrage and continue to fill their own pockets (Applause). He then gave an elaborate history of the great parties who had in turn ruled the country, and reminded his hearers that the abolition of slavery was brought about by the teachings of such Democrats as Thomas Jefferson and Martin Van Buren. The colored people had been misled into the belief that Democracy meant slavery, and it was done for the purpose of dividing the races. In response to a request from one of the audience to "tell us something about the Freedmen's Bank,"[1] he entered into an elaborate history of the founding of that delectable swindling machine. As early as 1870, he had warned the president and cashier of the bank that there was something wrong, but they paid no attention to him. Such was the confidence of the colored people that no one dared say anything against the bank. It was necessary now, he said, to have a government in this state that would have responsibility, and possess the confidence and respect of the people—such a government as would induce capital to came to the state, build up our waste places, and increase the prosperity of laborers as well as capitalists. To do this, the blacks and whites of the state must clasp hands and know no difference or mistrust of each other. Gen. Hampton and his followers were the first men to restore the principles of pure Jeffersonian Democracy in South

---

1. Freedmen's Bank, also known as Freedmen's Saving and Trust Company, was a private corporation in Washington, DC, chartered by the US government to enhance the economic development of blacks in the post–Civil War period. It lasted from 1865 to 1876 and was the leading financial institution specifically for freedmen.

Carolina. Look at the character and intelligence of the Democratic leaders. They had made pledges and promises that they would not dare fail to carry out. Further than that, nobody who knew them would for a moment suspect them (Applause). When a Democrat gives his word you may trust him (Applause). Did not a band of white men surround poor Isaac Rivers and Sawyer and protect them with their lives when they were hunted down by a mob of their own race? (Applause, and cries of Yes! Yes!). I say, then, that the men who are endeavoring to keep us apart are the enemies of both races. He wanted to see colored men be as proud of their principles as Republicans.

SOURCE: *News and Courier* (Charleston), October 14, 1876.

DOCUMENT 5

UNION OF THE TWO RACES: WHAT PREVENTS IT?

Major M. R. Delany gives excellent reasons for his declaration for Hampton and good government. As a colored man of intelligence, cherishing due regards for his race, he sees that their safety and prosperity lie only in the direction of good relations with the white people. The grounds of this belief Major Delany has frequently set forth with fine power and effect. He is, by all odds, the most original, correct and forcible thinker among the Negroes in this country. His publications always command respect. In a recent letter, he reaffirms his position, restates the grounds upon which it rests, and declares for the movement which will best tend to bring about a union of the two races, white and black, in one common interest. After quoting the language of General Hampton used at several public meetings, in which the fullest and amplest protection of the rights of colored people is guaranteed, he says that he will not hesitate to take him, representing the Democrats, at his word, and will give his own aid in supporting the state movement and voting the state Democratic ticket.

But Major Delany says something more that is instructive. He deplores the disorders which prevail in certain parts of the state, referring to the riots on the Combahee and Ashepoo, the memorable attack on free speech in Charleston on the 6th instant, and to the bloody scene recently witnessed on the Port Royal Railroad. He says truly that this condition of things is most anomalous and alarming in the extreme. "I cannot, nor will not," he says, "believe otherwise than that political motives, by unscrupulous leaders, have induced it. It evidently is intended to prevent a union of the two races in one common home or state interest." This is a terrible indictment of unscrupulous leaders coming from the source it does. Are the lives of colored men only fit to be offered as a sacrifice to the ambition and greed of such vile wretches as John Patterson? Ames said in Mississippi that fifteen or twenty dead Negroes would be of great service to the Republican Party there, and Patterson has declared the necessity of "raising hell" as he phrased it, "with the nigger" and so get additional troops into the state, or they would lose the election.

Colored people, turn your backs on John Patterson, and the smaller rascals whom he employs to manipulate you for his infamous purposes. Heed Martin R. Delany, who has put forth the words of truth and soberness, and indicated by precept and example how you may best secure your rights and interests, and all the blessings of peace and prosperity.

SOURCE: *Daily Register* (Columbia), September 28, 1876.

DOCUMENT 6

NEGATIVE REPORT ON DELANY BY ATTORNEY ST. JULIAN JERVEY

Law Office of Memminger, Pinckney and Jervey
17 Broad Street,
Charleston, S.C.,
Feb. 15, 1878.

S. J. Robinson, Esq.,
Summerville, S.C.

Dear Sir,

Yours of 5th inst. was received while I was too busily engaged in the Court of Sessions to find time to answer you immediately . . . you will therefore please pardon assuming discourtesy.

The matter to which you refer was referred to me by the late Atty. Gen. . . . shortly before his retiring from the office. I investigated the matter thoroughly, and made a formal report to the atty. Gen, reporting Delany as unfit for the office he holds. This report is now in the atty. Gen's Office, and has not been acted on . . . that I know of.

Very respectfully,
St. Julian Jervey

SOURCE: Gov. Wade Hampton Papers, Letters Received, Box 9, Folder 39, South Carolina Department of Archives and History, Columbia.

DOCUMENT 7
Petition to Dismiss Delany as Trial Justice

Charleston, S.C.,
March 18, 1878.

To His Excellency
  Gov. Wade Hampton,
  We the undersigned citizens of Charleston do earnestly petition that M. R. Delany be removed from the position of Trial Justice for this city, and that R. U. Smith be appointed in his stead. Because the office is conducted by the said M. R. Delany in a manner discreditable to the present administration of the State of South Carolina and repugnant to the feelings of both races in this community.

B. N. Rutledge	Geo. L. Buirt
R. B. White	Bernard O'Neil
... F. Fickens	R. Melchers
C. E. Flemings	D. W. Enoirs
W. B. Hacker	Roth D. White
S. C. Eckhard	Jack Blanshers
E. O. Hall	S. C. McKewn
A. Burnet Rhett	M. Aiken Kelly
W. H. Dawson	B. Rottmans
W. S. Frazers	...
A. F. Sterling	W. K. Steadman
J. D. ...	John Jones
A. Cameron	...
J. C. Ferguson	Julius ...
B. K. Kimlock	H. Harper
W. Hampton ...	...[2]

SOURCE: Gov. Wade Hampton Papers, Box 10, folder 14, South Carolina Department of Archives and History, Columbia.

---

2. There were thirty-two signatures. It is difficult to decipher some of them as they were not clearly spelled out.

DOCUMENT 8
DELANY TO GOV. WADE HAMPTON

Charleston, S.C.,
April 2, 1878

To His Excellency
Gov. Hampton,

Governor,

I have the honor to state to you that the Charleston Delegation has selected my name for removal from office; I know of no cause to merit this, and I hope, sir, that this shall not be done without giving me an opportunity of vindicating myself.

I have the honor to be, Sir,
Your Obedient Servant
M. R. Delany, Trial Justice.

SOURCE: Gov. Wade Hampton Papers, Letters Received, Box 10, Folder 29, South Carolina Department of Archives and History, Columbia.

DOCUMENT 9
COUNTER-PETITION TO RETAIN DELANY AS TRIAL JUSTICE

Charleston, S.C.,
April 3, 1878.

His Excellency
Wade Hampton
Governor of South Carolina.

We the undersigned citizens of Charleston city and county, do most earnestly recommend to your excellency the retention of Major M. R. Delany in office as a Trial Justice in and for said city and county.

We know that Maj. M. R. Delany is a man of coolness, deliberateness and broad experience, which enabled him to differ widely with many persons of his own race and party, and especially with the extravagant and ultra men....

His record speaks louder than this paper.

J. E. Hayne	Jas. H. Wheeler
H. N. Bouey	H. D. Lesesne, Snr.
B. F. Porter, Jr.,	W. W. Shackelford

F. J. Pugh
W. G. Brode
R. Nesbith
Macon Ballow
W. E. . . .
P. C. Gailliard
N. H. Crafee
F. J. M. Garey
W. G. Eason
. . .
J. K. Blackman
E. M. Brawley
N. Priston Dowking

Dan Talmadge . . .
William Roack
. . . Harterton
Arthur Darnelly
W. G. Courtney
E. C. Jones
Pas Macbeth
J. B. Motte
. . .
C. B. Nell
Ruidan & Dawson, "News & Courier."
W. H. Thompson
Jos Blackman[3]

SOURCE: Gov. Wade Hampton Papers, Letters Received, Box 10, Folder 30, South Carolina Department of Archives and History, Columbia.

DOCUMENT 10
DELANY TO HON. H. R. LATROBE

Charleston, S.C.
July 8th, 1878.

Hon. Jno. H. R. Latrobe
Prest. Am. Col. Society
Baltimore, MD.

My Dear Sir:

I write you as Chairman of the Committee on Finance of the Liberia Exodus Joint Stock Steamship Co., and a chairman of a special Committee with the Treasurer and another member to make a special negotiation. (I am one of Governor Hampton's Magistrates for the City of Charleston).

The contingencies which carried our vessel into Sierra Leone on the 28th of May last have incurred liabilities of sixteen hundred and eighty dollars ($1680.00) for supplies and towage, the drafts for which reached us Saturday from Boston through the First National Bank, Charleston, payable ten days after sight.

---

3. There were also thirty-two signatures here. Again, some of them were unclear.

We have asked through the Bank for thirty (30) days in which to make the payment, the reply to which is expected to be received in one week from this time.

My object in writing is to enquire whether or not there is to be found among the liberal contributors to the Colonization Movement some one or more gentlemen who would loan us that amount for about four (4) months, which would bring us to November the midst of our harvest season, when moneys will be coming in plentifully on the sale of stocks.

We solicit no money or donations as our movement is intended to be self sustaining in order to make our people self reliant.

Among the whites here we have no friends to our movement who would aid us by loan; but would rather contribute to prevent success.

We would not have these drafts dishonored under any consideration. Our prospect is very encouraging and we desire that nothing should impede our progress.

We hope to have a large and commodious vessel as soon as a sufficient amount of stock is sold to accomplish the design; but in accordance with your excellent advice, we are obliged to "hasten slowly."

What we ask sir, be pleased to remember, is as a loan to be paid back at a specified time.

A reply to this at your earliest pleasure will be thankfully received.

By, very respectfully Sir, on behalf of the Committee.

Your most obedient servant,

M. R. Delany

Chmn. Com. Warehouse & Transportation

P.S. Sir, I forward you by this mail some documents explanatory of our movement.

M. R. Delany

Chmn. Com. Warehouse & Transportation

NAMES OF CANDIDATES:
Of Board of Directors, L.E.J.S.S. Co.
B. F. Porter
Wm. H. Thompson
H. N. Bouey
F. J. Pugh
M. R. Delany
J. E. Hayne
E. M. Brawley
B. C. Singleton

Aaron Logan
C. J. Tolberts
Richard Nesbit
Peter W. Gibbs
B. F. Smalls
N. S. Robertson
J. J. Lesesne.

Source: American Colonization Society Papers, Library of Congress, Washington, DC.

DOCUMENT 11
DELANY TO WILLIAM COPPINGER

Charleston, S.C.,
Aug. 18, 1880.

My Dear Mr. Coppinger,

I am indebted to you for continual favors, and your last, the "African Repository" was rich in African intelligence. I perceived that you have been laboring under the false impression that I am at the head of the Exodus Emigration Movement here. I never was at the head of that movement, and all that I did, was at the earnest request of the friends engaged, to aid in its progress. All the operations named as occupied by me, were simply temporary and "Acting" officially.

I would have willingly taken hold permanently to conduct the company's affairs as its President, but as you might suppose, could not do so with the composite material of the Board, being of inexperienced and unbusiness trained men. As it was, I gave them eight months gratuitous service after litigation commenced, from the 18th of April 1879 till the last of November—to aid in managing affairs by which we had the false claims reduced from upwards of six thousand to two thousand and five hundred dollars ($2,500.00) upon which decree of court the vessel was sold, and bought in for us, all by a management of my own, when after which I quit, though I allowed the use of my name on their official circulars till May last 1880, when I withdrew my identity entirely from the transactions,—I mean as an official of the company. I have not resigned from the company as a member, because it would seem like desertion and thereby too discouraging to them, and I only attend such meeting as may require the most judicial considerations.

I am bound for Africa, and never intended when returning to remain, but the war coming on for the time being changed everything. When I returned from my exploring tour, my children were all young, my eldest (son) being but fifteen years old 1861. My children consisted of seven (7); six sons and one daughter, two; a son and a daughter being born since my return. I lost a son last December by drowning in the Savannah river at Savannah, Ga.

At 15, my eldest son I permitted to leave school in Canada where my family then resided, and enter the Army by joining the Mass. 54th. Determining to enter the Army myself, I took my family from Canada to Wilberforce, and there under care and guardianship of their mother, placed them in school (the eldest being in the Army) where four finished their education; and two, a son and daughter—the youngest—are now finishing theirs. So soon as they finish, they will all be ready for the great work before us.

In the mean time, my course has been laid out, and my work in Africa all fixed and clear before me. My expenses in supporting my family and educating my children very great, and as I could not be a corrupt politician, you see that I found no favor with those in influence and authority. Hence, I have made no money since I have been in the South. All the positions I have held politically was Inspector of Customs given me by a personal friend worth then $1,400 a year which I held one year, but had to resign to accept of the nomination of Lieut. Governor offered me by my friends; and the Trial Justiceship under Gov. Chamberlain which they (the corrupt politicians) made him take from me after eight months, and Trial Justice under Governor Hampton which I lost so soon as they got rid of him by sending him to the U.S. Senate, as he was too liberal for the rank and file of the party leaders.

I am at my old profession of Medicine, as the best I can do for the present. And I have been thus particular, and in letting you know something about myself and my interests in this greatest, and, to me, all absorbing to the Blackman, movement of Africa's future.

If I could get some one of the many government favors worth from $2,000 to $3,000 a year for about two years, this would give me the command of available means sufficient, so as to enable me to leave my family, and children at school, and go at once to Africa, the field of my destined labor. I am, dear Mr. Coppinger, your friend.
M. R. Delany.

N.B. Dear Sir:
I omitted to say, that after being mustered out of the Army at the end of '69, being disappointed by Gov. Scott in an appointment in S. Carolina, and also in the Liberian Mission—as Minister—all through the chicanery of wily politicians—I went into the Land and Note Brokerage in Charleston. This,

too, they conspired against, as I paid the poor employees fifty per cent cash on their salary certificates, where they were only receiving actually ten and fifteen percent from the "corner groceries" in goods, who were the agents of the officiaries both State and county, who were combined.

It was in this business that I received from the Collector of the Port on his appointment, the office of "Duty Inspector" one of the best positions in his gift. This was general H. G. Worthington, who appointed me in defiance of opposition of State politicians.

After the election in '74, I tried the business of general Auctioneering which did not pay.

Now to obtain the means as stated in my letter, could I get an appointment at Washington such as Superintendent of the Freedman's Hospital which I suppose pays a reasonably good salary (or any other). I would accept it to facilitate my designs for Africa.

I have desired to place my position fairly before you as a personal friend. I am, Dear Sir,
M. R. Delany.

P.S.: I must still add here other facts, because while I was giving you information concerning myself, it should be full and clear.

It was I who first suggested to Gen. Saxton the importance of the Government safeguard over the Freedmen's money, which had accumulated in the keeping of Army officers of his appointment under him—before he was aware of it—to the amount of $475,000 (four hundred and seventy five thousand dollars).

After the establishment of the Trust Company (Freedmen's Bank), I watched it closely and was the first to call the official attention of Mr. Harris, its General Inspector, to fraud going on in the Beaufort Branch, which had been the original 'bank' under the officers of Gen. Saxton.

As I went considerably through the South where these banks existed after my muster out at the end of '69, I made it a point—indeed at the request of Mr. Harris, there at New Orleans—to visit and inspect these banks voluntarily or rather gratuitously.

In May 1870, reaching Washington from far South, I at once called on Gen. Eaton, Actuary, and reported to him, as well as to the cashier, the wrongs I knew and suspected as going on in some of the Banks, when Gen. Eaton thanked me and suggested that I would also import the same to the President of the Bank. But on doing so, he at once grew angry and flatly told me, that he "did not believe it." And from that time forth, I lost cast with him.

Mr. Stickney was also well informed as to my interest in the affairs of the Bank, and knowledge of what was going on, as I had made several important suggestions as to changes in some of the officials and management, all of which received the sanction of Gen. Eaton and others in the Bank; and is it not singular that after all this, that in the selection for new managers—even Commissioners—to aid in settling the affairs of the Bank, I, who knew more about the institution than another colored man not officially connected with it, was ignored entirely, and a gentleman chosen as a race representative in winding up the affairs who had never taken any interest whatever in the institution from its establishment.

I have thus brought these matters in connection with myself before you—as an old friend, that you may see how studiously and completely I have been ignored by my "friends" after all my services faithfully performed under the government, in the Army, during four years and ten months. Your friend,
M. R. Delany.

SOURCE: American Colonization Society Papers, Library of Congress, Washington, DC.

DOCUMENT 12
DELANY TO WILLIAM COPPINGER

Charleston, S.C.,
Dec. 18, 1880.

My Dear Mr. Coppinger,
Enclosed please find the promised circular. I place a portion of my Army Record before the Country in hope that according to my merit, I shall receive recognition from the incoming Government.

I expect to be in Washington about the 1st of February when I shall impart to you fully my desire as to an appointment. In the meantime, I shall anxiously solicit your aid and influence in my behalf for any eligible paying position according to merit.

I should like to obtain in the first place (and I think the integrity of the country can afford it as well as they could to make my friend Frederick Douglass Marshall of the District of Columbia), the office of Door Keeper of the U.S. Senate. This is my first solicitation. Excepting to Senators, I have imparted this to no one in Washington.

I hope that you will bring to my aid our Colonization friends such as the Hon. H. R. Latrobe and others, members of the society, and others who may not hold any official position among you.
I remain, Mr. Coppinger,
With great respect,
Your friend,
M. R. Delany.

SOURCE: American Colonization Society Papers, Library of Congress, Washington, DC.

SELECTED BIBLIOGRAPHY

WRITINGS BY MARTIN R. DELANY

"The Attraction of Planets." *Anglo-African Magazine* 1 (1859).
Blake; or, The Huts of America: A Tale of the Mississippi Valley, the Southern United States, and Cuba. Serialized in the *Anglo-African Magazine*, January–July 1859, and the *Weekly Anglo-African*, November 1861–April/May 1862.
"The Column of Fire." *Daily Republican* (Charleston), June 22, 1871.
"Comets." *Anglo-African Magazine* 2, 1859.
The Condition, Elevation, Emigration and Destiny of the Colored People of the United States. Philadelphia, 1852. Reprint, Baltimore: Black Classic Press, 1998.
"The Earth." *Daily Republican* (Charleston), June 8, 1871.
Eulogy on the Life and Character of the Rev. Fayette Davis. Pittsburgh: Benjamin Franklin Peterson, 1847.
Homes for the Freedmen. Charleston, SC: 1871.
"The Moral and Social Aspect of Africa." *Liberator*, May 1, 1863.
Official Report of the Niger Valley Exploring Party. New York: Thomas Hamilton, 1861.
The Origins and Objects of Ancient Freemasonry: Its Introduction into the United States and Legitimacy among Colored Men. Pittsburgh: W. S. Haven, 1853.
"Political Aspect of the Colored People of the United States." *Provincial Freeman* (Chatham), October 13, 1855.
"Political Destiny of the Colored Race on the American Continent." *Proceedings of the National Emigration Convention of Colored People*; Held in Cleveland, Ohio, August 24–26, 1854. Pittsburgh: A. A. Anderson, 1854
"Political Events." *Provincial Freeman* (Chatham), July 5, 1856.

Principia of Ethnology: The Origin of Races and Color, with an Archaeological Compendium of Ethiopian and Egyptian Civilization, from Years of Careful Examination and Enquiry. Philadelphia: Harper and Brother Publishers, 1879.

Trial and Conviction of Martin R. Delany. Unpublished pamphlet. Charleston, SC, 1876. Copy in the Charleston Historical Society Library, Charleston, SC.

University Pamphlets: A Series of Four Tracts on National Polity. Charleston, SC: Republican Book and Job Office, 1870. Dawson Pamphlet Collection, the Wilson Library, University of North Carolina, Chapel Hill.

Books and Articles

Adeleke, Tunde. "Afro-Americans and Moral Suasion: The Debate in the 1830s and 1840s." *Journal of Negro History* 80, no. 111 (Spring 1998): 127–42.

Adeleke, Tunde. "Black Biography in the Service of a Revolution: Martin R. Delany in Afro-American Historiography." *Biography: An Interdisciplinary Quarterly* 17 (1994): 248–67.

Adeleke, Tunde. "Black Radicalism and Black Conservatism as Complementary and Mutually Reinforcing: The Political Pragmatism of Martin R. Delany." *Polish Journal of American Studies* 8 (2014): 51–71.

Adeleke, Tunde. "Demythologizing Martin R. Delany." Odense American Studies International Series. Working Paper 5, April 2004.

Adeleke, Tunde. "Martin R. Delany's Philosophy of Education: A Neglected Aspect of African American Liberation Thought." *Journal of Negro Education* 63 (1994): 221–36.

Adeleke, Tunde. "'Much Learning Makes Men Mad': Classical Education and Black Empowerment in Martin R. Delany's Philosophy of Education." *Journal of Thought* 49, nos. 1 and 2 (Spring/Summer 2015): 3–36.

Adeleke, Tunde. "Race and Ethnicity in Martin R. Delany's Thought." *Journal of Thought* 29, no. 1 (Spring 1994): 19–49.

Adeleke, Tunde. "Religion in Martin R. Delany's Liberation Thought." *Religious Humanism* 27, no. 2 (Spring 1993): 80–92.

Adeleke, Tunde. "'Today Is the Day of Salvation': Martin R. Delany's Struggles against Providential Determinism in Early Nineteenth-Century Black Abolitionism." *Interdisciplinary Journal of Research on Religion* 13, no. 4 (2017): 1–23.

Adeleke, Tunde. *UnAfrican Americans: Nineteenth-Century Black Nationalists and the Civilizing Mission.* Lexington: University Press of Kentucky, 1998.

Adeleke, Tunde. *Without Regard to Race: The Other Martin R. Delany.* Jackson: University Press of Mississippi, 2003.

Bell, Howard H. "The American Moral Reform Society, 1836–1841." *Journal of Negro Education* 27, no. 1 (Winter 1958): 34–40.

Bell, Howard H. *Minutes of the Proceedings of the National Negro Conventions, 1830–1864.* New York: Arno Press, 1969.

Bell, Howard H. *Search for a Place: Black Separatism and Africa.* Ann Arbor: University of Michigan Press, 1969.

Bell, Howard H. *A Survey of the Negro Convention Movement, 1830–1861.* New York: Arno Press, 1969.

Blackett, Richard. "Martin Delany and Robert Campbell: Black Americans in Search of an African Colony." *Journal of Negro History* 62, no. 1 (January 1977): 1–25.

Bushong, Millard K. *A History of Jefferson County, West Virginia*. Charlestown, WV: Jefferson Publishing, 1941.
Chiles, Katy. "Within and Without Raced Nations: Intertextuality, Martin Delany, and *Blake; or the Huts of America*." *American Literature* 80, no. 2 (2008): 323–52.
Clymer, Jeffory A. "Martin Delany's *Blake* and the Transnational Politics of Property." *American Literary History* 15, no. 4 (2003): 709–31.
Crummell, Alexander. *Africa and America: Addresses and Discourses*. New York: Negro University Press, 1969.
Crummell, Alexander. *The Future of Africa: Being Addresses, Sermons, Delivered in the Republic of Liberia*. New York: Charles Scribner, 1862.
Curry, Tommy J. "Who K(new): The Nation-ist Contour of Racial Identity in the Thought of Martin R. Delany and John E. Bruce." *Journal of Pan African Studies* 1, no. 10 (November 2007): 41–61.
Dann, Martin E. *The Black Press, 1827–1890: The Quest for National Identity*. New York: G. P. Putnam's Sons, 1971.
Daut, Marlene. "Martin Delany's *Blake* in Black Atlantic Revolutionary Context." *American Periodicals: A Journal of History and Criticism* 28, no. 1 (2018): 82–84.
Davis, Julia. *The Shenandoah*. New York: Rinehart, 1945.
Doolen, Andy. "'Be Cautious of the Word 'Rebel': Race, Revolution, and Transnational History in Martin Delany's *Blake; or, The Huts of America*." *American Literature* 81, no. 1 (2009): 153–79.
Draper, Theodore. "The Father of American Black Nationalism." *New York Times Review of Books*, March 12, 1970.
Draper, Theodore. "The Fantasy of Black Nationalism." *Commentary* 48 (1969).
Draper, Theodore. *The Rediscovery of Black Nationalism*. New York: Viking Press, 1970.
Du Bois, William E. B. *W. E. B. Du Bois Reader*. New York: Scribner, 1993.
Ellison, Curtis W., and E. W. Metcalf Jr. *William Wells Brown and Martin R. Delany: A Reference Guide*. Boston: G. K. Hall, 1978.
Ernest, John. *Resistance and Reformation in Nineteenth-Century African American Literature: Brown, Wilson, Jacobs, Delany, Douglass and Harper*. Jackson: University Press of Mississippi, 1995.
Foner, Philip S. *Frederick Douglass: A Biography*. New York: Citadel, 1964.
Foner, Philip S. *The Life and Writings of Frederick Douglass*. Vol. 5. New York: International Publishers, 1975.
Foner, Philip S. and George E. Walker, eds. *Proceedings of the Black State Conventions 1, 1840–1865*. Philadelphia: Temple University Press, 1980.
Geffen, Elizabeth M. "Violence in Philadelphia in the 1840s and 1850s." *Pennsylvania History* 4 (October 1969): 381–410.
Gerrity, Sean. "Freedom on the Move: Marronage in Martin Delany's *Blake; or, the Huts of America*." *MELUS* 43, no. 3 (August 2018): 1–18.
Gilroy, Paul. *The Black Atlantic: Modernity and Double Consciousness*. Cambridge, MA: Harvard University Press, 1993.
Glasco, Lawrence Admiral, ed. *The WPA History of the Negro in Pittsburgh*. Pittsburgh: University of Pittsburgh Press, 2004.
Griffith, Cyril E. *The African Dream: Martin R. Delany and the Emergence of Pan-Africanist Thought*. University Park: Pennsylvania State University Press, 1975.
Harding, Vincent. "Beyond Chaos: Black History and the Search for the New Land." In *Amistad 1: Writings on Black History and Culture*, edited by John A. Williams and Charles F. Harris, 267–92. New York: Vintage Books, 1970.

Harding, Vincent. *There Is a River: The Black Struggle for Freedom in America*. New York: Vintage Books, 1983.
Hill, Robert, ed. *Walter Rodney Speaks: The Making of an African Intellectual*. Trenton, NJ: Africa World Press, 1990.
Hite, Roger W. "'Stand Still and See the Salvation': The Rhetorical Design of Martin R. Delany's Blake." *Journal of Black Studies* 5, no. 2 (December 1974): 192–202.
Holly, Theodore J. "In Memoriam." *AME Church Review*, October 1886.
Holt, Thomas. *Black over White: Negro Political Leadership in South Carolina during Reconstruction*. Urbana: University of Illinois Press, 1977.
Johnson, Andre E. *The Forgotten Prophet: Bishop Henry McNeal Turner and the African American Prophetic Tradition*. Plymouth, UK: Lexington Books, 2012.
Kass, Amalie M. "Dr. Thomas Hodgkin, Dr. Martin Delany, and the 'Return to Africa.'" *Medical History* 4 (October 1983): 373–93.
Khan, Robert. "The Political Ideology of Martin R. Delany." *Journal of Black Studies*, June 1984: 415–40.
Kirk-Green, A. H. M. "Americans in the Niger Valley: A Colonizing Centenary." *Phylon* 22, no. 4 (1962): 225–39.
Levine, Robert S. ed. *Martin R. Delany: A Documentary Reader*. Chapel Hill: University of North Carolina Press, 2003.
Levine, Robert S. *Martin Delany, Frederick Douglass and the Politics of Representative Identity*. Chapel Hill: University of North Carolina Press, 1997.
Lincoln, Eric, and Lawrence Mamiya. *The Black Church in the African American Experience*. Durham, NC: Duke University Press, 1990.
Litwack, Leon, and August Meier, eds. *Black Leaders of the Nineteenth Century*. Urbana: University of Illinois Press, 1988.
Martin, Josephine W, ed. *"Dear Sister": Letters Written on Hilton Head Island, 1867*. Beaufort, SC: Beaufort Book Company, 1867.
McAdoo, Bill. *Pre-Civil War Black Nationalism*. New York: David Walker Press, 1983.
McAdoo, Bill. "Pre-Civil War Black Nationalism." *Progressive Labor* 5 (June–July 1966): 31–68.
McCormick, Richard P. "William Whipper: Moral Reformer." *Pennsylvania History* 10, no. 111 (January 1976): 23–46.
Miller, Floyd J. *The Search for a Black Nationality: Black Emigration and Colonization, 1787–1863*. Urbana: University of Illinois Press, 1975.
Mitchell, Henry H. *Black Church Beginnings: The Long-Hidden Realities of the First Years*. Cambridge, UK: William B. Eerdmans, 2004.
Nwankwo, Ifeoma K. *Black Cosmopolitanism: Racial Consciousness and Transnational Identity in the Nineteenth-Century Americas*. Philadelphia: University of Pennsylvania Press, 2005.
Ogunleye, Tolagbe. "Dr. Martin Robison Delany, 19th Century Africana Womanist: Reflections on His Avant-Garde Politics Concerning Gender, Colorism, and Nation Building." *Journal of Black Studies* 28 (1998): 626–49.
Painter, Nell I. "Martin R. Delany: A Black Nationalist in Two Kinds of Time." *New England Journal of Black Studies* 8 (1989): 37–47.
Painter, Nell I. "Martin R. Delany: Elitism and Black Nationalism." In *Black Leaders of the Nineteenth Century*, edited by Leon Litwack and August Meier, 149–172. Urbana: University of Illinois Press, 1988.
Payne, Daniel H. *Recollections of Seventy Years*. Nashville: AME 1898.

Pease, William H., and Jane H. Pease. "The Negro Convention Movement." In *Key Issues in the Afro-American Experience*, vol. 1, edited by Nathan Huggins, Martin Kilson and Daniel Fox, 191–205. New York: Harcourt Brace, 1971.
Rabinowitz, Howard H., ed. *Southern Black Leaders of the Reconstruction Era*. Urbana: University of Illinois Press, 1982.
Redkey, Edwin S. *Respect Black: The Writings and Speeches of Henry McNeal Turner*. New York: Arno Press, 1971.
Reed, Harry. *Platform for Change: The Foundations of Northern Free Black Community, 1775–1865*. East Lansing: Michigan State University Press, 1994.
Reid, Mandy A. "Utopia Is in the Blood: The Bodily Utopias of Martin R. Delany and Pauline Hopkins." *Utopian Studies* 22, no. 1 (2011): 91–103.
Rollin, Frank (Frances). *Life and Public Services of Martin R. Delany* Boston: Lee and Shepard, 1868.
Rosenfeld, Louis. "Martin Robison Delany (1812–1885): Physician, Black Separatist, Explorer, Soldier." *Bulletin of the New York Academy of Medicine* 65, no. 7 (September 1989): 801–18.
Sajna, Mike. "Martin Delany: Father of Black Nationalism." *Greensburg Tribune Review*, February 25, 1990.
Shelby, Tommie. "Two Conceptions of Black Nationalism: Martin Delany on the Meaning of Black Political Solidarity." *Political Theory* 31, no. 5 (October 2003): 664–92.
Shreve, Grant. "The Exodus of Martin Delany." *American Literary History* 29, no. 3 (September 2017): 449–73.
Simkins, Francis B., and Robert H. Woody. *South Carolina during Reconstruction*. Gloucester, MA: Peter Smith, 1966.
Simmons, Adam D. "Ideologies and Programs of the Anti-Slavery Movement, 1830–1861." PhD diss., Northwestern University, 1983.
Sterling, Dorothy. *The Making of an Afro-American: Martin R. Delany*. New York: Doubleday, 1971.
Stuckey, Sterling. *Ideological Origins of Black Nationalism*. Boston: Beacon Press, 1972.
Stuckey, Sterling. "Twilight of Our Past: Reflections on the origins of Black History." In *Amistad 2: Writings on Black History and Culture*, edited by John A. Williams and Charles F. Harris, 261–96. New York: Vintage Books, 1971.
Sundquist, Eric J. *The Oxford W. E. B. Du Bois Reader*. Oxford: Oxford University Press, 1996.
Thomas, Rhondda Robinson, and Susanna Ashton, eds. *The South Carolina Roots of African American Thought*. Columbia: University of South Carolina Press, 2014.
Thompson, Henry T. *Ousting the Carpetbagger from South Carolina*. New York: Negro University Press, 1962.
Ullman, Victor. *Martin R. Delany: The Beginnings of Black Nationalism*. Boston: Beacon Press, 1971.
Washington, Booker T. *Booker T. Washington Papers*. 14 vols. Urbana: University of Illinois Press, 1972–89.
Yaure, Philip. "Deliberation and Emancipation: Some Critical Remarks." *Ethics: An Interdisciplinary Journal of Social, Political, and Legal Philosophy* 129, no. 1 (October 2018): 8–38.
Zuck, Rochelle Raineri. "Martin R. Delany and the Rhetoric of Divided Sovereignty." In *African American Culture and Legal Discourse*, edited by Lovalerie King and Richard Schur, 39–56. New York. Palgrave Macmillan, 2009.

Index

abolition, xii, 3–4, 13–15, 27, 91, 139, 146, 171, 178, 222
Africa, 12, 17–18, 23, 27, 40, 53, 99, 138, 157, 159, 217–18, 227–33. *See also* Liberia
African Education Society of Pittsburgh, 14
African Methodist Episcopal Church, 4, 14, 16
African Repository, 229
Aiken, William, 173
Allen, Richard, 14
American Colonization Society, 12, 23
American Missionary Association, 76, 80
Ashepoo River, 223
Avery, Mr., 4

Bacon, Major, 130
Barnwell (a scout), 35–36
Baynard, Telemachus, 197
Bird, Mr., 125
black enlistment, 10, 19, 27–30, 34–38
black leadership, 3, 5, 8, 11, 20, 90, 95–96
Black Man's Party, 96, 122, 125–26
Black Nationalism, 5, 7, 12, 22
black political aspirations, 10, 12, 91–93
black political representation, 95–96, 100–101, 105–11, 135, 137–38, 194–95

Blair, Frank, 179
"Bonnie Blue Flag," 172, 180
Bonnin, John, 202
Bowen, C. C., 122, 129, 185, 202, 205–7
Brown, Mr., 198
Bryan, Judge, 210
Bryant, William Cullen, 195–96
Burleigh, William H., 4
Butler, M. C., 123, 130

Cain, Richard H., 95, 100, 122, 130, 132, 147, 163–64
Calvert, William H., 72
Campbell, Mr., 199
Cardozo, F. L., 132
Carolus V (king), 53
Carpenter, Judge, 123, 125, 130
carpetbaggers, 141
Chamberlain, Daniel H., 21–22, 169, 183, 185–86, 206–7, 209–10, 212–13, 215, 221, 230
Chaplin, J., 220
Charleston Daily Republican, 141
Charles V (king), 40
Chase, Chief Justice, 41
Christian Herald, 15–16

Christian Recorder, 15–16
citizenship, 93–94, 113–16, 222
civil rights, 23, 93–94, 114–19, 156–57
Civil War, 5, 8, 10, 18–20, 27–29, 47, 55, 63, 89–90, 94, 102–4, 118, 120–21, 172, 180, 187, 189, 217, 229
Clark, Mr., 132
Clitz, Henry Boynton, 62, 81
Clons, J. H., 44–45
Colcock, Colonel, 62
Coleman, A. G., 199
Colored American, 15
Columbus, Christopher, 39–40, 53
Combahee River, 223
Condition, Elevation, Emigration, and Destiny of the Colored People of the United States, The, 17–18
Constitution, US, 20, 93–95, 118–20, 130, 135, 193, 218–20
Cooper, Peter, 196
Coppinger, William, 217–18, 229–33
cotton, 29, 40–41, 44, 48, 50, 57, 60, 71–72, 75–77, 146, 152, 178
Crowell, Dr., 62
Crummell, Alexander, 7
cumulative voting, 165–68, 195. See also voting
Cunningham, G. I., 173, 179, 201
Cunningham, James H., 97, 99, 138, 155, 159–60

Davis, T. A., 181
Delany, Martin Robison: as a black major, 10, 12, 19, 27–46, 50, 68, 89, 196, 230, 232; as a conservative Republican, 11–12, 20–21, 89–156; as a Democrat, 12, 215–33; on discord between darker skin and lighter skin blacks, 97–98, 126–27, 136–40, 144–45, 147, 150, 153–55, 157–60; and emigration, 12, 17–18, 23, 27, 217, 227–33; on executive appointment practices, 137–39, 144–45, 147–48, 154–61; family, 12, 15, 19, 23, 35, 230; fight against corruption, 6, 99–100, 169–72, 175, 193, 196, 221, 230–31; as Freedmen's Bureau sub-assistant commissioner, 10, 12, 19, 47–87, 89–90, 96, 129, 146, 189; grand larceny trial and conviction, 11–12, 22, 172, 179, 183–213; as an independent Republican, 12, 169–82; as Inspector of Customs, 196, 198, 230–31; as John

Brown Abolitionist, 171, 178; land and commission agency, 184, 197, 204, 230–31; loss of Delany papers, 8; opposition to black political power, 21–22, 93–94, 105–6, 108, 133–36, 141–43, 150, 188–89, 193; pardon, 22, 185–86, 205–7, 212; as a political candidate, 92, 109–10, 147, 169–72, 176–77, 189–91, 195–96, 230; as trial justice, 21–23, 183, 185, 196, 209–10, 216–17, 224–27, 230; triple alliance doctrine, 48–51, 62, 83, 215
DeLarge, Robert, 95–96, 122, 126–27, 129–30, 208–9
Democratic Party, 11–12, 21–23, 97, 111, 120, 124–26, 131, 138–39, 152, 155, 160, 171–72, 176, 179–81, 215–16, 220–23
Diane, Edward L., 74
Dingle, Mr., 202
discrimination, 13, 15–16, 84, 86, 98–99, 111, 126, 128, 130, 138, 144–45, 155–59
Douglass, Frederick, 4, 7–8, 16–19, 22, 27–28, 90, 96, 98–99, 101–2, 131, 133–46, 148–59, 169, 184–203, 232
Douglass, L. H., 101–2
Dover, Mr., 202
Downing, G. T., 101–2
Drane, Gaton I., 70
Draper, Theodore, 5–6, 11
Du Bois, W. E. B., 7

Earle, George, 160–61
Eaton, D. L., 49, 64–68, 231–32
education, 13–16, 50–51, 57, 61, 66–67, 76–77, 80, 86, 95, 97, 99, 107, 129, 131, 137, 141–43, 148, 157, 172, 181, 189, 192, 230
Elizabeth I (queen), 40, 53
Elliott, General, 213
Elliott, Mr., 167
emancipation, 19, 55–57, 61, 91, 94, 99–100, 107, 118–19, 139, 141–42, 145
enfranchisement, 90, 92, 94–95, 103, 111, 116, 118, 143, 190
England, 40, 53–56, 60, 94, 103–4, 114–15, 117–19

Faust, Brigadier General, 76
Fides (pseudonym), 92, 110–12
Fish, Hamilton, 138, 146, 155, 159
Foster, C. W., 28–29, 31–36, 45–46

Index

Fox, Mr., 124
France, 53–54, 115–17
Freedmen's Bank, 161, 222, 231
Freedmen's Bureau, 10, 12, 19, 47–87, 89–90, 96, 129, 146, 189
Freedmen's Cotton Agency, 71–72, 76
Freedmen's Hospital, 231
Freedom's Journal, 14–15
Fugitive Slave Act, 17–18, 27

Gailliard, S. N., 98, 146–48
Gailliard, S. E., 173
Garnet, Henry H., 18–19, 27–28, 91, 105–6, 187–89
Garrison, William Lloyd, 4
Gate, Thomas, 53
Gayer, Major, 210
Gleaves, Richard, 169–70
gradualism, 91, 169
Graham, Judge, 197–98
Grant, Nelson, 4
Grant, Ulysses S., 102
Green, Colonel, 62
Green, John T., 169, 176–80
Green, Sampson, 199
Gregorie, Peter, 173–74
Griffith, Cyril, 6

habeas corpus, 119
Haiti, 6, 138, 144, 146, 155, 159
Hamilton, John, 73, 78
Hampton, Wade, 22–23, 216–17, 220–27, 230
Hawkins, H. J., 29, 44–45
Hawkins, John, 53
Holly, Theodore J., 6
Houston, Robert L., Jr., 72, 76
Howard, C. H., 39, 42
Howard, O. O., 51, 87
Hunter, N. N., 185, 208–9

Independent Republican Movement (IRM), 11, 21, 169–72, 178–79, 181–82, 183, 196
Indians (Native Americans), 40, 43, 53
Ingraham, Captain, 119

James I (king), 40, 53–54
Jefferson, Thomas, 119, 222
Jervey, St. Julian, 224

Johnson, Andrew, 47–48, 90, 101, 103–4, 160
Johnston, George E., 185, 206–7
Jones, Absalom, 14
Jones, John, 30, 101–2
Jones, W. R., 185, 208–11
Juba (a freedman), 57

Kershaw, Joseph B., 180–82
Keteltas, Henry, 28, 32
King, W. G., 209
Kotzia, Martin, 119
Ku Klux Klan, 152, 203
Kush, 194

land redistribution, 47–50, 59–60, 63–68, 72, 174
Langley, L. S., 92, 109–10, 189–91
Latrobe, H. R., 217, 227–29, 233
Lee, Mr., 198
Lee, Robert E., 60
Lesesne, H. D., 173
Levine, Robert, 7–9
Liberia, 18, 23, 27, 97, 138, 155, 159, 217, 230
Liberia Exodus Joint Stock Steamship Company, 217, 227–29
Lincoln, Abraham, 19, 28, 30–31, 43, 61, 95, 121, 133
Logan, Aaron, 173, 185, 206–7
London Times, 61
Louis V (king), 61

Mackey, Sheriff, 198, 204
Magna Carta (Magna Charta), 94, 117–19
Magrath, G. G., 210
McAdoo, Bill, 6
McGowan, Samuel, 182
McIntyre, R. C., 76
Meade, George Gordon, 102
Meier, August, 3, 5, 11
Melton, Attorney-General, 178–79
Melton, Judge, 162
Miller, Floyd J., 6
Miller, Peter L., 123
Milshaw, Mr., 131–32
minority representation, 100–101, 165–68, 195
Moody, James M., 160
moral suasion, 14–17, 49
Morris, Mr., 132

Morton, Senator, 120
Moses, Franklin J., 99–100, 130, 161–64, 173, 184
Moses, Julius T., 208–9

Napoleon III (Charles-Louis Napoleon Bonaparte), 53, 114, 117
Nash, William Beverly, 111, 221
National Compact, 117–18
National Independent Organization of Colored Men, 215–16, 218
National Independent Party, 218–19, 221
national polity, 52, 93–95, 112–21
Negro National Convention Movement, 14–15
Neide, A., 79
New Departure, 144, 170–72, 174–75
Newman, C. D., 69
New National Era, 93, 113, 141
News and Courier, 148–59, 172, 180–82, 185
New South, 48, 51–61, 86
New York Times, 91, 101, 161–62
Nording, Judge, 70
North Star, 4, 8, 15–16

Palpitators, 123, 130
Patterson, John, 224
Payne, Daniel, 4
Pennsylvania, 13–17, 60, 111
Phillips, Wendell, 91–92, 105–6, 109, 188–90
Pittsburgh Mystery, 15–16
police system, 73, 77, 81
"Political Destiny of the Colored Race on the American Continent," 17–18
political economy, 48–50, 52–54, 58–59, 61–62, 75
political equality, 91, 100, 103, 108, 110, 140, 156, 158, 166, 176–77
political rights, 10, 20, 22–23, 49, 58, 90, 92, 94, 115–18, 121
Porter, Charles H., 99, 160–61
Portugal, 53–54
proportional representation, 98–100

racial reconciliation, 11, 20, 22, 91–92, 169–72, 181, 185, 215, 219, 223–24
Radical Reconstruction, 8, 10, 20–21, 23, 96, 98, 215

Radical Republicans and Radical Republicanism, 6, 10–12, 22, 92–93, 96–97, 99–100, 132, 150, 166, 168, 169–72, 184–87, 189, 191–92, 194, 216–17, 220
Rainey, Senator, 127
Ransier, Mr., 127
Reconstruction, 4–6, 8, 10–11, 20, 90, 94, 119, 133–34, 140–41, 146–47, 149–50, 158, 174, 177–78, 189, 192–93, 204
Redeemers, 23, 217
Reed, J. P., 185, 202, 206, 212
Republican, 131–32
Republicanism, 10, 96–98, 126–27, 132–33, 135–36, 139, 148, 151, 177–78, 187, 193, 195, 218
Republican Party, 19–22, 92, 95–99, 111, 122–28, 130–33, 135–36, 138–40, 145, 147–48, 150–52, 159–61, 164, 169–78, 180, 183, 187, 192–96, 204–5, 215–16, 221, 223–24
Rhett, Major, 35
Richards, Catherine A., 15
Richards, "Daddy Ben," 14
Richardson, Mrs. E. B., 184, 197, 199, 204–5, 209
Rivers, Isaac, 223
Rivers, Mr., 198
Robinson, S. J., 224
Rodney, Walter, 6
Rollin, Frank (Frances), 5–6
Romain, Colonel, 138, 146, 155, 159
Rothschild family, 60
Roy, J. P., 51, 62, 85
Russwurm, John, 14–15

Sawyer, 223
Saxton, Rufus, 28, 33–35, 41, 62, 68, 73, 231
Schimmelfennig, General, 132
Schwartz, E. G., 199
Scott, R. K., 51, 76, 87, 124, 163, 230
Seabrook, E. D., 173
Seabrook, E. E., 202, 208
secession, 93–95, 104, 120–21
Sherman, William Tecumseh, 72, 102, 179
Shim, William M., 4
Sickles, D. E., 85
Simms, Colonel, 210
Simms, General, 210

Simpson, Colonel, 220
slavery, 12–18, 27–28, 39–43, 48–49, 51–53, 56–61, 66, 81–82, 86, 90, 93–95, 98–99, 102–3, 117–19, 131, 133, 139–44, 148, 153, 156–57, 172, 180, 186–87, 216, 222
Smalls, Robert, 76
Smith, John, 53
Smith, R. U., 225
Smythe, A. T., 199
social equality, 10–11, 92, 95, 107–8, 124, 171, 175, 184
South Carolina: Charleston, 28, 34–37, 41, 71, 76, 94, 96, 122, 126–28, 130–32, 162–64, 178, 181, 184, 193, 195–96, 203, 226–27; Columbia, 179, 188; Greenville, 180–81; Hilton Head Island, 10, 19, 47–49, 51–61, 69, 146, 164; immigration, 100, 125, 164–68; politics, 8, 10, 20–23, 93, 133, 135, 138–40, 144, 147–52, 158, 161–68, 169–82, 183–87, 193, 195–96, 204, 216–17, 222–23; Saint Helena Island, 4, 29, 39–44, 102
Southern Relief Association, 81
Spain, 40, 53–54
Special Orders No. 372, 50, 68
Stanton, Edward M., 28, 30–31, 33–35
Sterling, Dorothy, 6
Stickney, Mr., 232
Stinson, Captain, 35
Stockton, J. P., 120
Stoeber, Edward M., 4, 29, 39–44
Stoney, Joseph J., 62
Stoney, Rev. Dr., 62
suffrage. *See* voting

Taggard, F. W., 32
taxes, 49, 59, 65, 70, 72, 74, 79, 151, 174–75
Taylor, L. J., 96, 129
Taylor, S. M., 39–44
temperance, 14, 77–78
Tharin, R. S., 185, 209–10
Theban Literary Society, 14
tobacco, 29, 41–42, 50, 84
Tonking, James H., 73, 78
Town, Mr., 43
Townsend, E. D., 68, 85
triple alliance doctrine, 48–51, 62, 83, 215
Turner, Henry McNeal, 7
Turner, Nat, 13

Ullman, Victor, 3, 6, 11
Underground Railroad, 172, 180

Vail, Henry C., 70, 73
Van Buren, Martin, 222
Van Duyer, Stephen, 79
violence, 15–17, 23, 42, 97–99, 134, 136, 149, 151–52, 184, 192, 223–24
voting, 81–82, 91–94, 103, 107, 110–11, 114–19, 130, 135, 141, 143, 187, 193, 195, 221, 222

Walker, Peter, 5
Washington, Booker T., 7
Webb, Charles Henry, 35–36
Webster, Alonzo W., 198–99, 202
Wesley Church, 198, 206–7, 212
Whaley, Mr., 199
Whig Party, 120, 139
Whipper, William, 14, 90, 101–2, 110, 132, 190
White, Garland H., 218–19
Whyte, A., Jr., 39
Wilberforce University, 93, 112–21
Wild, General, 41
Willard Movement, 194
Willoughby, Major, 124
Wilson, Henry, 49, 63–64
Winkler, Mr., 198
Woodson, Lewis, 14
Worthington, H. G., 196, 231
Wright, Jonathan J., 100–101, 164–67, 169

Xenia, OH, 19, 23, 35, 93

Young Men's Moral Reform Society of Pittsburgh, 14

About the Author

Tunde Adeleke is a professor of history and director of the African and African American Studies Program at Iowa State University. He researches and teaches in African and African American history. A scholar of global reputation, Adeleke has published extensively on the subjects of the African diaspora, Black Nationalism, pan-Africanism, black biography, Afrocentrism, and African American identity. His publications include the critically acclaimed *UnAfrican Americans: Nineteenth-Century Black Nationalists and the Civilizing Mission* and *The Case against Afrocentrism*.

www.ingramcontent.com/pod-product-compliance
Lightning Source LLC
Chambersburg PA
CBHW030617230426
43661CB00053B/2034